THE PROCEEDINGS OF THE 17th INTERNATIONAL HUMANITIES CONFERENCE

ALL & EVERYTHING 2012

John Amaral
George Beke
David Brahinsky
Keith Buzzell
Irv Givot
Will Mesa
Russell Schreiber
Derek Sinko

Published by All & Everything Conferences
2012

First Edition Published 2012

Published by All & Everything Conferences (on behalf of the Planning Committee)
© Copyright 2012 by All & Everything Conferences

The contents of this publication may not be reproduced or copied in whole or part in any book, magazine, periodical, pamphlet, circular, information storage or data retrieval system, or in any other form without the written permission of the Planning Committee.

Any profit from the sale of these Proceedings will be devoted to the funds for the organization of future Conferences of a similar nature.

Published by All & Everything Conferences

Website: www.aandeconference.org
Email: info@aandeconference.org

First Edition Print

**ISBN-10: 1-905578-34-2
ISBN-13: 978-1-905578-34-4**

Also Published as
First Edition eBook

ISBN-10: 1-905578-35-0
ISBN-13: 978-1-905578-35-1

Cover Photo © Copyright 2012 by Bonnie Phillips

Table of Contents

Foreword 5

Conference Program 6

Planning Committee 18

Speakers 19

Beelzebub's Tales and the Work 22
    Beelzebub's Tales and the Work - Questions & Answers 30

Visualizing Beelzebub's Tales 36
    Visualizing Beelzebub's Tales - Questions & Answers 56

The Dilemma of the Toof-Nef-Tef 70
    The Dilemma of the Toof-Nef-Tef - Questions & Answers 78

Seminar 1: Chapter 34 - Beelzebub's Tales 86

Gurdjieff and Steve Jobs 108
    Gurdjieff and Steve Jobs - Questions & Answers 131

Gurdjieff, Plato & Pythagoras: Roman Coins & Planetary Connection ... 137
    Gurdjieff, Plato & Pythagoras - Questions & Answers 143

The First Page of Beelzebub's Tales 146
    The First Page of Beelzebub's Tales - Questions & Answers 159

Gurdjieff's Concept of the Function of Sexuality in the Evolution of Consciousness 163
    Gurdjieff's Concept of the Function of Sexuality - Questions & Answers 177

The Inner Trauma of Kundabuffer 191
    The Inner Trauma of Kundabuffer - Questions & Answers 212

Seminar 2: Chapter 8 - Meetings with Remarkable Men 220

Seminar 3: Chapter 35 - Beelzebub's Tales 234

Seminar 4: Where Do We Go From Here? 238

Appendix 1: List of Attendees 239

Index 240

Foreword

The Planning Committee would like to take this opportunity of thanking all the Presenters for their help in producing these Proceedings. We have all done our best to produce a permanent record of what some of us believe to have been the sixteenth important and definite Conference under the title of All and Everything 2012.

It is hoped that this will lead to further creative interaction of those in the Work in the near future.

The 17th International Humanities Conference - All & Everything 2012 convened on Wednesday, 25th April to Sunday 29th April, 2012 at the Peery Hotel, Salt Lake City, UT, USA. The conference was attended by 64 delegates travelling from Australia, Norway, Germany, Canada, the Netherlands, the United Kingdom and the United States.

From the Conference's inception, it's members have worked toward making this *"gathering of the Companions of the Book"* to become more and more just that - a gathering of people from all over the world who come together for the purpose of *"fathoming the gist"* of Gurdjieff's writings, of sharing our insights and experiences, our questions, and our efforts to understand and grow into becoming remarkable men and women.

The final session of the conference on Sunday morning, traditionally entitled *"Where Do We Go From Here,"* provided an opportunity to discuss the achievements of the conference and the challenges facing its future editions. It was decided that A&E 2013 will be held at Best Western Abbots Barton Hotel, Canterbury, UK.

Conference Program

all & everything

the 17th international humanities conference 2012

Wednesday, 25th April to Sunday 29th April, 2012
Peery Hotel, Salt Lake City, UT, USA

Conference Program

> "As it later became clear to me, these two learned beings happened to meet in the city of Babylon and during what is called their 'Ooissapagaoomnian-exchange-of-opinions', that is to say during those conversations the theme of which was, which forms of being-existence of the beings can serve for the welfare of the beings of the future,…
>
> *All and Everything, "An Objectively Impartial Criticism of the Life of Man"*
> *or Beelzebub's Tales to His Grandson, P 818*

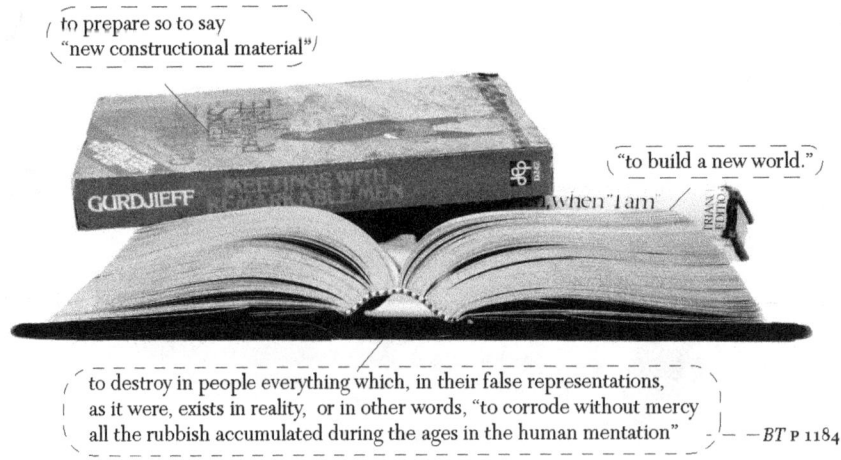

Conference Programme

8:00 AM - Each morning an unguided sitting / meditation / morning preparation room will be available.

Wednesday
- 1:00 PM - Planning Committee Meeting
- 2:30 PM - Informal Session: Getting to Know You, facilitator Farzin Deravi
- 3:30 PM - Coffee Break
- 4:00 PM - Paper: Will Mesa: *Beelzebub's Tales* and the Work
- 7:30 PM - Reading from *Beelzebub's Tales*
- Wednesday Evening – open

Thursday
- 9:15 - Opening Remarks – Paul Bakker
- 9:30 - Paper: Derek Sinko: Visualizing *Beelzebub's Tales*
- 10:45 - Coffee Break
- 11:15 - Paper: Keith Buzzell: The Dilemma of the Toof-Nef-Tef
- 12:30 - Lunch
- 2:30 - Seminar 1: Ch. 34 of *Beelzebub's Tales* - Russia - facilitated by P Bakker
- 3:45 - Coffee Break
- 4:15 - Seminar 1: continued
- 8:00 - Thursday Evening -Steffan Soule

Friday
- 9:15 - Opening Remarks – Farzin Deravi
- 9:30 - Paper: John Amaral: Gurdjieff and Steve Jobs
- 10:45 - Coffee Break
- 11:15 - Paper: George Beke: Gurdjieff, Plato and Pythagoras: Roman Coins & Planetary Connection
- 12:30 - Lunch
- 2:30 - Paper: Irv Givot: The First Page of *Beelzebub's Tales*
- 3:45 - Coffee Break
- 8:00 - Cultural Event TBA

Saturday
- 9:15 - Opening Remarks – Paul Bakker
- 9:30 - Paper: David Brahinsky: Gurdjieff's Concept of the Function of Sexuality in the Evolution of Consciousness
- 10:45 - Coffee Break
- 11:15 - Paper: Russell Schreiber: The Inner Trauma of Kundabuffer
- 12:30 - Lunch
- 2:30 - Seminar 2: Ch. 8 of *Meetings with Remarkable Men* – Ekim Bay – facilitator Russell Schreiber
- 3:45 - Coffee Break
- 4:15 - Seminar 3: Chapter 35 *Beelzebub's Tales* – "A Change In The Appointed Course Of The Falling Of the Transspace Ship Karnak" – facilitator Bob Godon
- 7:30 - Conference Banquet – toastmaster Steffan Soule

Sunday
- 9:30 - Seminar 4: Where Do We Go From Here – facilitated by Bonnie Phillips
- 11:30 - Conference Closes

Wednesday, 4:00 PM

Will Mesa
"*Beelzebub's Tales* and the Work"
"If you have not by nature a critical mind your staying here is useless." –
Aphorism inscribed above the walls of the Study House at the Prieuré.

The aim of this paper is to examine in details why Beelzebub's Tales, a book Mr. Gurdjieff wrote for humanity, cannot find its way into humanity through what is known in the Gurdjieff Community as the Gurdjieff Work or, simply, the Work. Several are the reasons that are given in order to fulfill this aim.

In order to establish a corresponding parallel with Beelzebub's Tales and to follow operation of the first cosmic law, the sacred Heptaparaparshinokh , the paper is structured in the form of six descents into the Living Teaching and the so-called Gurdjieff Work. The following is an outline of the six descents:
First Descent: Where I come from.
Second Descent: The Living Teaching.
Third descent: The Help from Above:
Fourth Descent: Why the Living Teaching cannot find its way through the Work
Fifth Descent: the Work in opposition to the Living Teaching
Sixth Descent: The Future of the Living Teaching

The paper then concludes with few remarks in relation to a statement of my mission for the future of the Living Teaching and its spreading to humanity, as Mr. Gurdjieff asked us to do and that the so-called Gurdjieff groups and Gurdjieff Foundations are not doing.

~Will Mesa received his Ph.D. in electrical engineering from the University of Florida. He spent three years with a group led by Henri Tracol in Paris, and six years with the groups of Nathalie Etievan in Venezuela, followed by four years with the New York Chan Meditation Center. He pursues a lifelong interest in the investigation of certain aspects of the Omnipresent-Okidanokh and the practical application of the Teaching of Ashiata Shiemash. He has published thirteen papers on Beelzebub's Tales to His Grandson. He is the author of A Treatise on Cosmic Engineering: A Book on Initiation and Transmutation Written According to the Law, a yet unpublished book.

Conference Programme

Thursday, 9:30 AM

~~~~~~

Derek Sinko
"Visualizing Beelzebub's Tales"
Beelzebub's Tales is rich in material relating to sight and seeing. Vision has its basis in light, which as Beelzebub explains, the great Chinese brothers Choon-Kil-Tez and Choon-Tro-Pel proved through their invention Alla-attapan to be constituted according to the Law of Heptaparaparshinokh. Aspects of Beelzebub's Tales can be shown to be structured in accordance with this Law as well, some of which relate to sight. This paper explores sight in Beelzebub's Tales in an effort to uncover some of the hidden patterns of the book.
I begin with an examination of two types of vision possessed by three-brained beings: Koritesnokhnian and Olooestesnokhnian. Along the way, some of the ideas falling under examination include: American fruit, chemicals invented by the Germans, the Amskomoutator, the ancient Egyptian observatory, Alla-attapan, Teleoghinooras and Korkaptilnian thought tapes, painting, devils and the path of the Karnak. I conclude by reflecting on the meaning of "being-sight" and finally suggest some aspects of Beelzebub's Tales for future study and possible application.

~Derek Sinko is an independent researcher and a graduate of Cleveland State University. His other interests include art, mythology, philosophy and the social sciences.

Thursday, 11:15 AM

Keith Buzzell
"The Dilemma of the Toof-Nef-Tef"
In chapter 45 "Electricity," Beelzebub presents the elements of a dilemma, the answer to which is of vital interest to each of us. The circumstances surrounding chapter 45 are important to note. Beelzebub is on his way back to Karatas, having received his full pardon. We are close to the end of The Tales, with the final stop on Saturn the conclusion of his time in the solar system. The Toof-Nef-Tef, the 'king' of Mars, is perplexed because he is unable to understand why in his subjects there is "a proportional diminishing of the intensity of their potency for the possibility of active mentation." His appeal to Beelzebub concerns beings of higher Reason and the fact that, in his return journey to Karatas, Beelzebub will meet such beings and that an answer to his dilemma might be forthcoming.

A number of essential questions flow from this dilemma. How does this dilemma concern each of us? What is the ultimate cause discovered by Beelzebub? What is 'Mars' in our individual 'solar system'? What is 'Saturn' in this metaphorical image of our individual solar system? And, most importantly, what is the solution to the dilemma of the Toof-Nef-Tef and how does it apply to us?

In our exploration of this mythical representation, we will posit a way of viewing our individual 'solar system' and the role played by the Earth, Mars and Saturn. The dilemma of the Toof-Nef-Tef will be placed in the context of our individual lives and we will make an effort to identify the critical efforts in the pursuit of 'higher Reason' that can resolve what is a very personal issue for each of us.

~Dr. Buzzell is a 1960 graduate of the Philadelphia College of Osteopathic Medicine. He is presently a member or the staff of Northern Cumberland Memorial Hospital in Bridgton and of clinical Medicine in Beddeford. Dr. Buzzell speaks from a broad perspective deriving from his life as a musician, musicologist, author, teacher, researcher, and physician. He is presently in Family practice in Fryeburg where he also serves as Medical Director of Hospice of Western Maine. He met Irmis Popoff (N.Y. Foundation) in 1971 and formed groups under her supervision into the 1980's. Dr. Buzzell met Annie Lou Staveley, founder of the Two Rivers Farm in Oregon, in 1988 and maintained a Work relationship with her up to her death. He continues group Work in Bridgton, ME.

Conference Programme

Thursday, 8:00 PM

~~~~~~

Steffan Soule

Steffan's magic is recognized with a Kennedy Center Award for the Arts. He has performed on National Television, twelve times for Bill Gates and in hundreds of corporations nationwide. His show entitled "The Magic of Recycling" is sponsored by the Department of Ecology. Steffan presents the Process Magic Experience to demonstrate the enneagram and the Nine Term Symbol principles from his book "Accomplish The Impossible". He gives corporate audiences a practical stimulating approach to process transformation. As designer and co-producer of two million-dollar-magic theatres custom built for his shows Steffan Soule performed the longest running magic show on the West Coast, "Mysterian". The show's five year run featured some of the greatest magic in the world according to magicians, critics and magic historians.

Steffan and his wife, Barbara are based in Seattle where their performances are well known in the arts scene. They have worked with the Seattle Symphony, Pacific Northwest Ballet, Seattle Repertory Theatre, The Fifth Avenue Theatre, Village Theatre, and Seattle Children's Theatre. Currently, Steffan Soule performs for theatres, corporate events and private parties while creating new works with artist Cooper Edens and their magic ensemble.

Friday, 9:30 AM

John Amaral – "**Gurdjieff and Steve Jobs**"
George Ivanovich Gurdjieff's whim "to live and teach so that there should be a new conception of God in the world" includes the striving to understand and reconcile Okidanokh, known to us variously as The Great Ray of Creation', 'The Emanation from the Sun Absolute', 'The Big Bang', or the entire EM spectrum of photonic emanation, whose 'heavenly' province began to be spirited away from the Church and scientifically imaged in the collective Western mind by James Clerk Maxwell's equations first published in 1861 and promoted by Heaviside in 1884, approximately coinciding with the time of Gurdjieff's birth. The publication was followed in a very short time (as little as 15 years) by two-way radio telegraphy and telephony, followed by broadcasting, electrical generators and motors, DC and AC artificial light, spark coils and plugs, transformers, mechanized factories and mass production assembly lines, relativity theory, particle physics, atomic energy and weapons, x-ray photography, satellites, moon landers, personal computers, cellphones, radiosonde bankcards, and so on. One particular inventive use of Okidanokh-based technology, arguably the largest construction ever by Man, which has the potential to reconcile, in a very big way, his second functional brain, the 'brain' which Gurdjieff observed as atrophied and a cause of lopsided 'topsy-turvy' imaging and unbalanced mentation, is… the internet. There has been no greater perfected utilization of this invention than in the products offered by Apple Inc., conceived, nurtured, selected, marketed and delivered in 'differently thought-out' ways by Steve Jobs. The subject of this paper is to place those products and Mr. Jobs' manifestations in the perspective of Mr. Gurdjieff's ideas. In this light, and considering Beelzebub's statement to Hassein at the end of *The Tales*:

"The sole means now for the saving of the beings of the planet Earth would be to implant again into their presences a new organ ... of such properties that every one of these unfortunates during the process of existence should constantly sense and be cognizant of the inevitability of his own death as well as the death of everyone upon whom his eyes or attention rests. Only such a sensation and such a cognizance can now destroy the egoism completely crystallized in them."

Perhaps there is no more striking and apropos statement by Steve Jobs than "Remembering that I'll be dead soon is the most important tool I've ever encountered to help me make the big choices in life. Because almost everything — all external expectations, all pride, all fear of embarrassment or failure – these things just fall away in the face of death, leaving only what is truly important. Remembering that you are going to die is the best way I know to avoid the trap of thinking you have something to lose. You are already naked. There is no reason not to follow your heart."

~John Amaral: born in Long Beach, CA, raised by nuns, trained in Electrical Engineering/Music, taught at Berklee College, directs USSchoolOfMusic.com. As Apple Developer #1234 in 1984, he exhibited at MacWorlds, attending keynotes from '84 to '09. He met Steve Jobs thrice and aims to improve the learning process and disrupt (reconcile) the learning business via iOS and OSX apps. He has studied Gurdjieff with students of Mr. Nyland, Mrs. Staveley, Mrs. Popoff, and Mr. Bennett and began to attend A&E in 2003.

Conference Programme

Friday, 11:15 AM

George Beke ~~~~~~
"Plato & Pythagoras: Roman Coins & Planetary Connection"

In February 2002, Dushka Howarth brought a very special audio recording to a celebratory meeting at Lillian Firestone's apartment on the upper West Side of Manhattan. It was a recording of the talk that her father, George Ivanovich Gurdjieff, had given at Christmas time many years earlier, in a hotel suite when he was visiting New York. Hearing Gurdjieff's own voice was mesmerizing and galvanizing.

In broken English, he gave the people assembled there a Christmas cadeau, a special holiday gift. There is a "point" in the heavens, Gurdjieff said, to which universal prayers were addressed, where the collective efforts of countless saints and sages were stored over the eons. From this special location in the heavens, a striving person could "suck, borrow, or steal" a finer substance, and with it coat one's inner bodies through the "I Am" exercise, through self-remembering.

Where could this point in the heavens possibly be located? That is a most absorbing journey from Pythagoras himself, to Plato, thence to Cicero, and finally arriving at Macrobius, who reveals that the Gates of Heaven lie at the intersections of the path of the Planets (along the Zodiac) and the Milky Way, which was seen as the heavenly abode of souls.

Have you seen the Milky Way recently? Have you seen the Zodiacal Light along which the Planets construct the stairs to the heavenly abode (Parabola Fall 2011, p. 74), and which intersects the Via Galactica at the celestial gates?

It's quite a thrill, which reveals Gurdjieff's connection to Plato's X (Chi) in the sky, and through Plato to Pythagoras himself, who paved this ancient road.

And the coins of Roman emperors bear witness to Plato's celestial intersections over hundreds of years, from Domitian to Antoninus Pius, to Marcus Aurelius, to Licinius and Constantine, etc.

Articles I've written:
Parabola (Spring 2011, 'Intentional Suffering')
Parabola (Fall 2011, 'Dionysos: The Mysteries Made Visible')
The Celator numismatic magazine (June 2011: 'Celestial Symbols on Roman Standards'),
Coin News UK ('Plato's X on Roman Coins,' to be published)
Books available on Amazon.com:
The Greek Roots of Gurdjieff's Esoteric Ideas
Visible Celestial Gates in the Pagan Skies

Friday, 2:30 PM

Irv Givot
Irv Givot first met the Work in 1973 when he joined a group in Colorado led by Elizabeth and Walter Van Renen, former students of Lord Pentland. In 1976 he moved with his family to Oregon, where he and his wife, Winnie participated in the activities at Two Rivers Farm – a Gurdjieffian community led by Annie Lou Staveley – for over 15 years, while pursuing his career as an alternative medical provider. Since then he has lived in Sisters, Or. and he and Winnie work with a fourth-way group in Bend (the Metanoia society, whose teacher is Cari Kimler) and he has continued his clinical practice.

Irv has been a Beelzebub reader for various groups for the last 27 years, and is the author of three books relating to the Work and his personal experiences. These are, Seven Aspects of Self Observation, Two Rivers Press, 1998; Healing in China, a Doctor's discovery of Chi Gong, Xlibris, 2004; and The Enneagram of Healing, Atom Press (To Be Published in 2012).

Conference Programme

Saturday, 9:30 AM

David Brahinsky
"Gurdjieff's Concept of the Function of Sexuality in the Evolution of Consciousness"

Gurdjieff, as far as I can tell from his writings and statements he is quoted as having made, believed that a healthy sex life is of fundamental importance for the process of spiritual evolution. He is quoted as having said, for example, that those whose sexual lives are governed by "constantly working buffers, fears and strange tastes" must eliminate them if they wish to get far in the Work. He says that the sex center plays a crucial role in creating a "general equilibrium;" is central in the formation of a "permanent center of gravity;" and that when it works properly, the sexual function represents the chief possibility of Liberation.

My paper will focus on how, according to Gurdjieff's understanding, this process works. Because Gurdjieff often speaks of the evolution of higher consciousness in terms of the formation of "higher-being bodies," the paper will explore how the proper functioning of the sex center relates to the formation of at least the Higher Emotional Body and so will include a discussion of such ideas as Gurdjieff's concept of sex energy, how it relates to formation of this body via what he called "the Second Conscious Shock" and how this relates to his concepts of energy density, vivifyingness, buffers, identification and a number of other ideas that he discriminated. The paper will discuss what it means for the sex center to function properly and will argue that when it does so, it brings in impressions, or "third-being food," that is required for crystallization of the Higher Emotional Body to occur.

My research indicates that Gurdjieff himself did not explain this process in other than symbolic terms and there is very little in the literature on it. For this reason, and because I am interested in trying to understand this process more concretely, I have attempted locate the relation of sexuality to the formation of higher being bodies within the realm of contemporary scientific investigation via the work of Wilhelm Reich, one of the few researchers who has attempted to study sex energy. At the end of the paper I will touch on this topic.

The paper is a condensation of some of the ideas that I explore in my book "Reich and Gurdjieff: Sexuality and the Evolution of Consciousness"

~David M. Brahinsky has been a student of the Fourth Way and the work of Wilhelm Reich since the mid-1960s. Akhaldan II, his school for Fourth Way studies, opened in the early 1970s. He received a Ph.D. in Philosophy in 1976 from the State University of New York at Binghamton and has been teaching philosophy and comparative religion at various colleges since 1969, currently at Bucks County Community College, in Newtown, Pennsylvania.

Saturday, 11:15 AM

Russell Schreiber
"The Inner Trauma of Kundabuffer"
This paper will address three interlinked psychological strands that G. I. Gurdjieff presents in All and Everything. In the first strand of this weaving, I examine deeper psychological repercussions of the introduction into humanity of an organ represented by Kundabuffer. We need a more complete understanding of the inner psychological trauma produced by Kundabuffer. Gurdjieff presents the foundational negative behavioral changes he observes in humanity due to Kundabuffer. However, there are important psychodynamic repercussions to be explicated that can help us understand the impressions we receive in our self-study. The second strand is the unexamined relationship of the psychological trauma produced by Kundabuffer to the subsequent design of religions or "ways" to correct for unexpected negative changes following Kundabuffer's removal. The third strand involves the inadequacy of these "ways" to foresee, understand, or compensate for the psychological, homeostatic dynamics created by Kundabuffer and the inherent difficulties of trying to correct humanity's negative, violent emotional behavior through "ways." We need to better understand the interactive mechanism of these three strands. A new approach to working with our negative emotions is needed and I will outline this in my presentation.

~Dr. Russell Schreiber has been involved in the Gurdjieff work since 1968. He studied with Willem A. Nyland from 1968 till Mr. Nyland's death in 1975, and was active in the Nyland group until 1980. He met Annie Lou Staveley in 1982 and was in contact with her until her death in 1996, visiting her on a regular basis. He has led and worked in groups since the 1970s. He currently teaches and works with a group in northern California.

Dr. Schreiber is also a California Licensed Clinical Psychologist at the Lomi Psychotherapy Clinic in northern California. As a staff psychologist, he supervises and trains psychologists and psychotherapists. He works with individuals who wish to unfold their full potential and who have either current or past material that is blocking them. To do this, many different psychotherapeutic modalities are useful and must be integrated in a manner that fits the unique needs of each person. He specializes in cognitive behavioral therapy and depth psychology for individuals. He combines cognitive behavioral therapy, depth psychology and exposure therapy to treat social phobias. Dr. Schreiber focuses on treating the following disorders: depression, covert depression in men, life transitions, PTSD, bipolar disorder, dissociative disorders, social phobias and OCD. He is also certified in somatic psychotherapy. He has been involved in individual and group process to develop the deeper aspects of human potential for over 40 years and helps individuals achieve integration of mind, body, and spirit.

Degrees granted as follows: B.A. Psychology, UC Berkeley, M.A. Counseling Psychology, Professional School of Psychology, Doctorate Clinical Psychology: Meridian University.

Professional Licenses held: Clinical Psychologist, Marriage and Family Therapist.

Conference Programme

~~~~~~

Peery Hotel
110 West Broadway
Salt Lake City, UT 84101, United States
Reception tel: 801 521-4300, fax 801 364-3295
contact email: wpowers@peeryhotel.com
Website: http://www.peeryhotel.com

ADVISORY BOARD
Nick Bryce, Dr. Keith A. Buzzell, Seymour B. Ginsburg,
Dimitri Peretzi, Prof. Paul Beekman Taylor

READING PANEL
Dr. Stephen Aronson, Rev. José Tirado, Terje Tonne
Music advisor: John Amaral

PLANNING COMMITTEE
Stephen Aronson, Paul Bakker, Marlena O. Buzzell, Farzin Deravi, Ian
MacFarlane, Clare Mingins, Robert Ormiston, Bonnie Phillips, Arkady Rovner

Visit the All and Everything Conference website at: www.aandeconference.org

Planning Committee

Paul Bakker - Netherlands
Marlena Buzzell - USA
Farzin Deravi - UK
Ian MacFarlane - UK
Clare Mingins - UK
Robert Ormiston - UK
Bonnie Phillips - USA

Reading Panel

Stephen Aronson - USA
José Tirado - Iceland
Terje Tonne - Norway

Advisory Board

Seymour B. Ginsburg - USA
Dr. Keith Buzzell - USA
Dimitri Peretzi - Greece
Prof. Paul Beekman Taylor - Switzerland
John Amaral - USA (Music Advisor)

Speakers

John Amaral
John Amaral: born in Long Beach, CA, raised by nuns, trained in Electrical Engineering/Music, taught at Berklee College, directs www.USSchoolOfMusic.com. As Apple Developer #1234 in 1984, he exhibited at MacWorlds, attending keynotes from '84 to '09. He met Steve Jobs thrice and aims to improve the learning process and disrupt (reconcile) the learning business via iOS and OSX apps. He has studied Gurdjieff with students of Mr. Nyland, Mrs. Staveley, Mrs. Popoff, and Mr. Bennett and began to attend A&E in 2003.

George Beke
Articles I've written:
Parabola (Spring 2011, 'Intentional Suffering')
Parabola (Fall 2011, 'Dionysos: The Mysteries Made Visible')
The Celator numismatic magazine (June 2011: 'Celestial Symbols on Roman Standards'),
Coin News UK ('Plato's X on Roman Coins,' to be published)
Books available on Amazon.com:
The Greek Roots of Gurdjieff's Esoteric Ideas
Visible Celestial Gates in the Pagan Skies

David M. Brahinsky
David M. Brahinsky has been a student of the Fourth Way and the work of Wilhelm Reich since the mid-1960s. Akhaldan II, his school for Fourth Way studies, opened in the early 1970s. He received a Ph.D. in Philosophy in 1976 from the State University of New York at Binghamton and has been teaching philosophy and comparative religion at various colleges since 1969, currently at Bucks County Community College, in Newtown, Pennsylvania.

Keith Buzzell
Dr. Buzzell is a 1960 graduate of the Philadelphia College of Osteopathic Medicine. He is presently a member or the staff of Northern Cumberland Memorial Hospital in Bridgton and of clinical Medicine in Beddeford. Dr. Buzzell speaks from a broad perspective deriving from his life as a musician, musicologist, author, teacher, researcher, and physician. He is presently in Family practice in Fryeburg where he also serves as Medical Director of Hospice of Western Maine. He met Irmis Popoff (N.Y. Foundation) in 1971 and formed groups under her supervision into the 1980's. Dr. Buzzell met Annie Lou Staveley, founder of the Two Rivers Farm in Oregon, in 1988 and maintained a Work relationship with her up to her death. He continues group Work in Bridgton, ME.

All & Everything Conference 2012

Irv Givot

Irv Givot first met the Work in 1973 when he joined a group in Colorado led by Elizabeth and Walter Van Renen, former students of Lord Pentland. In 1976 he moved with his family to Oregon, where he and his wife, Winnie participated in the activities at Two Rivers Farm - a Gurdjieffian community led by Annie Lou Staveley - for over 15 years, while pursuing his career as an alternative medical provider. Since then he has lived in Sisters, Or. and he and Winnie work with a fourth-way group in Bend (the Metanoia society, whose teacher is Cari Kimler) and he has continued his clinical practice.

Irv has been a Beelzebub reader for various groups for the last 27 years, and is the author of three books relating to the Work and his personal experiences. These are, Seven Aspects of Self Observation, Two Rivers Press, 1998; Healing in China, a Doctor's discovery of Chi Gong, Xlibris, 2004; and The Enneagram of Healing, Atom Press (To Be Published in 2012).

Will Mesa

Will Mesa received his Ph.D. in electrical engineering from the University of Florida. He spent three years with a group led by Henri Tracol in Paris, and six years with the groups of Nathalie Etievan in Venezuela, followed by four years with the New York Chan Meditation Center. He pursues a lifelong interest in the investigation of certain aspects of the Omnipresent-Okidanokh and the practical application of the Teaching of Ashiata Shiemash. He has published thirteen papers on *Beelzebub's Tales to His Grandson*. He is the author of A Treatise on Cosmic Engineering: A Book on Initiation and Transmutation Written According to the Law, a yet unpublished book.

Russell Schreiber

Dr. Russell Schreiber has been involved in the Gurdjieff work since 1968. He studied with Willem A. Nyland from 1968 till Mr. Nyland's death in 1975, and was active in the Nyland group until 1980. He met Annie Lou Staveley in 1982 and was in contact with her until her death in 1996, visiting her on a regular basis. He has led and worked in groups since the 1970s. He currently teaches and works with a group in northern California.

Dr. Schreiber is also a California Licensed Clinical Psychologist at the Lomi Psychotherapy Clinic in northern California. As a staff psychologist, he supervises and trains psychologists and psychotherapists. He works with individuals who wish to unfold their full potential and who have either current or past material that is blocking them. To do this, many different psychotherapeutic modalities are useful and must be integrated in a manner that fits the unique needs of each person. He specializes in cognitive behavioral therapy and depth psychology for individuals. He combines cognitive behavioral therapy, depth psychology and exposure therapy to treat social phobias. Dr. Schreiber focuses on treating the following disorders: depression, covert depression in men, life transitions, PTSD, bipolar disorder, dissociative disorders, social phobias and OCD. He is also certified in somatic psychotherapy. He has been involved in individual and group process to develop the deeper aspects of human potential for over 40 years and helps individuals achieve integration of mind, body, and spirit.

Speakers

Degrees granted as follows: B.A. Psychology, UC Berkeley, M.A. Counselling Psychology, Professional School of Psychology, Doctorate Clinical Psychology: Meridian University.

Professional Licenses held: Clinical Psychologist, Marriage and Family Therapist.

Derek Sinko

Derek Sinko is an independent researcher and a graduate of Cleveland State University. His other interests include art, mythology, philosophy and the social sciences.

Beelzebub's Tales and the Work

Will Mesa

Abstract

The Aim of the Paper

The aim of this paper is to examine in details why *Beelzebub's Tales*, a book Mr. Gurdjieff wrote for humanity, cannot find its way into humanity through what is known in the Gurdjieff Community as the Gurdjieff Work or, simply, the Work. Several are the reasons that are given in order to fulfill this aim.

Structure of the Paper

In order to establish a corresponding parallel with *Beelzebub's Tales* and to follow operation of the first cosmic law, the sacred Heptaparaparshinokh, the paper is structured in the form of six descents into the Living Teaching and the so-called Gurdjieff Work. The following is an outline of the six descents:

First Descent: Where I come from.
Second Descent: The Living Teaching.
Third descent: The Help from Above:
Fourth Descent: Why the Living Teaching cannot find its way through the Work
Fifth Descent: the Work in opposition to the Living Teaching
Sixth Descent: The Future of the Living Teaching

Statement of Mission

The paper then concludes with few remarks in relation to a statement of my mission for the future of the Living Teaching and its spreading to humanity, as Mr. Gurdjieff asked us to do and that the so-called Gurdjieff groups and Gurdjieff Foundations are not doing.

Beelzebub's Tales and the Work

> *"If you have not by nature a critical mind your staying here is useless."*
> (Aphorism inscribed above the walls of the Study House at the Prieuré.)

Introduction: The Pointing Finger

I open my presentation by telling you all that I am very happy to be a full time disciple of what I designate as the Living Teaching found in the Legominism *All and Everything* and very specifically in *Beelzebub's Tales*. I have no teaching of my own nor do I want to have a teaching of my own. The sense and aim of my existence on Earth is to bring attention to the material in the Legominism, of course according to my own individuality because I am also working on myself as I do this, and one of the most important aspects of my inner work is to attain the degree of self-individuality or sacred Martfotai. I consider myself to be in the tradition of how Zen monks and teachers describe themselves as pointer fingers. So, please, look to where the finger is pointing and do not stay with the finger.

Structure of the Paper: The Sacred Heptaparaparshinokh

In order to follow closely the six descents of Beelzebub to Earth, which I consider to be the Law of Seven of the book, I have also structured my paper in terms of six descents and will immediately proceed to start reading from them. In a paper I presented at the 2008 A&E Conference in England I also addressed the matter of the six descents of Beelzebub to Earth and raised the question of why only six and not seven descents when according to the Law of Seven every integral whole must contain seven centers of gravity. I did not answer my own question and let everybody to come out with his or her answer. I now ask the same question here; why only six descents presented in this paper and what would be the seventh and last descent? I will now go into each and every descent in my paper. I will try to be brief so that we will have time for discussions.

First Descent: Where I Come From

In the summer of 1975 I found myself with my family in Paris searching for one of the disciples Mr. Gurdjieff left in that city after his death in 1949. Why I was there is rather long to say and if you Google Will Mesa you will find that I describe the events that led me there in great details. Suffice is to say that on my trip from Caracas to Paris, we stopped at New York to visit my parents and it was there that I bought the three little booklets with the title *Beelzebub's Tales to His Grandson*. The first thing I read was this paragraph printed on the back cover of one of the books:

"To possess the right to the name of "man," one must be one."

"And to be such, one must first of all, with an indefatigable persistence and an unquenchable impulse of desire, issuing from all the separate independent parts constituting one's entire common presence, that is to say, with a desire issuing simultaneously from thought, feeling, and organic instinct, work on an all-round knowledge of oneself - at the same time struggling unceasingly with one's subjective weaknesses - and then afterwards, taking one's stand upon the results thus obtained by one's consciousness alone, concerning the defects in one's established subjectivity as well as the elucidated means for the possibility of combating them, strive for their eradication without mercy towards oneself." (BTTHG, p 1209)

That really impressed me because I have always wished with my whole being to be a man.

After two months in Paris seeking here and there, I finally found one of the groups led by Henri Tracol. By then I have already read the first book completely and the more I read, the more passionate I became. I was with his group for three years and for me personally the most significant event was that we never read *Beelzebub's Tales*, although every Saturday we met to read Ouspensky's *In Search of the Miraculous*. I asked Tracol why we were not reading the book and he replied that one day we may read it but that day never came. In 1978 I went back to Venezuela and joined the group of Nathalie Etievan, the daughter of Jeanne de Salzmann. What I also found of interest is that we never read *Beelzebub*, except once we read the chapter 'The-Terror-of-the-Situation.' The funny thing is that a friend of mine, who was member of a Gnostic group around and knew of my great interest for the book, invited me to give six talks on the material in *The Tales*. I remember that only few people attended the first talk. By the sixth and last talk, there were no chairs and almost no space left for attendees. I asked myself how come these people who are not in the Work are so interested in the book and all those who claim to be in the Work are not. It was then 1985 and I moved from Venezuela to New York. I had with me a letter of introduction by Nathalie to her daughter Marie at the New York Foundation. I did not even bother to take the letter with me. It was the end for me of all contacts with the so-called Gurdjieff Foundations and with any Gurdjieff group for that matter. I then knew what was more or less the sense and aim of my existence on Earth; to dedicate my life to the study and spreading of the message in *Beelzebub's Tales*. Now you know where I come from.

Second Descent: The Living Teaching

What is the Living Teaching Mr. Gurdjieff brought to humanity in *Beelzebub's Tales*? I am sure that each person will have a different answer. I am now preparing to give mine. I already wrote about this in my WordPress blog 'Gospel According to Beelzebub'. For me personally, the Living Teaching is the true Fourth Way Mr. Gurdjieff brought to us in the Living Teaching. This Fourth Way is the way of Conscience. Here is how I put it in my blog:

If Mr. Gurdjieff were alive today, he would probably be very surprised to know that people who follow his teaching describe themselves as followers of the Fourth Way. I am sure that he would have immediately set out to find where this expression came from because he did use the term fourth way, and only one time, but in very specific terms and not as a Way. If that had been the case, he would have determined that the expression refers to those who do not follow the way of the fakir, the monk, and the yogi. Following my train of speculative thoughts here, I think that Mr.

Gurdjieff would have said that he indeed spoke about the ways of the fakir, the monk, and the yogi at one time during the giving of his teaching in Russia and faithfully recorded by Ouspensky in his book *In Search of the Miraculous*, but that later he corrected himself and spoke of three other ways: The Ways of Faith, Love, and Hope.

And then he would have probably added:

"The Fourth Way is the Way of Conscience and that the Way of Conscience exists in the fakir, the monk, and the yogi, and in all of us because 'Conscience in three-centered beings is sometimes called the REPRESENTATIVE OF THE CREATOR.'"

The true Fourth Way is the Living Teaching.

Third descent: The Help from Above

"When you get to ME, you will receive help," said Mr. Gurdjieff. Since I have structured my paper according to the sacred Heptaparaparshinokh, I have assigned the third stopinder of the law of my paper to the first Mdnel-In, the interval between MI and FA if we use the music scale. All help at the interval comes from outside and from Above, from point 9 in the enneagram. Help for evolution of the first-being food comes from air, outside and above. Sometimes this help does no come, does not materialize. In the Law of my own life, I have seen again and again how help never came to me whenever I tried to make money; however whenever I tried to understand and live the Living Teaching, help indeed has come. What about the motion of the trajectory of the Living Teaching in *Beelzebub's Tales*? I am now convinced by certain events I have seen here and there that help for this trajectory has indeed already come. There have been a number of books and articles that have brought this help from outside and above. My favorite one is Orage's *Commentaries on Beelzebub's Tales*. Orage not only supervised the rendering of the 1950 original English edition of *The Tales*, but he was the person among the first generation of the Living Teaching who better understood the meaning of the book. It is well known that Ouspensky never read the book and even confessed to C. S. Nott that every time he tried to read it, it stuck in his throat. Nicoll never read it either. He was too busy dictating his six volumes of his Commentaries to his secretary. And it is quite obvious from Jeanne de Salzmann's *The Reality of Being: The Fourth Way of Gurdjieff* that it not only has anything to do with the true Fourth Way of Mr. Gurdjieff but it clearly shows that she had no idea of what *Beelzebub's Tales* is all about. Bennett's book *Talks on Beelzebub's Tales* is very good but never at the level of Orage's commentaries. There have been other sources that have served as help from outside and above. The important point is that the Living Teaching has received the help necessary and sufficient in order to bring the trajectory of the Living Teaching to the Harnel-aoot of its evolutionary movement.

All & Everything Conference 2012

Fourth Descent: Why the Living Teaching cannot find its way through the Work

I will now give a complete spectrum with corresponding commentaries of why, according to my own understanding and subjective views, the Living Teaching cannot find its way to humanity via the Work. Here are the seven components of this integral spectrum:

1. The Work is not interested in *Beelzebub's Tales*. This is quite obvious by the fact that the book is studied by only a minority within the so-called Gurdjieff groups and Foundations. During my ten years in the Foundations it was read only one time. I know things have changed since then but I also know that reading and study of the book is not encouraged among group leaders and some of these leaders have not read the book even one time, let alone three times.

2. The Work is secretive. It took me two whole months to find the Work when I was in Paris and I found it through what Mr. Gurdjieff calls a conjury. Now, it is easier to find but if you look at the websites of all of the so-called big Foundations and little Foundations around, you will notice how secretive these sites are. This contrasts with finding Mr. Gurdjieff who was always sitting at Cafe de la Paix and Child's cafes. This man lived in the streets and cafe of life. The Work lives in hiding.

3. The Work does not bring help from Above. There is more help for the spreading of the Living Teaching in life than in the Work. One of the conditions imposed by the Foundations is not to talk about *Beelzebub's Tales* outside the Beelzebub's groups. There is very little interest in the Foundations for this kind of event we are here gathered for around what is called the companions of the book, the book being *Beelzebub's Tales*. These kinds of events are what I call help from Above and were it not by the founders of this International, we would not be here.

4. The Work is absorbent. I understood this in relation to my experience with a Gurdjieff group I used to frequent. For three consecutive years we gathered to study *Beelzebub's Tales*, that is to say, exchange on the book. But little by little this spirit of exchange on the book was taken by other aspects of the Work such as morning sitting, movements, exercises and all those favorites of the Work. Last time I attended one of those gatherings, *Beelzebub's Tales* was hardly discussed. That is why I stopped going to those gatherings. I am aware that I am a pain in the neck but I spent four years at a Chan meditation center and one thing I learned is that it is the intention that is what counts. My intention here is certainly not to offend anyone but to expose the views of my Conscience. But if any if you are offended by my remarks, then remember that teaching of Saint Buddha: "The best form of intentional suffering is to bear the unpleasant manifestations of others."

5. The Work is anti-unitarian. The spreading of the Living Teaching into humanity will be founded on Unity. However, the Work cannot find unity. I understood that when I attended a week-end work period at the Two Rivers Farm group. There were about ten people from the Foundations and they were complaining about how the morning sitting was being conducted and that it was different from that of the Foundations. One of these person told me something about

that and I told this person that there was no morning sitting in Paris when Mr. Gurdjieff was alive and that according to what Dushka Howarth, one of the daughters of Mr. G., has told me, to direct a sitting was anti-spiritual. I remember that when she told me that, I thought about my four years in a Chan (Zen) meditation center in Queens, New York. I never saw a zazen sitting being directed. So, I told this person that maybe both the Foundations and the Two Rivers Farm were wrong. Then I concluded saying that there was only one morning preparation in *Beelzebub's Tales* and that it was standing and with the eyes open (page 78 of the book). In any case, there is no hope the Work will ever unite because each and every group thinks that what they are doing is the correct approach, particularly among the Foundations which think they were anointed by Mr. Gurdjieff himself.

6. The Work is hierarchical. Within each Work group there is established a well-defined hierarchy not necessarily according to being but according to time and favoritism. If a member is a relative of a group leader, this member may be on the top. I saw that when I was in the group in Venezuela. Yes, it is true that there is a hierarchy of Being in *Beelzebub's Tales* but it is all according to being and what makes a leader in the organization of Ashiata Shiemash is the meritorious being of the person, that is to say, how much the person has worked consciously and suffered intentionally.

7. The Work is selfish. On page 1185 of *Beelzebub's Tales* we read this: "The highest aim and sense of human life is the striving to attain the welfare of one's neighbor", and that this is possible exclusively only by the conscious renunciation of one's own. This statement, if I well remember, is quoted in Bonnie's project The Golden Rule. The Work does not live by this statement. They seem to be worried only about their own welfare. There is not possibility of Antkooano between the Work and humanity.

Fifth Descent: the Work in opposition to the Living Teaching

We now come to the Harnel-Aoot of this octave of descents. This is the most critical Stopinder because of its asymmetry between the third and the last. One of its major characteristics is that it can give "*results opposite to each other*". That is why during the fifth descent of Beelzebub to Earth we find the teachings of Ashiata Shiemash and that of Lentrohamsanin. Both teachings oppose each other. One is evolutionary and the other is involutionary. It is the same with what I designate as the Living Teaching and the Work. The former is involutionary and the latter is evolutionary. The former is the system of the Archangel Hariton and the latter is mainly the system of Mme. De Salzmann. In fact, and according to the Law of Three, the Work is the holy-denying and the Living Teaching is the holy-affirming. The holy-reconciling will come from what humanity or a part of humanity does with Living Teaching.

All & Everything Conference 2012

Sixth Descent: The Future of the Living Teaching

I will say nothing of my own. I will simply quote here what I consider to be the best review among the sixty reviews of *Beelzebub's Tales* in Amazon.com. I too have a review there but this one is better than mine. Here it is:

"A JAVALIN HURLED INTO THE FUTURE, March 25, 2001
By Steve Adams (Denton, North Carolina) - This review is from: *Beelzebub's Tales to His Grandson: All And Everything: 1st Series* (Compass) (Paperback)

When Gurdjieff discovered that his institute would fall short of accomplishing his aims and his condition after a severe automobile accident forced - or bookmarked - a re-evaluation of what he must do, he turned to writing and produced this *"Magnum Opus."* He remarked that it was a javelin hurled into the future. I have read the book 3 times, and portions repeatedly, and contrary to the remarks of certain reviewers, I and others giving favorable reviews are not gullible. It took me three decades to see this issue in its true light, and the more I understand, the more I see I have a long way to go. The book is a Legominism, to use Gurdjieff's own technical term defined in the text. It exists on several levels, and on occasion I have been able to verify that for myself by the perceptivity of its deeper currents. Actually I will be the first to confess that you cannot tell much about this book by the reviews. The reviews - pro and con - tell much more about their authors than they do about this book. That should be expected. Even my own review reminds me of Beelzebub's description of our species as those unfortunate three-brained beings that breed and multiply upon the face of that ill-fated planet Earth. Gurdjieff held up a mirror, and reviewers - including myself - seem eager to show our faces in it. Without question this is the most important work ever written on the issue of stopping wars, and that singular observation alone among many other comparable ones is sufficient to validate Leary's comment that this is the most important work produced in the twentieth century. But because of its inaccessibility to many audiences, I would also include Ouspensky's account of Gurdjieff's teaching, *In Search of the Miraculous*, on a par with it. Ouspensky's book may actually be more important immediately, but ultimately Gurdjieff's *Beelzebub's Tales* will emerge to its true stature among segments of our posterity. Gurdjieff knew and stated that there was no hope for current generations. Without this javelin hurled into the future, there would be no hope at all."

Mission Statement

My mission statement is very simple: "To spend the rest of my life until I die bringing the attention I put in *Beelzebub's Tales* to my life first and then to the lives of others. For the fulfillment of my mission statement I am now following a series of activities involving posting in my WordPress blog with the title of 'Gospel According to Beelzebub'. Traveling next month to Buenos Aires in Argentina and to Santiago en Chile where I have been invited to give talks about the Book. Then in October I will attend the large International gathering in Moscow to celebrate the one hundred years of the arrival of Mr. Gurdjieff to that city. I will be presenting a paper inspired on a comment from Orage to his friend Nott about Mr. Gurdjieff: "He is a god walking among us". I also hope that my book project that Bonnie was going to publish and that is now in stand still will be re-initiated again. That book had the title *Views on Beelzebub's Tales*. Then about a year ago, I changed the title to *Life with Beelzebub*. I hope and wish my book will be a testimony of my 37 years living with Mr. Beelzebub.

Concluding Remarks

In Mathew 6:24 the Divine Teacher Jesus Christ said: *"No man can serve two masters: for either he will hate the one, and love the other; or else he will hold to the one, and despise the other. You cannot serve God and mammon"*. Now rephrasing Him, I say: *"We cannot serve two masters, either we serve the Living Teaching or we serve the Work"*.

And finally, concerning the sense and aim of my existence on Earth, I conclude with the words of the Most Most Saintly Ashiata Shiemash at the end of his Legominism, *"The Terror-of-the-Situation"*:

"May the blessing of our almighty OMNI-LOVING COMMON FATHER UNI-BEING CREATOR ENDLESSNESS be upon my decision, Amen."

© Copyright 2012 - Will Mesa - All Rights Reserved

Beelzebub's Tales and the Work - Questions & Answers

Q1: Just to put it in perspective, I agree with everything you have been saying.

WM: Thank you.

Q1: But, the question I have is what is that word that I have read in *The Tales* but I don't follow it, it somehow means spreading of sacred ideas into humanity. Could you please spell that word for me and say it very slowly.

WM: Antkooano. I should have made a reference. Antkooano is the natural process by which beings of a planet share cosmic truth around the planet, and that improves the formation of Divine Objective Reason. And what happens there is a superfluity of the Holy Reconciling when that happens. It is not happening now of course. It is not happening in this society we are living. Well, it's happening in small groups. Little bits here and there.

Q1: And we need to intensify that?

WM: Yes, well, I think we do, because you know there is something that is discovered by biology in England, maybe you read him, Sheldrake, he says something that is called morphogenetic, maybe you've read about it. He says that if you work on something then for the future generations it will be easier to work on that. And you know how he tested this? He asked people to solve the crossword in London at 9 o'clock, and they could do it better than the people at 7, because the people at 7 worked on that. Very ingenious idea. So if we work on this now, future generations are going to work on this more. So we have to do it now. We have to do it. I believe in that.

Q2: Will, I believe it's in the chapter right in the middle of the book, A Change in the Appointed Course of the Falling of the Transspace Ship *Karnak*: could you comment on the statement that in order to get from Purgatory to Deskaldino, the home planet of the great teacher, one has to pass through a solar system Salzmanino.

WM: I spent three months writing about that, and I've sent it to Toddy, and sent it to about nine people around the world, and then I stopped because it was eating me alive inside. Because the whole thing is what is the meaning of Deskaldino? What is the meaning of Zilnotrago? What is the meaning of Salzmanino? What is the meaning of Trogoautoegocrat? You know. It is all in that paragraph that you mentioned. And for me the conclusion is that the Living Teaching, okay, which is the *Karnak* - you know what the word *Karnak* means, tomb of the body in Armenian, one of the meanings; I got that from Orage by the way, it doesn't come from me - and what is the *Karnak*? The *Karnak* is the embodiment of the teaching. The *Karnak* cannot go to Holy Purgatory and the planet Deskaldino, where the great teacher is waiting, through the solar system Salzmanino because this solar system emanates Zilnotrago. And you know what Zilnotrago is? It's a cosmic poison. And once you get in contact with ?.... That's one of the meanings.

And now, a question that Bonnie raised in a private exchange we had: it is possible, and I think about this, that Mme de Salzmann did this consciously, she initiated this in conjunction with Mr Gurdjieff, to create the Holy Denying. Because in the dynamic of the Law of Three which is the law of phenomena, you always begin with the Holy Denying. You never begin with the Holy Affirming. You always being with the Holy Denying. And that's why *Beelzebub's Tales* of the three series is the Holy Denying. The *Meetings* is the Holy Affirming and the last is the Holy Reconciling. You have to begin with *Beelzebub*, and he said it. Begin with this book, because it is the Holy Denying.

So, Mme de Salzmann had to create the Work for the Work to become the Holy Denying, for the Law of Three to advance. So I'm not blaming her really, and you know it's something that maybe she had a large ?..., and maybe she did that on purpose.

Q3: Will I want to say thank you again for coming to Baltimore a couple of times at your own expense to speak to and work with my group there.

WM: You say own expense, you know when I am invited to go to Buenos Aires, all things are paid, so I'm improving. But that was good to travel there. Oh by the way, I had a big experience going to Baltimore one day on the train from New York. I was giving a talk on the terrible situation to the group in Baltimore, and I was sitting in the train, I love to travel in trains, and then suddenly I look out of the window and we are entering Philadelphia. And I see three streets coming together to a main street. And the moment I look out of the window the conductor came through the hall, 'Philadelphia, Philadelphia.' And then right there I understood what Mr Gurdjieff said, 'All ways of the ?.... are different but they all lead to Philadelphia.' And all the streets were leading to one street. And Philadelphia, we know what it is, the brotherly love. Okay.

Q3: Yes. And my question has to do with a comment you made in your talk about sitting. Because I've been associated with several groups, and we sit. And you alluded to G.'s comments about standing. And I'd like you to please comment further on that. And my question is what's wrong with sitting, since most of us associate sitting with meditation?

WM: No there is nothing wrong with sitting. What is wrong according to Dushka, as I understand, is *guided* sitting.

Q4: So how do you make the distinction? I was with you when she said that, but I didn't understand.

WM: It's when you sit and somebody is telling you, 'Now you go to the right arm, now you go to the right leg, now you go to this, now you go to that, and where are you going? You are going where they tell you to go. But what if you want to go to ?.... instead of to the right leg? You see.

And this is Dushka., she told me. And I did not realise this until she told me. And then I compared with my four years in meditation centres. I tell you, they never told me what to do. Only six hours on the Saturday the introduction: how to breathe. For instance, breathing, if you see that you breathe, after seven months more or less - I did it, I'm not talking here, I stopped it because I don't do it any more - you enter into what is called the fourth state of breathing. And you enter by yourself. …..wow, what's going on here? I'm no longer breathing. And you are breathing more than ever. But I found it myself. Nobody told me. Do it, and you'll find something. So that's the point of the sitting. It's not that sitting is wrong. Look, two thousand years of Zen tradition, and yes maybe in some places they do a directed sitting, but not there. In Zen you sit, you sit there, and you are doing there.

Q4: Thank you for that clarification.

Q5: I was very struck by what you were saying about the separateness of different groups, and there is an interesting diagram which I have, which I gave to Mrs Staveley many years ago, it came from Mr Nyland, and it shows the progression of possibilities of mankind or of a human being. And the upper octave that can be achieved, the highest note, is love of mankind. And that's very much I would say almost an affirming part, but it seems that the Zilnotrago has to do with the opposite of that, which comes from, in *All and Everything*, which I see repeatedly, is it's a book about egotism. I just wanted to bring that up. That seems to be the missing piece in terms of what you're contrasting with the living teaching versus the Work. The piece that has somehow been captured by certain levels and certain people who are involved in Buddhism. Compassion, in other words they're living compassion. There's a being there and people pick it up. And it's not about words, it's about experience of the person. That piece, that compassion piece, it seems to be held for me in that upper note, love of mankind. Does it make sense what I'm saying?

WM: Yes, it makes sense. And there are seven aspects of love. The first three are love of body, that depends on type and polarity, sex; love of feeling, that evokes the opposite; love of consciousness which evokes the same. And then comes all the other up to love of God, which is the highest commandment from Jesus. And it says, Love your God. Not love God. Love *your* God. And what is your God? I know what my God is. I had it in my childhood. And that is why Mr Gurdjieff said that changing the religion of another human being is immoral, from the point of view of objective morality, because you have this from essence, from your childhood. And yes, the second, Love your brother as you love yourself.

Q5: That seems to be what's missing. It's missing in the sense of the unity. In other words, it has become the specialness.

WM: The best article I ever read on this is by Joseph Azize. Joseph Azize I have tremendous respect for him because he's a monk. This man is a monk. He wrote a paper, *Where are the Gurdjieff groups heading?* You can read it if you go to his WordPress. He said that they are leading nowhere. Why? Because all the great beings died already, including George Adie who was his teacher in Australia. They have all passed away. What is left? Imitation. But this compassion, this love, is lost.

Q6: Given what you have just said, what is the source of your hope for humanity?

WM: You know, Ashiata Shiemash means ray of light, when you translate from the Persian. Ashiata is one of the hopes. Bennett asked Mr Gurdjieff, 'Are you Ashiata?' And Mr Gurdjieff did not answer yes or no. Now there are three faces of Mr Gurdjieff in *Beelzebub*. One is Gornahoor Harharkh, the other is Saint Buddha, and the other is Ashiata. The three faces of Gurdjieff. He was Gornahoor, he is Saint Buddha - Buddha in the book is not the historic Buddha, it's Mr Gurdjieff; if you read you will see it has nothing to do with Saint Buddha, with the teaching of Buddha. And Ashiata is hope.

Q6: I wanted to share with you an insight I had a while ago about Ashiata's teaching and it just came to me in the middle of the night when I was in that state when I could see things a little more clearly. Because you referred to this. And he had, as I recall, I haven't read it recently, but he had everybody trying to convert hundreds of people. One person would convince a hundred and they would convince a hundred. Pretty soon you had this Ashiatean epic where everyone was more or less enlightened. But in two generations Lentrohamsanin came along and destroyed it all.

WM: Seven generations.

Q6: Okay. But maybe what he was trying to tell us under the surface there was, that doesn't work. The way Ashiata went about it doesn't work. It only lasted a few generations and it was gone. And when Gurdjieff himself died his directive was to create a small nucleus of people who would be able to carry on his work. And he didn't try to convert large numbers of people. So I'm just wondering, it raised a question for me whether he's trying to tell us something about that. He buried the dog pretty deep but maybe he's trying to tell us something there about why Lentrohamsanin succeeded.

WM: I don't know. Lentrohamsanin is the way of the Greeks. The Greeks came and followed the way of Lentrohamsanin instead of the way of Ashiata. But there was a way of Ashiata.

Q6: But if Ashiata had gone about it differently, maybe his teaching would have persisted and not have been destroyed.

WM: Well, it's difficult because it's the Law of Seven. There is involution. It's going to involve. I mean, look, the Divine Teacher Jesus says, Love your neighbour, and then we have the Spanish Inquisition. You see the Law of Seven going around and around, you know. But Ashiata has renewals. The renewals of Ashiata Shiemash. He means that we can renew now. Now Ashiata is not a prophet from the past, he is from the future. I show this in an intuition I had; it says Ashiata came after the way of love, faith and hope, and he said these ways are no longer valid.. Well how can Ashiata be after that, if the way of love is Jesus, the way of faith is Saint Lama, and the way of hope is Mohammed? How can Ashiata find out before? So he is a prophet of the future not of the past.

Somebody said that *Beelzebub's Tales* is a failed experiment. Somebody said it, an experiment that failed. Maybe it failed, I don't know. I don't think so.

Q7: Thank you Will for your paper. I just wanted to come back to the egoism and love of mankind and something you quoted from the last chapter about the highest sense and aim of man's existence being the welfare of one's neighbour and this being exclusively at the sacrifice of one's own. But this is a very difficult page because it is preceeded by Gurdjieff saying that he is disappointed in these ideals which were instilled in him in his childhood. And there is this very difficult approach he has to being selfish, as it were, that to be a true altruist one has to be an egoist first. So I just wanted to bring that up.

WM: Yes. And we have to. I think we have to. We have to isolate ourselves for a period. I remember I worked for twenty years studying *Beelzebub* by myself and other people, very close people, and then after twenty years I published my first paper. It was 2000, and the first person who responded was Bonnie, because it was regarding the Stopinders. I remember Bonnie sent an email. Some people say, Who is Will Mesa? Nobody knew me. Because I was working twenty years. I wrote a book called *A Treatise on Cosmic Engineering - A Book of Initiation and Transmutation According to Law*. Now I spent twenty one years working on that book. I never published it, even though it is copyrighted in the Library of Congress twice. Because I wrote the book only to understand *Beelzebub's Tales*, or to try to work on that. So that is *egoismo*. And then you come out and you do whatever you have to do.

Q8: I'd like to bring up this problem maybe with *Beelzebub's Tales* is a failed experiment, or maybe the Lentrohamsanins in this world continue to destroy what is created. What I'd like to understand is where in the Third Striving we're asked to learn more and more about the laws of World-creation and World-maintenance. Now it's been my experience, and I think of many people here, that we have all this enthusiasm when we're creating. Now that we've built the house or painted the painting, whatever we've done, we become more divorced from it and we forget that it needs maintaining. So I wanted just to bring that up because in my own experience I look so much more to creation, but day to day I recognise that maintenance goes along with that creation. So now we have this experiment of *Beelzebub's Tales*, and you're raising the question, other people will raise the same question in their talks here and there, but how can we maintain? We get so excited with creativity, but golly, you get out the broom, you know the floor needs to be swept.

WM: For me it's very simple you know. We have to work with people who are working on this. That is my conclusion. That is why I went to work with a group in Chile, in Argentina, and everywhere. We have to work with people who are working on this. And you said it, the third striving is the most important, not the most important but the one that is the bridge between the personal and the cosmic. The first two are personal, the last two are cosmic. This one is the bridge. And we have to work. That's what I do, I get together with people and we go. I gather now a new group in Russia, in Moscow. We have a group in Moscow. And I have a group called *Bringing Beelzebub's Tales to Life*. That's my group. And it's amazing what people are doing. We are working there, I mean working through the internet.

You know something, if Mr Gurdjieff had been alive he would have been using the internet. There is absolutely no question for me. Because he was a bodhisattva. And in the four vows of the bodhisattva, the third one is, I vow to master an endless approach to dharma. So I use all the approaches to dharma. What did he do? He sent his music into the world. He was in New York, and he was giving a demonstration of Movements, and Olga de Hartmann asked him, 'Are we wasting our time here?' He said, 'How do you know we are wasting our time? What do you know if one person sitting there is going to awake right now? We don't know. We don't. So what did Mr Gurdjieff do? He went through the streets of Paris giving bonbons and candies to everybody in the street. Of course we are not him and we cannot do that. If I give a bonbon in Florida they will put me in jail, because maybe it's poisoned, you know. So we don't do that. But Mr Gurdjieff did it. And one guy asked him, 'Why did you give a candy to that woman?' 'You never know when she's going to need me.' You see, it's out there, out there where we have to do this, and try to live it. I'm sorry but I get emotional. A gringo, an American, told me, 'Only a Latino can understand *Beelzebub* because you are passionate.' So I get excited.

Visualizing Beelzebub's Tales

Derek Sinko

Abstract

Beelzebub's Tales is rich in material relating to sight and seeing. Vision has its basis in light, which as Beelzebub explains, the great Chinese brothers Choon-Kil-Tez and Choon-Tro-Pel proved through their invention Alla-attapan to be constituted according to the Law of Heptaparaparshinokh. Aspects of *Beelzebub's Tales* can be shown to be structured in accordance with this Law as well, some of which relate to sight. This paper explores sight in *Beelzebub's Tales* in an effort to uncover some of the hidden patterns of the book. I begin with an examination of two types of vision possessed by three-brained beings: Koritesnokhnian and Olooestesnokhnian. Along the way, some of the ideas falling under examination include: American fruit, chemicals invented by the Germans, the Amskomoutator, the ancient Egyptian observatory, Alla-attapan, Teleoghinooras and Korkaptilnian thought tapes, painting, devils and the path of the Karnak. I conclude by reflecting on the meaning of *"being-sight"* and finally suggest some aspects of *Beelzebub's Tales* for future study and possible application.

Visualizing Beelzebub's Tales

INTRODUCTION

Because of the advice given to readers by Gurdjieff to read *Beelzebub's Tales* *"Secondly - as if you were reading aloud to another person"* and because of the many neologisms, some of which are difficult to pronounce out loud, it seems that more attention has focused on the audio rather than the visual aspects of the book. While I do not wish to deny that the sonic aspects are an important element of the book - and indeed there is much interesting and informative material in *The Tales* relating to sound and language - *Beelzebub's Tales* is also a highly visual narrative work. This is as much because of what is not there as it is because of what is there. There is a notable lack of visually descriptive elements in terms of what characters and places look like. Much more consideration is given to how things, such as the numerous inventions and machines, work than what they look like, and it is left to the reader to create their own picturings and sketches. The descriptive emphasis is more on the behavioral and informational aspects of things rather than their surface effects.

The Alla-attapan, for example, is purported to demonstrate the commonalities of the structure of light, sound and opium: *"these three results in respect of the causes of their arising and outer manifestations have nothing in common with each other, yet the inner construction and* functioning are nevertheless exactly alike down to the smallest detail." (827) Interwoven in this device is "the Sacred Triamazikamno" (138) in its three parts and in terms of the "inner construction and functioning" of the "three results," reducible to "the law of Heptaparaparshinokh" (750) which is defined as "'The-line-of-the-flow-of-forces-constantly-deflecting-according-to-law-and-uniting-again-at-its-ends.'" (750) The reader, like Hassein, is directed to look beyond "outer manifestations" and into the essences of things.

With its great complexity, it can be difficult to discern the incredible orderliness of *Beelzebub's Tales*. Much of this paper is the result of trying to figure out how *Beelzebub's Tales* could be exact in the manner in which Gurdjieff described "real art" (*In Search of the Miraculous*, 26-7). My strategy has often been to identify various 'idea clusters' and attempt to cross-reference and compare where they occur elsewhere in the book. I have therefore tried to rely as much as possible on the internal evidence of *Beelzebub's Tales* itself. As should already be apparent, unless otherwise noted all citations refer to the 1950 Penguin edition of *Beelzebub's Tales*.

KORITESNOKHNIAN & OLOOESTESNOKHNIAN SIGHT

There are at least three types of vision in *Beelzebub's Tales*. Two relate to the organic functioning of the eye. They are: 1. The vision common to the three-brained beings of the Earth (especially contemporary humans), which has gradually been deteriorating - Beelzebub calls this type of sight "'Koritesnokhnian,' that is to say, into the sight proper to the presences of one-brained and two-brained beings" (305); 2. The vision of three-brained beings of the Earth who exist in a more "becoming" (1105) fashion than their contemporaries, and shared by three-brained beings of other planets - this type of sight is then that which is proper to the presences of three-brained beings. This type of sight can be thought of as an extension of the first type, attainable by humans through self-perfecting (469), and as a more complete form of sight from which the first devolved. It is manifested as an extra or super functioning of Koritesnokhnian sight. "'Olooestesnoknian sight'" (469) is one variety of this kind of sight. Another type of vision in *Beelzebub's Tales*, and perhaps the most essential for approaching it, is 3. what Beelzebub calls "being-sight." (151,161,585)

American Fruit Preserves & German Chemicals

Koritesnokhnian sight has to do with surfaces. To illustrate, let's look at some genuine advice given to readers of *Beelzebub's Tales*, said to be "the fundamental commandment given to three-brained beings from Above, namely, 'strive to acquire inner and outer purity.'" (948) Beelzebub says that of the seven aspects of this saying, Americans have taken one aspect "and in a distorted form have made [it] their ideal" (948-9) to "Help everything around you, both the animate and the still inanimate, to acquire a beautiful appearance." (949) "American fruit preserves" (949) are shown to be characteristic of such an ideal - according to Beelzebub "You have to see them for yourself to experience in your common presence the degree of the impulse of 'rapture' to which one can be carried on perceiving with the organ of sight the external beauty of these American fruit preserves." (949) However, when Beelzebub presents them to his companions, "all that was needed was to see their grimaces and the change of color on their faces to understand what effect these fruits have upon the organism of beings." (951) Significantly, Beelzebub uses the *"color on their faces"* to describe the reactions of his companions to American fruit preserves. Of all the possible ways to describe the disagreeable taste, it seems that this description was carefully chosen to emphasize the idea of sight via color and so connect this passage with other material related to vision.

To continue with American fruit preserves - Beelzebub relates it to two *"chemical substances"* (950) invented by Germans, *"'aniline' and 'alizarin'"* (950), appropriately recalling the chemical inventions of Germans in the chapter *"The Fruits of Former Civilizations."* Three of the five chemicals described by Beelzebub relate directly to the function of sight. Aniline *"is that chemical coloring substance, by means of which most of those surplanetary formations can be dyed from which the three-brained beings there make all kinds of objects they need in the process of their ordinary being-existence."* (428-9) The downside of this invention is that, unlike the *"simple vegetable dyes, which they had learned during centuries how to maintain"* (429) and used by humans to color objects and materials and which *"would formerly last from five to ten or even fifteen of their centuries"* (429), objects dyed with *"aniline, or to dyes of other names into which this same aniline enters as the basis, there remains of the objects dyed with the new colors at most, after about thirty years, only perhaps the memory of them."* (429) This rapid destruction of objects dyed with aniline is in keeping with one of the larger concerns of *The Tales*, "the transmission of true knowledge to distant generations." (459)

The second chemical, alisarine or alizarin *"is used there chiefly by what are called 'confectioners' and other specialists who prepare for the other beings of that planet most 'tasty' articles for their first food."* (431) This is done *"for that purpose which has already finally become the ideal for the whole of contemporary civilization"* (431); this time Beelzebub uses one of the sayings of Mullah Nassr Eddin to illustrate: *"'As-long-as-everything-looks-fine-and-dandy-to-me-what-does-it-matter-if-the-grass-doesn't-grow.'"* (431)

The third chemical invented by Germans which has a direct relationship to seeing, and possibly the most symbolically interesting since it deals directly with the eye, is atropine which when it is *"in a certain way introduced into the eyes of beings the pupils become dilated and darker; and because of this, most of them introduce atropine into their eyes, in order that their faces may appear good and pleasing to others."* (431) Like the two other chemicals, the results are counter-productive: *"so far there has never been a case there when a being using this means could see and still continue its use after the age of forty-five."* (431) When a pupil dilates it takes in more light, and in cases where the pupil dilates from atropine, the end result is blindness from trying to look good.

A correlation between the degradation of human eyesight and a naïve preference for surface appearances is also at play in the Egypt sequence where Beelzebub explains the loss of Olooestesnokhnian sight by humans, which had enabled them to perceive stars during the day (305). After Nature altered the eyesight of humans to the Koritesnokhnian variety, in addition to being able to view stars only at night, *"they perceive the visibility of objects only when almost* next to them." (305-6) This tragi-comic portrayal of the deterioration of human sight foreshadows a superficially unrelated account of the practical difficulties Beelzebub and his companions had in mooring the spaceship *Occasion*: "We had, it is true, the possibility of making our ship *Occasion* invisible to their organs of perception of visibility, but we could not annihilate its presence, and without this it could not remain stationary on the water because of the constant danger that their ships might bump into it." (528) These excerpts combine to create the image of humans unintentionally running into things which they do not have the visual acuity to perceive, while also connecting the theme of sight to the theme of space travel.

The unifying theme of Koritesnokhnian sight in *Beelzebub's Tales* is what Gurdjieff called "a growth of personality at the cost of essence" (*ISM*, 309). Because this first kind of sight is the degenerated sight possessed by most contemporary humans, it is ironic, and somewhat of a hidden joke in *The Tales* that the three-brained beings with the poorest eyesight have the most esteem for surface appearances. In this sense we can more fully appreciate Beelzebub's disparagement of contemporary art as "something which, although it continues to consist of, as it is said, 'complete vacuity,' yet has gradually collected about itself a fairylike exterior, which now 'blinds' every one of these favorites of yours who keeps his attention on it only a little longer than usual." (493) We can also more fully appreciate *Beelzebub's Tales* as something different, a true work of art that rewards "every one of these favorites of yours who keeps his attention on it only a little longer than usual." If contemporary art can be compared to American fruit preserves, then *Beelzebub's Tales* can similarly be compared to the spaceships *Occasion* and *Karnak*: the first are physically appealing on the outside but vacuous and even harmful on the inside; the others are at times invisible on the surface but consistently possess mass. Furthermore, the spaceship *Karnak* has transparent elements: "At the time of this narrative, Beelzebub with Hassein and his devoted old servant Ahoon…were seated on the highest "Kasnik," that is on the upper deck of the ship *Karnak* under the "Kalnokranonis," somewhat resembling what we should call a large "glass bell," and were talking there among themselves while observing the boundless space." (55)

By characterizing ordinary sight in this way, and through the clustering of such ideas in *The Tales* that refer back to similar themes in different contexts, we are directed to other kinds of seeing.

The second kind of vision depends on the work of self-perfecting to achieve a higher degree of being and therefore sight, since faculties or their absence are often presented as dependent on the degree of one's 'being-Reason,' as for example Gornahoor Harharkh's inability to "manifest himself in an absolutely empty space" (160). In the explanation of the degradation of human eyesight, three degrees of seeing are described which are superior to the ordinary vision of contemporary humans. Most contemporary humans can perceive 7 to 49 different colors, sometimes less (474). Of the total number of 5,764,801 tonalities of color "all the ordinary beings on whatever planet of our Great Universe they arise" (469) can perceive "a third" (469) of them. This was the kind of sight proper to humans before it was downgraded by Great Nature to the Koritesnokhnian variety. "But if the three-brained beings complete the perfecting of their highest part, their perceiving organ of visibility thereby acquires the sensibility of what is called 'Olooestesnokhnian sight,' then they can already distinguish two-thirds of the total number of tonalities existing in the Universe" (469). Olooestesnokhnian sight figures in other areas of *Beelzebub's Tales* such as the observatory of the ancient Egyptians, the Alla-attapan and Teleoghinooras.

The highest level of sight occurs when a being perfects "*their highest being-part to the state of what is called 'Ischmetch'*" (469-70) and thereby "*become able to perceive and distinguish all the mentioned number of blendings and tonalities*" (470) except for the one color that only HIS ENDLESSNESS can see (470). As we find out at the end of *The Tales*, Beelzebub has perfected his Reason to the degree of Podkoolad, the fourth highest possible degree of Reason (1177) and higher than the degree of Ischmetch - this is deduced because Ischmetch is described as a state that all three-brained beings can reach (1148) therefore it is not the degree of Reason that is higher than Anklad, these being the only two degrees besides that of HIS ENDLESSNESS that are higher than Podkoolad (1177). So, Beelzebub can see every color in the Universe except for one; this amounts to a sight that is around 100,000 to over 800,000 times more sensitive than the sight of most contemporary humans in terms of perceiving color. However, even with what from our perspective is greatly superior vision, Beelzebub and other three-brained beings with higher degrees of Reason occasionally make use of inventions to further enhance their vision.

The Amskomoutator

When Beelzebub was a participant in the experiments of Gornahoor Harharkh (pronounced as a raven's caw, the Saturnian neologisms being onomatopes for raven sounds) he was highly impressed by "*the connector created by that great scientist Gornahoor Harharkh to enable the 'organ-of-sight' of ordinary beings to perceive the visibility of all kinds of surrounding objects in an 'absolutely-empty-space.'*" (160) Beelzebub goes on to explain how "*this astonishing connector was fitted in a certain way, also by means of appliances on the helmets of our temples, while the other end was joined to what is called the 'Amskomoutator,' which in its turn was joined in a certain way by means of what are called 'wires' to all the objects with the Hrhaharhtzaha as well as to those outside, namely, to those objects whose visibility was needed during the experiments.*" (160-1) The Amskomoutator can be pictured as either a set of eyepieces or glasses, or as a kind of interface that causes objects to appear directly in the minds of the wearer, behind their eyes: "*these connectors and the said special 'magnetic-currents' had, it seems been created by that truly great scientist Gornahoor Harharkh in order that the presences of learned three-brained beings - even those not perfected to the Sacred Inkozarno - might, owing to one property of the 'magnetic current,' be 'reflected' for their own essences and that, owing to another property of this current, the presences of the mentioned objects might also be 'reflected,' so that thereby the perception of the reality of the said objects might be actualized by their imperfect organs of being-sight in a vacuum*" (161).

What Beelzebub seems to be describing here is a system of holograms used to circumvent the inability of beings to see in a vacuum. If this invention was included in early drafts of *Beelzebub's Tales* it would mean that Gurdjieff anticipated the 1947 invention of holography; the Amskomoutator almost certainly predates other ideas of electronically induced virtual reality.

Beelzebub's participation in Gornahoor Harharkh's experiments also connect to what was mentioned earlier about contemporary art on one hand and *Beelzebub's Tales* on the other, as in the experiments of Gornahoor Harharkh he and Beelzebub are in an artificially created vacuum.

The Ancient Egyptian Telescope & the Alla-attapan

The sequences of *Beelzebub's Tales* relating to Egypt have a strong visual component even though, as is characteristic of *The Tales*, we are not presented with descriptions of what people looked like, how they dressed or the aesthetics of their culture. We are however given descriptions of an ancient Egyptian observatory and the Sphinx. Since the present theme is visualizing *Beelzebub's Tales*, let's take a closer look at what Beelzebub has to say about the ancient Egyptian observatory, the more so as it "proved to be exceedingly ingenious and provided data for the enrichment of [Beelzebub's] common presence by a great deal of productive information for [his] consciousness." (304) Construction of the observatory "had begun long ago by one of what are called there 'Pharaohs'" (286) and was being "completed by his grandson, also a Pharaoh." (286) Similarly, Hassein is the heir to Beelzebub's legacy, and the observatory was being built "on the initiative issuing from the Reasons of the remote descendants of the member beings of the learned society Akhaldan." (306) The fact that the observatory was still under construction but was being completed by the grandson of the Pharaoh who started it mirrors Hassein's continuing education. This is also in accord with the Egyptian temples built over multiple generations, and a further connection is thus established with the spaceship *Karnak*.

Beelzebub goes out of his way to view the observatory under construction, the form of which although not explicitly stated, was probably a Pyramid since, according to Beelzebub, the Pyramids were used for observing cosmic concentrations in addition to weather control (308,311). Beelzebub tells more about how the observatory worked than what it looked like: "they placed this Teskooano very deeply within the planet, and they carried out their observations of cosmic concentrations found beyond the atmosphere of their planet through specially bored, pipelike hollows. The observatory, I then saw, had five of these hollows. They began, in relation to the horizon, from different places of the surface of the planet occupied by the observatory, but they all met at a small underground common hollow that was something like a cave." (307) The use of five hollows from which to gather light probably had the practical purpose of enabling the Astrologers (the operators of the observatory) to have a longer period of time to observe a particular cosmic concentration; one of the hindrances to observing "the cosmic points seen from their planets through their 'child's toys' called telescopes" (290) was that "they could see from the surface of their planet only those suns and planets which to their good fortune do not very quickly change the course of their falling in relation to their own planet and thus give them the possibility during a long period of time - of course long as compared with the brevity of their own existence - to observe them" (291). That the hollows penetrate the surface of the planet connects to the aforementioned surface level viewing of most of contemporary humanity.

Beelzebub compares his own observatory, which had a telescope designed by Gornahoor Harharkh (151) and incorporated elements of the ancient Egyptian observatory (307), with the one under construction by the ancient Egyptians and states that *"my seven long pipes were fixed not within the planet but on it."* (307) Beelzebub's observatory is on the planet Mars, so he has a bird's eye view of Earth - he descends from Mars to Earth (109) and ascends from Earth to Mars (206) - while the learned beings of Earth must utilize the Earth to the best of their abilities. Also, Mars is the red planet, and as we shall see, the color red is important in understanding the use of colors throughout *The Tales*.

It is interesting that Beelzebub draws a distinction between the number of apertures used in the ancient Egyptian observatory and his own because there is the same discrepancy between the Chinese (seven restorials) and Greek (five restorials) divisions of sound (860-1), and the relationship of light and sound recalls the Alla-attapan. These two inventions, the ancient Egyptian observatory and the Alla-attapan, also share the distinction of not being *"child's toys,"* (290,835) unlike two related inventions. As we have already seen, contemporary telescopes are considered by Beelzebub as *"child's toys"*; he uses the same phrase to describe the prism relative to the *"two crystals"* (835) that were parts of the *"'Loosochepana'"* (834) which was the *"fore part"* (834) of the Alla-attapan. Obviously both telescopes and prisms have the function of collecting and refocusing or dispersing light; Beelzebub's disparaging remarks concerning them suggests contemporary humanity's ignorance of light.

A deeper relationship emerges between the ancient Egyptian observatory and the Alla-attapan through the concept of Olooestesnokhnian sight. In addition to the utility of its five underground hollows, the ancient observatory also enabled humans with their degenerated, Koritesnokhnian sight *"to perceive freely at any time, as they say, 'of the day and night,' the visibility of all those remote cosmic concentrations which in the process of the general 'cosmic harmonious movement' come within the sphere of the horizon of their observation."* (306) The Alla-attapan utilized two crystals *"of special form"* (834) with *"which the great scientists obtained"* (835) what Beelzebub calls *"'positive colored rays'"* (835) in contrast to the prism from which *"only what are called 'negative colored rays'"* (835) can be obtained. Positive colored rays refer to light that lies outside of the visual spectrum; Beelzebub says that obtaining them is necessary *"in order to understand any other cosmic phenomena connected with the transitory changes of this white-ray."* (835) Like the light that is outside of the visual spectrum, star light during the daytime is invisible to humans with Koritesnokhnian sight. Based on these connections, through the use of *"child's toys,"* it can be deduced that Choon-Kil-Tez and Choon-Tro-Pel (the inventors of the Alla-attapan) could see stars during the day.

Also significant and *"in the highest degree an interesting and curious circumstance"* (823-4) is that the brothers Choon-Kil-Tez and Choon-Tro-Pel were the great grandsons of King Konuzion, who invented a *"'religious teaching'"* (824) to keep his subjects from chewing poppy, and the great twin scientists took the composition of opium as one of the three phenomenon to be studied with the Alla-attapan. As I will show, King Konuzion's 'religious teaching' figures in other material relating to sight.

After comparing the ancient Egyptian observatory with his own observatory on Mars, Beelzebub says that *"nevertheless all their innovations were so interesting in detail that, for any case that* might arise, I even made, during my stay there, a detailed sketch of everything I saw, and later even used something of it for my own observatory." (307) Might it not be the case that Gurdjieff is making a suggestion to readers to make their own sketches of *The Tales*? "Why not take example from what is good?" (654)

Teleoghinooras and Korkaptilnian Thought Tapes

The ideas of sight in *Beelzebub's Tales* are often transcendent of ordinary vision, leading to surprising patterns within *The Tales* themselves. One interesting example is that of Teleoghinooras and Korkaptilnian thought tapes, which were the means whereby Beelzebub learned about the origins of the society Akhaldan (293). A Teleoghinoora is defined as "a materialized idea or thought which after its arising exists almost eternally in the atmosphere of that planet on which it arises" (293) and Korkaptilnian thought tapes are "the sequential series of being-ideas, materialized in this way" (293). Beelzebub explains that these "being-ideas" can only be formed by three-brained beings who have perfected their Reason to a certain degree ('Martfotai') and can be "perceiv[ed] and cogniz[ed]" (294) by "every three-brained being in whose presence there has been acquired the ability to enter into the being-state called 'Soorptakalknian contemplation'" (294).

One of the connections between Teleoghinooras and Korkaptilnian thought tapes elsewhere in *The Tales* is the sympathetic and learned Hamolinadir who warned the citizens of Babylon that they were building the Tower of Babel in their debates about the soul, and who "became learned in Egypt where the highest school existing on Earth at that time was found, and which was called the 'School of Materializing-Thought'" (332). The name of this Egyptian school calls to mind the creation of Teleoghinooras and Korkaptilnian thought tapes, as well as by association the Egyptian Pyramids, used to view cosmic concentrations.

Teleoghinooras and Korkaptilnian thought tapes acquire another layer of meaning in relation to Beelzebub's descriptions of advertising. When Beelzebub first travels to New York City, he is in need of learning what he calls the "'American English language'" (932) and sees an advertisement for the "SCHOOL OF LANGUAGES BY THE SYSTEM OF MR. CHATTERLITZ" (932) which was "reflected on the sky, by projectors" (932), a description reminiscent of Teleoghinooras and Korkaptilnian thought tapes. Beelzebub refers to advertising as a "maleficent invention" (938) which replaced "that being-function which is everywhere called 'the sane instinct to believe in reality'" (928) with "a continuous doubt about everything" (938). This treatment of advertising, valid as it is on its own, is deepened if we imagine that advertisements projected in the sky might obscure the Teleoghinooras and Korkaptilnian thought tapes "deliberately fixed" (293) there by initiates. We can infer that the beings who perfected their Reasons to Martfotai were initiates and that access to the state of Soorptakalknian contemplation is a relatively rare occurrence because of Beelzebub's account of the invention of art as a method of transmitting information across generations through non-initiates. Such a method would not be required if non-initiates could place materialized thoughts in the sky or if past images could frequently be seen.

Also in connection with art, the advertisement for Mr. Chatterlitz's school was not the first advertisement that Beelzebub had come across in his travels on Earth. When he was in Babylon and needed to *"practice the Hellenic speech"* (435) Beelzebub *"saw on a large building which [he] had already many times passed, what is called an 'Ookazemotra,' or as it is now called, on the Earth, a 'signboard' which had been just put up and which announced that a club for foreign learned beings, the 'Adherents-of-Legominism,' had been newly opened in that building."* (452-3) The Adherents-of-Legominism (AOL) were, of course, the collective inventors of art, so that a simple comparison of Teleoghinooras and Korkaptilnian thought tapes with an advertisement projected on the sky over New York City gives us an interesting commentary on the distinctions between art and advertising, often conflated in today's world. Such an interpretation is reinforced by the fact that when Beelzebub encountered the advertisement for the AOL and the advertisement for Mr. Chatterlitz's school he was in both instances attempting to learn how to better speak the local language.

PAINTING & COLOR

Painting & the Law of Sevenfoldness

Beelzebub's account of the seven branches of art practiced by the AOL follow Gurdjieff's exposition of *"the discontinuity of vibrations"* (*ISM*, 123). The first interval of the seven tone scale occurs between mi and fa (*ISM*, 127 fig.13) and by substituting the seven notes with the seven branches of art in the order of the days on which they are presented, this interval occurs between Wednesday and Thursday - between *"the 'day-of-painting'"* (464) and *"the 'day-of-religious-and-popular-dances.'"* (464)

In Beelzebub's description of the first day, Monday, *"the 'day-of-religious-and-civil-ceremonies'"* (465) we are presented with a relatively concise account of what occurred: *"'fragments-of-knowledge' that had been previously selected for transmission, were indicated by means of inexactitudes in the Law of Sevenfoldness, chiefly in the inexactitudes of the lawful movements of the participants in the given ceremonies."* (465) And *"by a conventional what is called 'alphabet,' those ideas which they intended should be transmitted through these ceremonies to the men-beings of their remote descendants."* (465) In the description of the second day, *"the 'day-of-architecture,'"* (465) the architects of the AOL practiced the same technique of using lawful inexactitudes in the Law of Sevenfoldness to transmit information, although obviously in this case the knowledge was passed on through buildings rather than through the participants of dances and ceremonies. However, instead of giving one example as in the description of what was done on Mondays, Beelzebub gives two examples (466) and then explains a new concept, *"Daivibrizkar"* (466), before briefly mentioning that it *"utterly failed to reach the contemporary three-brained beings of that planet"* (466) and finally gives an example of its utilization by the architects of the AOL. (This gradual imparting of more information possibly relates to the different ratios *"or the frequency of vibrations"* (*ISM*, 123 fig.11) of the notes in an octave.)

It becomes more apparent that Gurdjieff has interwoven the structure of the octave into *The Tales* in Beelzebub's lengthier account of *"Wednesdays - the-day-of-painting - [which] were devoted to the combining of different colors."* (467) After substituting the seven notes of an octave with the seven branches of art, it is seen that the day-of-painting corresponds to the note mi, the note before the first interval or gap. Beelzebub describes the objects and materials used by the painters of the AOL and then interrupts the flow of the narrative he had established to discuss the gradual deterioration of the eyesight of humans (468). Next he says, *"I am speaking about what is called the 'common-integral vibration of all sources of actualizing,' namely, about that which the learned being Aksharpanziar, of whom I spoke, called the 'white ray' and about the perceptions of impressions from separate 'blendings of gravity center vibrations' which are distinguished by beings as separate what are called 'tonalities-of-color."* (468) This statement nicely bridges the gap between the subject of painting and the subject of eyesight, the *"white ray,"* or light, being the common element - the medium - between them.

To sum up: the flow of the narrative deviates from the different branches of art of the AOL to a discussion of sight, light and color precisely where we would expect to find an interval in the seven tone scale after substituting the seven musical notes with the seven branches of art in their given order. (A detailed analysis of the remaining branches of art in the program of the AOL and their relationship to a sevenfold structure is beyond the scope of the present paper; it is hoped that enough internal evidence has been presented to convey something of the patterns at play.) Since *Beelzebub's Tales* is itself a work of art, one might expect the chapter titled *"Art"* would contain important information relating to its structure. Several elements of *The Tales* lead one to conclude that the *"sacred 'Heptaparaparshinokh'"* (84) is an important element of its structure. One is the emphasis that Beelzebub places on teaching Hassein about its details: *"Try very hard to understand everything that will relate to both these fundamental sacred laws, since knowledge of these sacred laws, particularly knowledge relating to the particularities of the sacred Heptaparaparshinokh, will help you in the future to understand very easily and very well all the second-grade and third-grade laws of World-creation and World-maintenance."* (755)

There is also a key passage in the chapter *"Purgatory"* where Beelzebub begins his explanations *"about the fundamental cosmic laws by which our present World is maintained and on the basis of which it exists"* (748) by describing the origin of the *"'Megalocosmos,' i.e. our World."* (749) Beelzebub says that *"In the beginning, when nothing yet existed and when the whole of our Universe was empty endless space with the presence of only the prime-source cosmic substance 'Etherokrilno,' our present Most Great and Most Most Holy Sun Absolute existed alone in all this empty space, and it was on this then sole cosmic concentration that our UNI-BEING CREATOR with HIS cherubim and seraphim had the place of HIS most glorious Being."* (748-9) In this sentence there are seven elements: 1. time (*"In the beginning, when"*); 2. *"empty endless space"*; 3. *"'Etherokrilno'"*; 4. the *"Most Holy Sun Absolute"*; 5. *"our UNI-BEING CREATOR"*; 6. *"HIS cherubim"*; and 7. HIS *"seraphim"*. The CREATOR *"with HIS cherubim and seraphim"* indicate *"the sacred Triamazikamno"* (750) while the seven elements obviously indicate the Law of Heptaparaparshinokh. If the CREATOR, cherubim and seraphim are taken together as one element, then the Laws of Triamazikamno and Heptaparaparshinokh themselves are the two remaining elements in the origin of the Megalocosmos.

The interval between the day-of-painting and the day-of-religious-and-popular-dances corresponds to the lengthened *"Stopinder between its third and fourth deflections."* (754) By making use of this *"lawful inexactitude,"* Gurdjieff, like the learned painters of the AOL *"indicated various useful information and fragments of knowledge"* (475). In this instance the information has to do with color, light and seeing. For example there is a correspondence between the materials used by the painters of the AOL - *"colored threads"* (475) - with Hassein's statement to Beelzebub that *"the need of periodically occupying themselves with the destruction of each other's existence, runs like a crimson thread through all your tales."* (1055-6) The *"crimson thread"* as symbolic of blood also relates to the cross-generational transmission of knowledge, which was the purpose of the formation of the AOL (459-60).

These considerations taken together with what can be gathered from Gurdjieff's teachings regarding *"objective art"* (*ISM*, 296-7) leave little doubt that the patterns in *Beelzebub's Tales* are intentional. Even the capitalizing of the word *"THIS"* (449) at the beginning of the chapter *"Art"* is significant because *Beelzebub's Tales* is a work of art utilizing the same principals as those used by the AOL - it is *"At THIS place of his tales"* (449) that the self-referential, fractal structure based on lawful inexactitudes in the Law of Sevenfoldness becomes clearly visible. This may seem frivolous; however, no other chapter of *The Tales* begins in such a way, with a seemingly randomly capitalized word in the first sentence.

Finally, consider this statement by Beelzebub, made prior to his explanation of the methods and program of the AOL: *"A brief interval was then allowed for eating, after which they all assembled again, and the second general meeting of that day continued throughout the night."* (463, italics added) This statement accomplishes at least three things in addition to helping to explain how the AOL organized themselves: it plays off of the connections between appearances and food in other parts of *The Tales*; it suggests Gurdjieff's teachings on the types of food and the processes of nutrition (*ISM*, 181-92), particularly impressions; and it alerts the attentive reader to the use of the octave in the structuring of the chapter *"Art."*

Color

Color is used sparingly and deliberately in *Beelzebub's Tales*. There are entire chapters which have no mention of colors: this is partly because of the author's distaste of 'bon ton' writing that also contributes to the lack of visual descriptions of characters and places, and partly because he is following the program of the AOL in its use of *"colored threads"*. *"So, whenever the Babylonian learned painters wove or embroidered with colored threads or colored their productions, they inserted the distinctions of the tonalities of the colors in the crosslines as well as in the horizontal lines and even in the intersecting lines of color, not in the lawful sequence in which this process proceeds, in accordance with the Law of Sevenfoldness, but otherwise; and in these also lawful 'otherwises,' they placed the contents of some or other information or knowledge."* (475) One of

Visualizing Beelzebub's Tales

the things this means for *Beelzebub's Tales* as a work of art is the repetition of similar themes in different contexts (as with for example, angels and devils) throughout the book. This methodology is used by Gurdjieff in the furtherance of the stated purpose of the book and also suggests a self-referential, fractal structure (based in some measure on the Laws of Three and Seven), indicating that writing can be thought of as an eighth branch of art. This technique works very well for a detailed narrative as a yarn is a synonym for a tale, and one often hears of writers spinning or weaving them. So, when colors do appear in *Beelzebub's Tales* they are like signs pointing the way to what Hassein calls *"new and interesting information"* (59). To illustrate, let's examine some of the colors in *The Tales*, how they are used and what information they point to.

Perhaps the most striking example is the aforementioned *"crimson thread"* running through *The Tales*. In addition to its connotations of war and blood and therefore the cross-generational transmission of knowledge - as for instance the importance of *"the voluntary undertaking of an obligation, especially when signed with his blood"* (114) to a member of Beelzebub's tribe - there are in light of the methodology of the painters of the AOL several further connections. If one were to mix the first color of the visible spectrum, red, with the last, violet, one would obtain a shade of crimson. In this way the color crimson in a sense traverses the rainbow, just as it traverses *The Tales*. Another link is established through the chemical compound alizarin which itself is crimson and is used in crimson pigments. So the *"crimson thread"* running through *Beelzebub's Tales* literally stitches together the ideas of sight, color and the cross-generational transmission of knowledge.

Another example of the deliberate use of colors in *The Tales* occurs in the chapter *"Art"* in the context of what at first glance appears to be three arbitrary and perhaps chauvinistic punishments for women in the Tikliamishian civilization who had shown one of four manifestations. *"Namely, if all her neighbors noticed, and the seven mentioned elderly women confirmed it, that the woman had behaved without due regard to and negligently towards her family duties, then according to the law she had for a definite term to appear everywhere with painted lips."* (510-11) Note that the word *"painted"* is used, in the same chapter in which Beelzebub tells about the program of the painters of the AOL, and that seven women presided over the enforcement of the punishment.

Next, *"if the various women noticed that she had begun to manifest toward her children with a weakening of her maternal impulses, then under the same conditions those around her condemned her to go about everywhere, also for a definite term, with the left half of her face made up and painted white and red."* (511) White and red mix together to create the color pink, usually thought of as the quintessential feminine color. So why *"white and red"* instead of 'pink'? Beelzebub uses the same way of referring to a color as two colors elsewhere - the color red, as the color of an *"abnormal orange-crimson growth of a peculiar strange form"* (1079) on the *"left paw"* (1079) of a flea that bit *"the neck of a certain historical King Nokhan"* (1079) and causing it to *"swell"* (1079) according to an *"expert in fleas"* (1079). Both of these instances refer back to *"the Babylonian learned painters"* who knew that *"one of the separate colors of the white ray always ensues from another and is transformed into a third, as, for example, the orange color is obtained from the red, and further itself passes in its turn into yellow, and so on and so forth."* (475) Since the color red is implicated in both instances, in the first as one of two colors creating a third, and in the other as the result of two other colors, is also one of the colors specifically mentioned by Beelzebub as an example of the combination of colors, and furthermore relates to the planet Mars and thus the sequences having to do with observatories, there can be little doubt as to the precise use to which colors are used in *Beelzebub's Tales*.

Before passing on to the color orange ourselves, other connections regarding the punishment of Tikliamishian women are worth mentioning. Being made to wear pink paint on the left side of their faces was the second punishment for the second infraction. The third and fourth infractions applied to "*a woman who attempted to violate her chief what is called 'wifely duty,' that is who deceived her legal husband or who attempted to destroy a new being conceived in her*" (511) and incurred the third punishment, being "*obliged by the same procedure to be always and everywhere, also for a definite term, made up and painted white and red, this time over the whole of her face.*" (511) The use of three punishments for four different infractions indicates the law of seven. That the punishments are made manifest plays off of the concepts of Koritesnokhnian sight and American fruit preserves - instead of covering up supposed flaws, they are made explicit. That the punishments are made manifest in different sequences, on the face, suggests the program of the sculptors of the AOL: "*The facial dimensions of every three-centered being in general, and also the facial dimensions of the three-centered beings of the planet Earth who have taken your fancy, are the result of the dimensions of seven different fundamental parts of the whole of his body, and the dimension of each separate part of the face is the result of seven different dimensions of the whole face.*" (477)

If Beelzebub calling pink "*white and red*" and red "*orange-crimson*" are significant, perhaps the contexts in which he uses them relate to one another? They do. Despite being wildly different on their surfaces, both have to do with moral indignation. Seven women "*who had earned respect by their previous conduct*" (510) enforce the punishment of pink face painting on Tikliamishian women. I suspect many women would be indignant at the injustice of what amounts to public humiliation for deceiving their husbands or getting an abortion (though "*a new being conceived in her*" may just as well relate to higher being-bodies), especially since these punishments are described as "*a very sensible what is called 'measure-of-justice'*" (510). The moral indignation of the "*expert*" who claims that the flea that bit King Nokhan had a red growth on its left paw is more explicit: "*if this expert in fleas there will write his voluminous work or if he will read for a whole evening his popular lecture on the 'orange-crimson growth' on the mentioned flea, then if anyone will express his doubt to his face, he will not only be offended but even greatly indignant; and he will be indignant chiefly because this somebody is such a what is called 'ignoramus,' that he has even not yet heard anything about the 'truths' communicated to him by this 'expert.'*" (1079) Before finishing his tale about the punishment of pink face painting exacted upon Tikliamishian women for what "*were considered there, for women, as the greatest laxity and immorality*" (510), Ahoon interrupts Beelzebub, which brings us to the color orange.

Lucifer, a Karatian like Beelzebub, is mentioned seven times in *Beelzebub's Tales* (*Guide & Index*, 366). This conforms to the well-known sense of his name, the light-bringer. Of these seven

Visualizing Beelzebub's Tales

times we hear of the *"Arch-cunning Lucifer"* (338) two of them relate to color and both instances suggest the gap between the day-of-painting and the day-of-religious-and-popular-dances. (Note that 7 divided by 2 is 3.5, indicating the gap between the 3rd and 4th days.) These instances leave no question as to the masterful use of color in *Beelzebub's Tales*, and additionally reinforce one another. In regards to the question of *"whether they had a soul and whether it was immortal"* (804), *"they having fallen under the influence of this psychosis, mixed into the Legominisms concerning the holy planet Purgatory and handed down such a "Kha-boor-Chooboor' that the tail of our Lucifer from pleasurable emotion turned a shade of what is called the color 'tango.'"* (804) Tango is both a color and a dance, further indicating the interval between the day-of-painting and the day-of-religious-and-popular-dances. Also the mixing of *"the Legominisms concerning the holy planet Purgatory,"* is suggestive of the skies of Purgatory, which *"reflected, as it were the radiance which recalls the radiance of the famous and incomparable 'Almacornian turquoise.'"* (746) Turquoise is a mixture of blue and green and if mixed with the color tango would, since blue and orange are complementary colors, produce a shade of gray. This leads to the other instance of Lucifer the light-bringer and colors.

In reference to the limited experiencings of *"the caste of the bureaucrats"* (1088) Beelzebub remarks that *"It is said that about this same puzzling question, that is, about how these terrestrial types manage to exist on the surface of the planet, even the great cunning Lucifer once grew very thoughtful, and he grew so intensely thoughtful that all the hairs of the tip of tail turned quite gray."* (1088) In the gap between the day-of-painting and the day-of-religious-and-popular-dances, we hear about a strand of Babylonian painters: *"This peculiar movement of the painters of that time had the following program: 'To-find-out-and-elucidate-the-Truth-only-through-the-tonalities-existing-between-white-and-black,"* (472) and by the time Beelzebub knew of these painters *"its followers were already using for their productions about fifteen hundred very definite shades of the 'color gray.'"* (472)

Back to the color orange, it figures prominently in the last chapter of *The Tales* proper, *"The Inevitable Result of Impartial Mentation."* The casket containing the sacred rod which, through Beelzebub's kinsmen, restores his horns *"radiated...something orange."* (1174) Recalling the relationships between Lucifer and the color orange, the means whereby Beelzebub gets his horns back acquires deeper meanings than would be apparent through a surface level reading of the narrative. Beelzebub's horns are restored through the sacred rod held by Beelzebub's kinsmen *"and on the length of time the handle of the sacred rod is held will depend on the amount of active elements passing from your own horns for the formation of the corresponding horns on this pardoned being of your nature."* (1175-6) Why is the instrument a sacred *rod*? It could just as well have been a staff or a wand, or an altogether differently shaped instrument. Rods, along with cones, are parts of the eye which absorb and transmit light to the other parts of the eye.

To establish that the particular use of a rod is not merely a happy coincidence, since English was far from being Gurdjieff's first language, consider that other puns and plays on words occur in *The Tales*. For example, the beings existing in drops of water have *"even 'periods-of-thirst-for-self-perfection,'"* (126) indicating that perfection can be conceived of as a dissolution in a higher cosmos. There is also the relationship between tales and tails which we will explain shortly. And the Alla-attapan, a device intimately connected with light, *"The first part which was named Loosochepana had a special cone-shaped pipe, the wide end of which was hermetically fitted into the frame of the sole window of that room where the experiments were made"* (834). A *"cone-shaped pipe"* transmitted the light into the other parts of the machine, initiating its functioning. So we have both rods and cones connected with light.

Taken together, the process of the restoration of Beelzebub's horns - their being made visible - by his kinsmen, beings of his nature, constitutes an elegant summation of *The Tales* as a work of art. The longer the rod is held - the longer one pays attention to it - the more active elements go into restoring Beelzebub's horns, the more his wisdom is made manifest - the more one partakes of his nature. Beelzebub's horns are described as having *"forks"* (1176) and *"by their number the gradation of Reason to which Beelzebub had attained according to the sacred measure of Reason would be defined."* (1176) Forks can be thought of as branches, and Beelzebub refers to *"special branches of knowledge"* (298) of the society Akhaldan, different means of artistic expression as branches (519) as well as *"independent branches of their what is called 'exact science'"* (859). Similarly, the achievements of Choon-Kil-Tez and Choon-Tro-Pel can be understood as a different branching of Akhaldan from some of the Egyptians who were *"the remote descendants of the members of the great learned society Akhaldan"* (313).

DEVILS

Beelzebub doesn't get around to explaining why his name has been confused by humans with some kind of a demonic entity until near the end of his tales starting on page 1143 in the tale I call "Those Karatian Devils." In this brief but detailed story Beelzebub tells how a religious teaching based on the notion of external good and evil coincided with most of the Karatians departing from Earth. Because members of Beelzebub's tribe live longer than humans, they were thought to be immortal. When HIS ENDLESSNESS requested that as many of the Karatians as possible leave Earth (1142), it was suggested by followers of the said religious teaching that the Karatians were really 'Devils,' or spirits that cause humans to perform evil deeds. In the notions of the believers of this religious teaching, these devils became invisible because of the removal of the power of suggestion in the faithful - they were unaware that the Karatians had actually left Earth at the request of HIS ENDLESSNESS - and they didn't see them leave.

In this tale there are many elements that refer back to other parts of *The Tales*: invisible spirits, the power of suggestibility (and therefore the organ Kundabuffer), varying lifespans amongst three-brained beings, space travel and the cross-generational transmission of knowledge. One sense in which sight in this tale relates to the idea of devils is that they are supposed to only be visible when not under the power of suggestion and *"just these same Devils who, foreseeing the arising of a true religious teaching and fearing that people in consequence would perhaps 'find them out,' made themselves invisible but continued in reality to exist among them."* (1143) In relation to Beelzebub's many other tales, just the opposite was the case: the Karatians weren't really devils, when they were on Earth they were visible, and most of them had left Earth.

Beelzebub goes on to explain that *"It was then that the real names of many beings of our tribe, which also chanced to reach in the said manner the beings of the period when this mentioned religious teaching appeared, acquired a greater special meaning and, passing from generation to generation, these names even reached to your contemporary favorites."* (1143) The most infamous of these names is Lucifer which we have seen leads us back to the familiar themes of light, vision and color. The reader can infer why Beelzebub and Lucifer are thought of as devils and why the horns, tails and hoofs of their species (64) are considered physical and symbolic characteristics of devils.

Although Beelzebub doesn't explain until near the end of his tales how the beings of his tribe came to be misconstrued by humans as devils, the origin of the idea of devils can be traced to the teaching King Konuzion invented in an attempt to stop the people of his community from ingesting opium through the character "Mister God" (216). In this teaching it is described how there *"exist many 'spirits' attendant upon Him, who walk among us in 'caps-of-invisibility,' thanks to which they can constantly watch us unnoticed and either inform our Mister God of all our doings or report them to Him on the 'Day-of-Judgement.'"* (217) In this iteration of the tales of invisible spirits, the spirits invented by King Konuzion who report misdeeds with the possible result of a sentence to the small island "Hell" (218) are prototypical devils. They do not however try to influence people as was the case in the Babylonian dualistic teaching where *"it was said that as soon as a man is born, two invisible spirits immediately perch upon his shoulders. On his right shoulder sits a 'spirit-of-good' called an 'angel,' and on his left, a second spirit, a 'spirit-of-evil' called a 'devil,'"* (339) and that *"Among the duties of these two spirits is that of suggesting and compelling a man to do more of those manifestations which are in their respective domains."* (340) In King Konuzion's tale, the invisible spirits merely record and report their observations, whereas in further elaborations of the premise of invisible spirits they suggest and compel, eventually leading to *"a 'world view' [which] is formed in them based exclusively on that maleficent idea about external Good and Evil."* (1141)

A further twist is added to the tales about angels and devils when Beelzebub inserts his own invention into the religious teaching of King Konuzion. *"I invented that those spirits in 'caps-of-invisibility' who, as it was said in that great religion, watch our deeds and thoughts in order to report them later to our Mister God, are none other than just the beings of other forms, which exist among us."* (220) Beelzebub did this in order to further the cause of his second descent - the Angel Looisos, inventor of the Kundabuffer (88) suggested to him that it would be *"a great service to our UNI-BEING ALL-EMBRACING ENDLESSNESS"* (183) if he were to help rid the Earth of animal sacrifices by humans.

Appropriately, the organ Kundabuffer was "caused to grow in the three-brained beings there, in a special way, at the base of their spinal column, at the root of their tail - which they also at that time, still had, and which part of their common presences furthermore still had its normal exterior expressing the, so to say, 'full-ness-of-its-inner-significance'" (88-9). The organ Kundabuffer is thus an antecedent to Beelzebub's religious invention; both are deliberate deceptions inserted into tails and tales for what is supposed to be the greater good. About his own tail, Beelzebub says that (when facing potential examination by a physician) *"if I had bared myself, I should inevitably have betrayed my tail which there on your planet I skillfully hid under the fold of my dress."* (608) Beelzebub's clothing can be read as the surface level of *Beelzebub's Tales*.

THE PATH OF THE FALLING OF THE KARNAK

When we first meet Beelzebub, Hassein and Ahoon they are traveling from their home planet Karatas to the planet Revozvradendr to attend a *"special conference."* (51) They arrive there at the conclusion of Beelzebub's and Ahoon's tales about art (523) whereupon they begin their journey home. Most of the information relating to the places that the *Karnak* travels through and its periodic stops on the way back to Karatas is detailed in the chapter *"A Change in the Appointed Course of the Falling of the Transspace Ship* Karnak*"* (657-9).

There are a couple of considerations suggesting that the path taken by the *Karnak* is not frivolous or arbitrary, the obvious being that if it were there would be little sense in devoting a chapter to its change of course. Another is Beelzebub's request to the Captain of the *Karnak* that they stop at the planet Deskaldino to visit Beelzebub's first teacher before going to Karatas. Beelzebub tells the Captain *"that I am giving you no easy task"* (658) indicating that the path of the *Karnak* has some significance which has to be uncovered by the reader's ingenuity.

In fact, by making this suggestion to the Captain, we are able to situate Deskaldino between Purgatory and Karatas, since Beelzebub's request is to visit that planet *"after the visit to the holy planet Purgatory."* (657-8) The difficulty, as explained by the Captain, is that *"in the present case, on the direct route between the holy planet Purgatory and the planet Deskaldino, there lies the solar system called Salzmanino, in which there are many of those cosmic concentrations which, for purposes of the general cosmic Trogoautoegocratic process, are predetermined for the transformation and radiation of the substances Zilnotrago; and therefore the direct falling of our ship Karnak, unhindered, will scarcely be possible"* (659); thus, Salzmanino is situated between Purgatory and Deskaldino.

Earlier in their conversation, the Captain tells Beelzebub that *"we shall soon be passing through the solar system Khalmian, and if having passed this system we do not direct the falling of our ship immediately more to the left, we shall greatly lengthen the path of its falling"* (657); the Captain mentions this because of Beelzebub's wish to visit Purgatory on his way home. Therefore the solar system Khalmian is between Revozvradendr and Purgatory.

One further episode, in the final chapter, relates to the path of the *Karnak* - the encounter with the Egolionopty (1173), which like the namesakes of the ships *Occasion* and *Omnipresent* also happens to be an event. Situating the meeting of the Egolionopty with the passengers of the *Karnak* gives seven points including the point of departure (Revozvradendr) and the destination (Karatas). We are now in a position to plot the path of the *Karnak* on its journey back to Karatas.

Visualizing Beelzebub's Tales

Although the Law of Falling makes a vertical or horizontal path arbitrary since *"Everything existing in the World falls to the bottom. And the bottom for any part of the Universe is its nearest "stability," and this said "stability" is the place or the point upon which all the lines of force arriving from all directions converge"* (66), I have chosen to plot the points horizontally since *"falling"* generally has the connotation of moving from up to down, and because the various lists of seven aspects of a phenomenon, such as days of the week (464) and colors (474) are presented in such a manner in the text. So now let's plot the path of the *Karnak* on its return journey accordingly:

1. Revozvradendr
2. Khalmian
3. *"immediately more to the left"* - Purgatory
4. Salzmanino
5. Deskaldino
6. Egolionopty
7. Karatas

There are a few things to be observed here. One is that the structure doesn't exactly mirror that of the program of the AOL because the gap indicated by steering the *Karnak* to the left takes place between the 2nd and 3rd points, and not between the 3rd and 4th. The structure does however correspond to the structure of a lateral octave within a descending octave wherein the lateral octave begins after the note fa. (ISM, 139) Adopting this schema, the planet Revozvradendr corresponds to the place where *"sol of the cosmic octave, begins at a certain moment to sound as do, sol-do."* (ISM, 139) This allows us to make sense of the initial journey from Karatas to Revozvradendr as well, as here there are only two points mentioned as being between the two planets: *"the solar system 'Vuanik'"* (56) and *"the great comet belonging to that solar system and named 'Sakoor' or, as it is sometimes called, the 'Madcap'"* (56) so that Karatas is do of the initial octave, Vuanik is si, the comet Madcap is la and Revozvradendr is sol in the initial journey, and turns to do on the return journey.

The directive of steering the ship *"immediately to more the left"* allows us to picture the path of the *Karnak* as circular, spiral and three-dimensional in accordance with the omni-directional nature of the Law of Falling and the statement that *"there are no straight lines in nature."* (ISM, 127) Intriguingly if, for the sake of symmetry, we picture points 5 through 7 as steering back to the right, with point 4 as a fixed in the middle, we would obtain the familiar s-shaped curvature of the yin-yang symbol. This seems satisfactory as it can also model *"The System of Archangel Hariton,"* (70-2) the *"'perpetual motion'"* (73) machine which propels the *Karnak* through space, in which *"the lid of the cylinder-barrel alternately opens and shuts."* (71) The directive of steering *"immediately more to the left"* means that the *Karnak* was already going to the left, further conforming to this schema.

CONCLUSIONS

Being-Sight

Beelzebub uses the phrase 'being-sight' three times in his tales (*G&I*, 552). The first time it is used it is in reference to his ability to *"relatively easily see and observe the processes of the existence occurring on the surfaces of those parts of the other planets of that solar system which, in accordance with what is called the 'common-cosmic Harmonious-Movement,' could be perceived by being-sight at the given moment."* (151)

The second time this phrase is used it is in reference to the Amskomoutator enabling visibility in a vacuum. The third time it is used is in reference to Beelzebub's recollections regarding his impressions of Egypt: *"But now, as I was speaking, of this contemporary Egypt and there was revived before my 'being-sight' pictures of certain localities of that part of the terra firma surface of the planet which had once pleased me, the faint impressions I had previously of this said event there became gradually coated in me into a definite awareness and to be clearly recollected in me."* (586)

It should be clear that in all three instances where Beelzebub uses this phrase, it indicates visibility where ordinarily there would be none. All three instances are also tied in with sequences of *The Tales* that are connected with vision in additional ways: Beelzebub's observatory on Mars, the experiments of Gornahoor Harharkh and the sights of Egypt. 'Being-sight' thus refers to sight attained with a being's *"entire," "total,"* or *"whole presence"* (*G&I*, 477).

Suggestions for Further Study & Applications

In this paper I have only scratched the surface of the depths of *Beelzebub's Tales*. Particularly in regards to color I hope to have shown that a complete and thorough study of its use in *The Tales* is in order. For instance, I did not touch upon the color green and its possible connections to the taste sensations of the passengers of the *Karnak* (742-3, 917) and the use of *"green tea"* (194, 889). The points on the path of the *Karnak* may relate to a color schema - if this can be shown, it will be because the inner structuring of *Beelzebub's Tales* relates to a conception of *"the universe as consisting of vibrations. These vibrations proceed in all kinds, aspects and densities of the matter which constitutes the universe, from the finest to the coarsest; they issue from various sources and proceed in various directions, crossing one another, colliding, strengthening, weakening, arresting one another, and so on."* (*ISM*, 122) The Alla-attapan, the Lav-merz-nokh, and the scientific experiments of Hadji Asvatz Troov all suggest this to be the case. A similar study could be undertaken in respect to the numbers (many of which are divisible by 7) used in *Beelzebub's Tales*.

More fancifully, there is the possibility that *The Tales* contains a hidden musical score. There are numerous references to sound and sound producing instruments, beginning with Gurdjieff's assertion that *"this new venture of mine will now proceed, as is said, "like a pianola.""* (3)

Plotting out Beelzebub's travels through the universe, our solar system and the planet Earth looks eerily similar to musical scales. Other material suggestive of this are the few occasions where Western artists are referred to in *The Tales* - Pythagoras (an original member of the AOL), Ignatius (521), Leonardo da Vinci (522), Bocaccio (936) and briefly Shakespeare (142), Beethoven (1015) and Chopin (1015). Beelzebub spends the most time discussing Pythagoras, then Ignatius and Leonardo da Vinci and then Bocaccio, whose *Decameron*, like *Beelzebub's Tales*, has a frame story in which other stories are told. It has been speculated by others that Leonardo's painting *The Last Supper* contains a hidden musical score, so I don't think it improbable that *Beelzebub's Tales* could.

Finally, the experiments of Gornahoor Harharkh would, if done well, make for an amazing animated short film with the numerous *"special and very strange"* (153) apparatuses, Gornahoor Harharkh's intriguing manner of pointing *"with a particular feather of his right wing"* (153), and the perches of the Saturnian beings *"carved with all kinds of figures"* (1155). When Gornahoor Harharkh speaks, it could be done in raven song, with subtitles underneath.

WORKS CITED

Guide & Index to Gurdjieff's All and Everything: Beelzebub's Tales to His Grandson. 3rd ed. Toronto: Traditional Studies Press, 1979. Print.

Gurdjieff, G.I. *Beelzebub's Tales to His Grandson: An objectively impartial criticism of the life of man.* 1950. New York: Penguin Arkan, 1999. Print.

Ouspensky, P.D. *In Search of the Miraculous: The Teachings of G.I. Gurdjieff.* Orlando: Harcourt, Inc., 1949. Print.

© Copyright 2012 - Derek Sinko - All Rights Reserved

Visualizing Beelzebub's Tales - Questions & Answers

Q1: Well thank you, that was very good. I like it. Now I have one question, because you said in the beginning that your interest is in art, and I see that you've done a lot of work with the chapter *"Art"*...

A: Mm-hmm

Q1: ...and the club of Adherents of Legominism.

A: Right.

Q1: Now, my question to you is this: have you been able to visualize inexactitudes in the book, or lawful otherwises?

A: I thought that the instance of utilizing the...if you read the chapter on art and the descriptions of the different branches of art practiced on each successive day, they start very simple and gradually become more complex, and where you'd look for the 1st gap, between the 3rd and 4th day, it just goes on and on with all this information about light and the deterioration of human sight. So to me the inexactitudes they were utilizing were the gaps in the octave.

Q2: I thought your presentation was genius...

A: Well thank you so much.

Q2: ...really engaging for me, it took me to a whole new way of looking at *The Tales* which I don't fully understand, I admit to.

A: I don't think anyone fully understands the book.

Q2: But I suppose they're to be studied which is what you're doing...

A: Uh-huh

Q2: ...and I have a question about the process. When, where, how did this come to you? What was the process in your mind, was it like in the wee hours or as a result of a course or professor or walks in the park, or how did all this start to take shape in your mind? And will you add to it? I think you ought to keep it going.

A: Well thanks. As far as the process, when I read the book for a 3rd time, I took note of every single possible category, everything I could think of, like I noted all of the characters, all of the places, every time Beelzebub repeats himself, and as many things as I could think of. And to me there's a lot of material suggesting that the structure of the octave would be one of the underlying structures of it, and kind of matching it up with material about vibrations and the octave in *In Search of the Miraculous*. So I was looking for that gap, for instance, in the chapter "Art". And then, you know, I think there's a statement somewhere about the book that the 'keys aren't by the doors,' so that's why I wrote everything down so that I could cross-reference, because material in one part gets recapitulated in another. So that was sort of my process. Thanks for the compliment.

Q3: So, also thank you for the great presentation.

A: Thanks.

Q3: Clearly there's a lot of grunt work that's needed with approaching *The Tales*. As far as this goes, I'm curious what your take is on why Gurdjieff structured *The Tales* to be broken down in this way. Like, why did he do that?

A: Well, my basic idea is that *Beelzebub's Tales* itself is a work of art based on the principles of the Adherents of Legominism and so he's using these divergences in the gap of the octave to put, you know, more and more information, and...what else do I want to say about that? The title itself, *Beelzebub's Tales to His Grandson*, the ship that they're in, the *Karnak*, which is an ancient Egyptian temple created over multiple generations, everywhere in the book it is just pregnant with the idea of transmitting to future generations. So, I mean, I think that was definitely one of the purposes of him doing that.

Q4: About this idea, the degradation of human sight, this is a small point, but I've always been interested in... there's got to be something other than a literal meaning to the idea that people used to be able to see hundreds of tonalities of a certain color; and it's degenerated to where we only can see seven colors, but obviously that has more than a literal meaning because we can see many more colors, so do the colors have an inner meaning? Do you know what he means by that, or did you study that part?

A: You know, I took note of some of the colors and I think there's a more sophisticated structure than I was able to pinpoint, but for instance the color green, the references I could find to the color green were about green tea, and when they're traveling on the *Karnak*, they'll be...sort of when they get somewhere, you know, there'll be something will activate their taste buds, or the wandering nerves of their stomach; and so if the path of the *Karnak* can be seen as an octave and the colors can be seen as an octave, I think there's a more sophisticated structure underlying that that I am not knowledgeable enough to grasp it yet. But with the use of the colors, that's what I was trying to say about the red paw of the flea that bit the neck of a certain king, and the red and white face, I think he was combining colors in the same way as the painters of the Adherents of Legominism.

Q4: Well one thing that made sense to me, someone suggested that the colors in the sense of our diminished capability of perceiving them has to do with emotions, that that's a symbolic meaning. So in other words, people used to be able to perceive a vast number of different shades of emotions and now we're so dull that we only perceive gross ones like fear and anger and so forth. So I don't know if you've ever studied that idea.

A: I didn't look at the emotions of the colors, but with the sight, the Olooestesnoknian sight, that's like you could see into the infrared and the ultra violet, that's how they could see stars, you know, during the day.

Q5: On the question of color. As children we may have experienced color more directly and the deterioration is the formatory apparatus. Instead of seeing the color it triggers the associations we've developed for that.

A: I'm sorry, I don't understand the question you're asking.

Q5: Well, he talks about the deterioration of sight.

A: Right.

Q5: And this deterioration, I was thinking it may have…if you look at the experience of a child and an adult, a child doesn't have this barrier of all those associations that we develop, that prevents us from seeing directly.

A: Well maybe so, I mean I think if you look at the text itself it has to do with nature altering the beings of humans because the quality of their vibrations weren't vivifying enough to properly feed the moon, so that nature had to shorten our life spans and overall diminish our capacities; so to me that was the sense of those two different types of sight. As far as being able to see more colors when you're a kid, I don't know, maybe.

Q6: I would like to ask a question concerning contemporary art. What exactly is the contemporary art that is referred to?

A: Well I think there's a lot of examples of bad art or art that doesn't have much content but maybe looks glossy on the surface.

Q6: Do you think about when this was written is the contemporary art?

A: He does talk about surrealism and a bunch of other movements of painting ending with 'ism' which he summarily dismisses.

Q6: What about art like Kandinsky?

A: I don't know, what about it? Do you think Gurdjieff admired Kandinsky's work?

Q6: No, but I think that Kandinsky made tremendous efforts in developing something that had not been done before, and I'm one of his admirers, and as well as other persons I can think of at that time period.

A: I just think that Beelzebub wasn't such of an admirer of them. He says that there's nothing new under the Sun, so when you talk about Kandinsky doing something new, I don't know, I'm kind of skeptical. And, back to Gurdjieff's ideas about objective art, it's, you know, exact, so that's what I was trying to do was to see how it could be exact. And I don't know Kandinsky's artwork enough to say whether they're exact in such a fashion.

Q6: I agree completely with your notion of Gurdjieff as an artist.

A: Thank you.

Q7 (same person as Q1):
I just want to make a final comment here, because as high as the organ of sight is, the organ of hearing is higher [in octave?]. And I'll give you two reasons why, in my opinion.

A: OK.

Q7: The first is that if you go to the chapter *"Art"* there is no description of the organ of sight as much as the description of the organ of hearing.

A: I think that might have been another gap though, too.

Q7: OK, maybe. I don't know, I'll have to think about that. But then, he recommends to read the 2nd reading as though you were reading aloud - that involves hearing, no seeing. And then of course is the final pronouncement from Jesus Christ: 'Those who have ears, let them hear.' It doesn't say 'Those who have eyes, let them see.'

A: I'm not like a follower of Jesus, but doesn't he say 'they have eyes but see not'?

Q: Yeah.

A: And the 3rd advice about reading *The Tales* is fathoming the gist of it, which includes sound or vision. I wasn't trying…I just think in past studies the audio aspects have been more privileged. I'm not saying they're more or less important; I think what's actually interesting is for instance with the device the Alla-attapan where it shows that sound and light have the same inner structure because they're both vibratory phenomena.

Q7: I'm sure you have seen the Harold Good videos on YouTube, he has the whole book on videotapes.

A: Yeah, I heard some of the chapters.

Q7: OK, now something I always do is block the images and just hear the words.

A: Yeah, I agree there's great value in that and there's a ton of information about languages and sound itself. But I think the underlying this is, you know, underneath…you've got vibrations of sound and light but underneath this you have the laws of three and seven which they're both based upon.

Q8: I liked your diagrams very much, thank you.

A: Thanks.

Q8: Especially the one with the threads, for instance, the crimson thread. Do you think the usage of these colors and particular places where they occur, that they might act as a key, or landmarks for unlocking something?

A: Yeah, that's how I was looking at it because there's not…actual mention of specific tonality of color by name occurs relatively infrequently so I think that when it is used that it's significant, and leads to the other information about sight and color. I mean, I feel like the book is so interconnected it's like itself a thread that you try to grasp a piece and unravel a bit and see the constituent elements of it.

Q9: I wonder if you had any impressions about…that are not specifically color but are very closely related to color, and that is in the characterization in Russia of the peacocks, the turkeys and the crows. Very distinct coloration involved in this and I just wonder if you have some impressions on that.

A: I hadn't thought of that, that's a good idea. You know, crows are relatives of ravens, leading us back to Gornahoor Harharkh.

Q10: You said that Gurdjieff summarily dismisses contemporary art. I wonder what you thought about how he spoke of certain new movements in painting, which he doesn't seem altogether negative about.

A: You don't think he was dismissive about it?

Q10: Because he talks about…there's one of his lists: surrealism, futurism, cubism. But he's introducing it by saying that certain beings amongst these painters had noticed a certain illogicality and they strove to find something, and so that doesn't seem to me negative, it seems to me he has possibly looked into these things, into this modern art.

A: You could be right. It might be interesting to go over that exact passage that we're talking about. I could've misinterpreted it or there could be multiple interpretations possible. But to me the evidence suggests that…Beelzebub describes contemporary art as 'blinding with a fairylike exterior' and so, to me that doesn't seem like a positive thing. And I contrast that too with the spaceships they're on that can be made invisible and have transparent elements. In one instance, Beelzebub talks about mooring his spaceship and he would've made it invisible but people would bump into it. So they are transparent but there's a mass to it. And then there's all these statements by Mullah Nassr Eddin where he says 'there's everything in him except for the core or even the kernel' and 'if everything looks fine and dandy to me what does it matter if the grass doesn't grow?' All of these things connect to a glittering surface that is like hollow at the center. As far as what you were talking about with the different movements of painting, maybe it's in a more positive light than I read it.

Q10: It's just a few paragraphs that had puzzled me.

A: Well it'd be interesting to go over it again.

Q11: Thank you, Derek.

A: Sure.

Q11: I'll carry the image of Gornahoor in his helmet with me to my last days, with pleasure.

A: Oh, that's great.

Q11: The deterioration of sight, to only see the surface, suggests to me, I think as [someone else] said, we need also to look beneath the surface and that what this deterioration leads to is a loss of insight, seeing all the shades and tonalities and colors of meaning inside of us. This is what Kundabuffer did - it focuses on the glittering sensory exterior and made us blind to the interior. Another association is all the conversation about the shiny bling-bling that people wear to cover up their nullity.

A: Yeah, where he talks about fashion.

Q11: Yeah, so it seems to me that certainly on the exterior level, if we're not paying attention, we miss all sorts of things outside, but what we really reed to see is what's going on inside. And being stuck on a superficial surface understanding and losing all of the shades of depth and the holographic nature of this multidimensional life that we have is what's missing.

A: Well yeah, I agree. I think that's almost a caution to too literal or dogmatic reading of *Beelzebub's Tales* because…that's what I was trying to demonstrate with the three punishments of Tikliamishian women - on the surface to me, and Beelzebub presents these as sensible and just punishments, but you know, that's just a surface level reading. If you look at the colors that make it up and the fact that it could make, especially women I think, morally indignant, that connects to the - I forgot to mention this in my presentation actually - the expert in fleas who said that there was a crimson-orange growth on this flea that bit someone's neck, Beelzebub says that, if giving his long-winded lecture, if someone were to express doubt to their face, he would become sincerely indignant. So that's why I think that that invites comparison between those two different things.

Q11: But also painting the face shows people what is on the interior, character, the quality of the being of the woman whose face is painted; and because we can't see into the depth of people, this is a way of demonstrating certain inappropriate qualities under the surface.

A: I think that's part of it, instead of a character…some sort of a defect being hidden, it is made manifest.

Q11: Mm-hmm.

A: But I also think that the painted face is more like a veil if you look beyond the punishments and so forth and compare that usage of color with the use of color with the flea. So I think it's calculated to make one morally indignant.

Q11: And one other question: Do you have any impressions about the Egyptians putting their observatory underground and having five tubes?

A: Yeah, I included this in the paper that I wrote, but I had to just focus on some things for a presentation. But that also relates to surface level and like a further level, right? So, similarly there's giant ants who have tunneled the moon and Beelzebub compares humans unfavorably with them. Because it's again surface level and we literally don't know completely what's underneath our feet like the ants who have been able to tunnel their whole planet. And then on Mars they're digging canals to conduct water from one place to another and elsewhere Beelzebub describes water as the blood of a planet. So I think all of those things are tightly interconnected.

Q12: What will happen to us if we become morally indignant? Why does he calculate to do that to me?

A: Well, I don't know, I think that's part shock tactics. Well, what I think is this: say that makes you morally indignant, and I'm troubled, I'm like 'these don't seem like just punishments for these offenses to me,' but I think it causes the reader to think 'why would this author who I esteem so much, you know, suggest something unjust like that, under the guises of it being just?' And then it makes you look beneath the surface to other things.

Q12: So by saying, 'I'm not what you think I am' - I'm the writer now - this writer: 'Hey I'm not what you think I am, you better look deeper' - is that kind of what you're saying?

A: I'm not exactly sure I know what you…

Q12: But you're sure he wants us to feel morally indignant, right?

A: Sure? No, I guess not.

Q12: But you see it as a calculation.

A: Yeah, but I also would say that 'destroying a being newly conceived in her' could also be like ideas of souls rather than necessarily a fetus, so that there's multiple ways to look at it, I think.

Q12: I feel you're right, it's just that I don't know exactly what do I do with that?

A: I think then that, that's why I was talking about the growth on the flea, because the expert in fleas would be morally indignant, and the way he uses colors is the same in both instances: white and red and pink; and crimson and orange is red, and all these colors are close to each other on the spectrum too, you know, combine two to make another one.

Q12: So in a way he's giving us a clue that says 'Hey reader, I wanted you to feel morally indignant'?

A: I think so.

Q12: Yeah.

A: I could be wrong, but I think so.

Q12: So then what do we do with that is my question, and it's not to be answered, it's just…

A: Yeah.

Q12: …what do we do once we feel that?

A: Yeah, that's a good question. I don't know the answer to that.

Q13: I think your presentation is great.

A: Thanks.

Q13: I think your digging deep is great. It makes me wonder a lot of things, including, because of this deep penetration into *The Tales*, have you been encouraged to look into anything else, or any other way that Gurdjieff taught, and a corollary to that is: have you looked at the other writing with the same kind of deep search?

A: I read *In Search of the Miraculous* fairly thoroughly. And I kind of look at *Beelzebub's Tales* as a narrative version of that work.

Q13: But not the 2nd series?

A: The 2nd series I read once. I mean I liked it, I just haven't gotten around to reading it more.

Q13: Yeah, I would just suggest that there might be almost as much in the 2nd series as in this, but very, very, more hidden, obscure.

A: You might be right, I mean, it would be cool to find it, right?

Q13: Yeah.

Q14: Hello, thank you very much, that was a really interesting presentation; especially I found your accompanying visuals were quite stimulating and the use of maybe some objective symbology was very nice, that yin-yang and such like that. I don't know about Gornahoor's helmet, but maybe. I'm wondering if I'm understanding this correctly and maybe not, which is why I'm asking: Regarding objective art, and you talked about exactitudes, and another aspect of objective art, as we know, and I'm roughly paraphrasing, 'invokes the same in all who view it or experience it'. And I'm wondering: Are some of these exactitudes that you're talking about, for example, using like you just talked about, crimson and orange, this is not red and yellow, it's very specific words and you said that those very specific colors with their particular frequencies add together in a certain way, crimson and orange, to make another very particular color. Are these some examples of the exactitudes of the objective art regarding color that you're talking about?

A: Well I think so, I mean, whatever 'objective' means, I don't have a great idea of what that means, but following the indications that objective works of art are exact, then my starting premise is that everything is significant, and that 'nothing is accidental' is another statement that Gurdjieff makes about objective art. So that's how I was looking at it, as nothing is accidental in it. Doesn't mean my interpretation is necessarily correct or anything, of course.

Q15 (same person as Q12):
Is an object work of art something new under the Sun?

A: Well, I don't know, it depends on how far you go back I guess. What the oldest work of objective art is? I guess it was new when it was first created, but there must have been other ones that preceded *Beelzebub's Tales*, right? Like probably some Egyptian temples and things like that.

Q16 (same person as Q11): Do you have any insight into an example of a lawful inexactitude and how one would place something into the lawful inexactitude in the arena in which you have been studying?

A: Yeah, I think I addressed that, where they [the Adherents of Legominism] were utilizing the gaps in the law of seven.

Q17 (same person as Q1 & Q7): The whole book is inexactitude, one after another. And that's where the knowledge is placed.

Q18 (same person as Q6): It seems to me that contemporary art in our generation is so full of all these inexactitudes that you do not know what it is inexact in relation to. Too many inexactitudes. So it seems to me that we have to be led some way to a logical or significant approach and then something interferes and we are led astray, and then we have work to do to figure it out.

Q19 (same person as Q4): I just wanted to clarify, inexactitudes have to do with Legominisms, not objective art, and they're lawful inexactitudes, that's why contemporary art…intentional *lawful* inexactitudes, so that's different than just something not according to law.

A: I think so, it's the difference between it being accidental or non accidental.

Q19: Mm-hmm, but objective art, I mean from my little tiny understanding, is a work of art that evokes something the same in everybody and in "The Bokharian Dervish" where there were certain vibrations that were played that made everybody cry. Everybody had the same response to that work of art, so it was objective because there was no subjectivity there; it effected everybody the same way.

A: I think what happens in that part of the book that you're talking about is that the dervish predicts that after he plays a sequence of notes a boil will appear somewhere on everyone, but it fails to appear on Beelzebub because he's of a different species, and so forth.

Q19: Well there was that but I was referring to another part where…I don't remember the idea…maybe this is something Mrs. Staveley talked about, that the idea of objective art is that it has the same effect on everyone.

A: Yeah, I think that's more from Gurdjieff's lectures than in…

Q19: OK

A: *Beelzebub's Tales.*

Q19: OK

A: But I think the common element there, or one of the common elements there, is transmitting knowledge from generation to generation, because that's how the Adherents of Legominism reasoned, was that the law of seven would be in existence for as long as the world was, so in these inexactitudes we'll hide knowledge and it'll theoretically last as long as our productions last, since the law of seven will exist for as long as the world; but they didn't count on everybody forgetting the significance of the law of seven.

Q19: That's a very good point, by the way.

A: Thanks.

Q20: Thank you very much for your presentation, I also enjoyed it. I thought the title was great, and also some of the images you created were very helpful. Do you think perhaps moving to a three-dimensional visualization of *The Tales* might also help? You used color and 2D…

A: Mm-hmm

Q20: …but you think there might be in the depth information of some of these scenes that are depicted, like the scene in Gornahoor's laboratory. Do you think…Can we do more?

A: Yeah, I think so. I mean, I think a great work of art can hopefully spawn other works of art, you know? And I make the point at the end of my paper that that would be a great animated film. But if holograms ever became advanced…that's pretty much what, essentially what they create in that vacuum since there's no light in a vacuum and they can't see, that's essentially what that device is…it's either like projecting images from objects outside of…that apparatus in which they're conducting the experiments, you know, in front of their eyes, or it's beaming them directly into their minds as, like, holograms. So I thought that was…I think holograms were invented in [19]47 and I think that kind of like predates that. I think there's a lot more, I really think I just scratched the surface.

Q21 (same person as Q2): Forgive me for pressing this a little bit; that's the academic in me I suppose…but where are you going with this next? Are you going to take it to another level? Obviously there's a lot of interest in it, and I can see you adding another twenty slides or more from some of the symbols that we've caught and talked about, such as the raven and the peacock, and I'd like to see your rendition on the Hasnamuss and so on.

A: On the what, sorry?

Q21: Hasnamuss, the shit-soul.
A: Oh, OK.

Q21: Yeah, just there's so many possibilities that could be brought to the screen and, as someone said just a moment ago, maybe even 3D and animation or something, so are you prepared to take this to another level? Or is this like a closed project for you? I'd like to see you come back in a couple years with it stepped up to another level.

A: Yeah, yeah, I…it really depends on my time and my life circumstances, so…You know, I just hope that maybe more talented people than me in the future will derive other great works of art from this great work of art [*Beelzebub's Tales*].

Q22 (same person as Qs 1,7,17): What I love about you is that young people are getting interested.

A: I'm not that young anymore.

Q22: Compared to us.

Q23: I thought it was very interesting, about this objective art conversation, I think that with contemporary art, that Gurdjieff really denigrates all the contemporary art.

A: That was my interpretation.

Q23: I think so too, but he has to do that because he's trying to smash our enamored view of art and current artists. But I think as individual artists, he doesn't denigrate them all and there have been many works of objective art that Gurdjieff puts out there, for example Mont St. Michel - that's not ancient - or the temple Karnak, or…I mean there's a number of them…

A: …Leonardo da Vinci…

Q23: …like the statues they saw with the Seekers of Truth and there are a good number of objective works of art and they came from somewhere. But that contemporary art thing, it's a little like when he denigrates the Greeks as a bunch of fisherman that were just making up tales and pouring from the empty into the void, but obviously he had some respect for the Greek traditions - I mean he's trying to smash our beliefs of buying in wholesale without discriminating. Gurdjieff was a discriminator, so I think that there is some value in contemporary art; there have been objective works of art before, and you're mentioning of Kandinsky - I know Thomas de Hartmann was a real collaborator with Kandinksy, bringing the tonality of music to the wavelengths of color and art. And I think that Gurdjieff would've had respect for those initiatives into it, you know, whether Kandinsky's is objective art, I doubt it, but he's moving in the right direction; so everything with Gurdjieff you have to take with a grain of salt - it's true on one level and not true on another level. So all contemporary art is trash, but not all contemporary artists are trash.

A: Yeah, I see what you're saying…I agree for the most part, I mean, I don't know if it's true because I wasn't there obviously, but didn't he supposedly have a collection of horrible paintings? So…

Q24 (same person as Qs 1,7,17,22): Jane Heap told him 'this no art, what you have here'.

Q25: In relation to the question of how he felt about art, I'm just wondering if in general he wasn't telling us, not telling us, but if he wasn't giving us an example of our attachment to things, our identification. In other words, that we like a piece of music, we like a piece of art, we like this color, whatever it may be, and we are identified with it, we're attached to it. The thing I'm saying right now, I'm attached to, I'm identified to. So I think a lot of his work is in the belief smashing, so to say, to get us to be able to dis-identify, to be able to say 'Oh yes, that is the way I feel about this,' or 'I'm moved by this' or 'I'm affected by this, but it's automatic, it's mechanical, I'm attached to it.'

A: No, I think you're right. At one point in *The Tales* he talks about...he sort of dismisses the idea of there being four pillars upholding the world, or the Universe, but then in another context he talks about these four All-Quarters Maintainers. So it's sort of the same thing, I think. It's like things get recapitulated in a different scale, and sometimes they undercut the other, I think designed to make people think for themselves.

Q26 (same person as Qs 1,7,17,22,24): The funny thing is that the word 'objective art' is never used in the book. Never, never. Objective science is used. So maybe objective art is just a branch of objective science. But the word that is used in the book is 'initiate art'. That's the word: 'initiate art'.

A: Initiates of art?

Q26: Yeah, initiates of art, and initiate art. Objective art is never used.

A: That's true. I wanted to go into that...that's something else that could be explored, the forks on Beelzebub's horns and then there's all these different branches of knowledge, you know, there's the seven activities that the society of Akhaldan was involved with, there's seven branches of art, so I think that has to do with...it's like this idea of branching. I don't know which precedes which though, as far as art and science.

Q27: There has been for quite a while, I think, a tendency to lionize artists. To see that, or to feel, often, regardless of how dissolute an artist might be in his personal life, that at certain periods he acts as a conduit to something higher. And so we can become attached to products of art with a reverence which is beyond what it actually merits. I think part of his discussion of objective art, and certainly part of what he's talking about here, is to dissolve that kind of attachment. He does the same thing with actors. But I think the fiction of art is something which has taken a very strong hold on contemporary society. And it's a distraction. That's essentially what he's saying.
A: And what?

Q27: It's a distraction.

A: Yeah, I'd agree with that for the most part, yeah.

Visualizing Beelzebub's Tales - Questions & Answers

Q28 (same person as Q8): In the description of the cave of the dervish Hadji Asvatz Troov, there is the usage of color and sound. My question, maybe quite vague, but is there anything you could say about vibrations issuing from the colors in this particular instance?

A: Yeah, that's something I thought about, I wish I could've presented something that was fully pieced together, but that would almost involve understanding a huge part of the book. But color is based on vibrations, right? So I think there's something there. I mentioned in my paper too - this could just be a fanciful idea - but there's like, if you were to map out where the *Karnak* and the *Occasion* go, and say assign the different areas, like the different planets to a note, and they go back and forth, and there could be a periodicity there, I think. Maybe it's a song or something. Which, you know, somebody that knows a lot about music might be able to find that.

Q29 (same person as Q13): You mention branches in art and science. And I just wanted to add, the connection with branches of Beelzebub's horns, which is at the end of the book, and the connection with the degrees of Reason. So it could be that, I mean there's nothing more to say about that, but I think we need to keep, when we talk about branches, we need to keep that in mind as well.

A: And also...I didn't address it when the gentleman asked me, the discrepancy between five and seven? And, the Egyptian observatory has five hollows from which they view the sky, and then that's the same in the Greek division of sound, there's five, and in the Chinese there's seven. And Beelzebub has five forks in his horns. I don't know, I haven't been able to exactly piece it together, I think there's something there though.

Q29: Well, as far as the Greek division, I think he's referring possibly to the octave. The Greeks have five divisions which are more pentatonic and it can go all the way up to la-si of an octave. They didn't have a seven note scale; they did have modes of these scales that they had, but…So in that sense, it's not rocket science to think of the law of seven as really something with more divisions in an octave than an octave with five notes in it. So if you want to look at it musically, you could say something like that. As for Beelzebub's horns, I don't know whether those horns are proceeding as an octave, maybe so, everything else is an octave, this might as well be.

A: My starting point is that everything's significant. So to me it's like there has to be something there; in all cases I can't figure it out though, you know. Sometimes I can figure out a bit of it, but…

The Dilemma of the Toof-Nef-Tef

Keith Buzzell

Abstract

In chapter 45 *"Electricity,"* Beelzebub presents the elements of a dilemma, the answer to which is of vital interest to each of us. The circumstances surrounding chapter 45 are important to note. Beelzebub is on his way back to Karatas, having received his full pardon. We are close to the end of *The Tales*, with the final stop on Saturn the conclusion of his time in the solar system. The Toof-Nef-Tef, the 'king' of Mars, is perplexed because he is unable to understand why in his subjects there is *"a proportional diminishing of the intensity of their potency for the possibility of active mentation."* His appeal to Beelzebub concerns beings of higher Reason and the fact that, in his return journey to Karatas, Beelzebub will meet such beings and that an answer to his dilemma might be forthcoming.

A number of essential questions flow from this dilemma. How does this dilemma concern each of us? What is the ultimate cause discovered by Beelzebub? What is 'Mars' in our individual 'solar system'? What is 'Saturn' in this metaphorical image of our individual solar system? And, most importantly, what is the solution to the dilemma of the Toof-Nef-Tef and how does it apply to us?

In our exploration of this mythical representation, we will posit a way of viewing our individual 'solar system' and the role played by the Earth, Mars and Saturn. The dilemma of the Toof-Nef-Tef will be placed in the context of our individual lives and we will make an effort to identify the critical efforts in the pursuit of 'higher Reason' that can resolve what is a very personal issue for each of us.

The Dilemma of the Toof-Nef-Tef

In chapter 45 of *The Tales*, the story of the dilemma of the Toof-Nef-Tef contains a number of points to consider. Among other things, it points to a personal *dilemma* facing each of us. How we confront and resolve this circumstance has great impact on the future of our individual and collective work.

The placement of chapter 45, *"Man's Extraction of Electricity,"* as the second to last chapter in *The Tales* is significant. Only *"Form and Sequence"* and *"The Inevitable Result of Impartial Mentation"* remain and, thus, chapter 45 stands as the last chapter which is focused on a theme concerning the three-brained beings of Earth.

The Dilemma of the Toof-Nef-Tef

It is also notable that *"America"* (chapter 42), *"Beelzebub's Opinion of War"* (chapter 43), *"Justice"* (chapter 44) and *"Electricity"* (chapter 45) are, singly and collectively, *stinging* criticisms and indictments of man's behavior. These criticisms have no 'silver linings'. The final two chapters are focused on entirely different concerns leaving, at the end of *The Tales*, a distinctly grim atmosphere concerning man's behavior and possibilities. More essential, perhaps for us, is the fact that the fate of the Higher Being-bodies that do arise on Earth is left in an indeterminate, if not impossible, situation.

Each of these points will be taken up in more detail as we explore the meaning(s) of the dilemma in which the Toof-Nef-Tef found himself.

The Solar System 'Ors'

From our first reading of *The Tales*, a host of questions arose concerning the meaning of the image of the solar system Ors, the comet Kondoor, the fractured planet Earth and its remnants, Moon and Anulios, and of the planets Mars and Saturn. Rather than a classical, astrological interpretation, we were struck by this new metaphorical image that in some way had to do with a human being. Finding an organic way to view this collective image became very important to us, because the entirety of *The Tales* unfolded from and within this broad 'stage'. Over several years, we considered a number of alternative ways to reconcile this multi-faceted image; settling on a view that appeared quite resonant with the developmental interstices of *The Tales*. We decided on the following.

The solar system Ors[1] is a metaphor for each of us - taken as a one or as a whole, its 'parts' being major functional aspects of a three-brained being. A Sun that *"neither lights nor heats"*[2] points to the absence of a Real I, that which should be the true source of a three-brained being's individuality and creativity. Kondoor is a *lawful* 'comet', entering from the outer boundary of the system *prior* to the emergence of 'responsible' life. The comet is an 'event' which shocks the immature Earth (a state of manifestation of its brained nature) and 'splits off' the Moon (first brain - physical) and Anulios (second brain - emotional) from the Earth (third brain - intellectual).

Analogically, we settled on Earth as the third brain because we were aware from our neurophysiological studies that the third brain (including its early developmental form in one- and two-brained beings) is the *initiator* of all experience with the outside and the inside worlds. Without that initiation into events, the first and second brains are not 'fed' (fulfilling the image that the planet Earth *"constantly send to its detached fragments, for their maintenance, the sacred

---

[1] Our etymology text defined *"Ors"* as *"buttocks or ass-end,"* a typical example of Gurdjieff's picturesque and meaningful language.
[2] Gurdjieff, *Beelzebub's Tales*, chapter 17, "The Arch-absurd: According to the Assertion of Beelzebub, Our Sun Neither Lights nor Heats," pp 134 - 48.

vibrations 'askokin'." In that image, 'askokin' is *experience*.³ The Moon is a reflected 'image' of the Sun; cold but having the *gravitational* power over movement on the *surface* of the Earth. It is a metaphor of moving center-automatic and only dimly reflecting the light of the Sun. It is 'external reality', as seen from Earth.

Anulios is a proper image of the role being played by the second (limbic or emotional) brain in modern man. The brain of feeling has become a much diminished carrier of force in the life of brained beings; leading to the comment that "no 'grandmother' ever told them that once upon a time any such little satellite of their planet was known."⁴

Taking Earth, Moon and Anulios as a metaphor for the third, first and second brains, we naturally turned to address the other 'planets' of the solar system Ors. We found it interesting that Jupiter, by far the largest planet, is never mentioned in *The Tales*. Venus and Neptune are each referred to once and do not appear to play any distinct role throughout *The Tales*. Mars and Saturn, however, play constant, essential roles. After a time, we concluded that Mars was a metaphor for Higher Emotional Center. The reasons for this were multiple:

Mars was assigned as the primary place of existence for Beelzebub during his exile and this assignment was made by endlessness.

Mars is 'separated from' Earth (in a 'higher' orbit) and Earth can be 'seen' from Mars - seen in great detail when we consider the power of the Teskooano Beelzebub constructs (with a magnification of seven million plus).

Of note here is that sight (and, in one instance, smell⁵ and touch) is the focal sense that enables Beelzebub to 'observe' events on Earth via the Teskooano. The implication of *impartiality* is clear.

Beelzebub's visits to Earth are named "*descents.*"⁶ A 'descent' is a motion from a higher state or place to a lower state or place.

The beings inhabiting Mars are always kind and courteous. They know, from the beginning, the nature of Beelzebub and the kinsmen and also know the reason why they were compelled to dwell on Mars.⁷ This is in marked contrast to the three-brained beings of Earth who remained ignorant of

---

³ Ibid., p 84. In much the same way, the river of life (in another of Gurdjieff's mythic images) provides the 'events' from which we can extract what we need. We cannot take everything from the river, but enough to build the Higher Bodies. In a three-brained being, it is the third brain that 'searches in the river' and creates opportunities from which we ourselves can profit.
⁴ Ibid., p 85.
⁵ Gurdjieff, *Beelzebub's Tales*, p 81.
⁶ Ibid., pp 108-09.
⁷ Ibid., p 1149.

The Dilemma of the Toof-Nef-Tef

the nature of Beelzebub and his kinsmen. In fact, they invented fantastic explanations (i.e., angels and devils[8]) for their presumed presence.

The beings of Mars are very ingenious and industrious; digging canals so that water could be brought to the arid half of the planet in order to increase the growth of *wheat*, the *"divine grain"*[9] (their *only* first being-food being bread). This is a powerful metaphor concerning the true nature of Higher Emotional Center.

The Toof-Nef-Tef, as the merited 'King' of Mars, is a Zirlikner (physician-tutor), dedicated to assisting his people. He is the embodiment of Conscience,[10] nearing the state of the sacred Ischmetch, after long service to his 'people'. We understand this as a metaphor for the I appearing within the Kesdjan Body.

After his full pardon, Beelzebub *ascends* to Mars from Earth and then *ascends* further to Saturn before his final departure from the solar system Ors.

Each of the six descents is made via the spaceship *"Occasion"* (an event or occasion[11]). In the context of an 'event', the descents represent opportunities to *communicate*[12] (recall that it is the *"transspace communication"* that is the means of 'travel').

The physical features of Martians highlight two functions: sight and flight. Their planetary bodies have:

"… a long broad trunk, amply provided with fat, and heads with enormous protruding and shining eyes. On the back of this enormous 'planetary body' of theirs are two large wings, and on the under side two comparatively small feet with very strong claws.

"Almost the whole strength of this enormous 'planetary body' is adapted by nature to generate energy for their eyes and for their wings.

"As a result, the three-brained beings breeding on that planet can see freely everywhere, whatever the 'Kal-da-sakh-tee', and they can also move not only over the planet itself but also in its atmosphere and some of them occasionally even manage to travel beyond the limits of its atmosphere.[13]

---

[8] Ibid., pp 1142-44
[9] Ibid., p 951.
[10] Ibid., p 1147.
[11] Date of Origin 14th c. Like English *befall*, *occasion* depends on a metaphorical connection between 'falling' and 'happening', further information in the glossary.
[12] communicare *"to share, divide out; communicate, impart, inform; join, unite, participate in," lit. "to make common,"* from communis.
[13] Gurdjieff, *Beelzebub's Tales*, p 61.

In this quotation, we feel that Gurdjieff is metaphorically pointing to particular capacities of Higher Emotional Center.

All of the above reasons support the notion that Mars metaphorically represents Higher Emotional (feeling) Center. It also provides possibilities for exploring Gurdjieff's characterization of this planet and its inhabitants as having parallels in the structure and function of Higher Emotional Center. The same is analogously true with regard to Higher Intellectual Center and the planet Saturn and its inhabitants, Gornahoor Harharkh and Gornahoor Rakhoorkh.

Once we saw the possibility of considering Mars as a metaphor for Higher Emotional Center, it was a direct step to explore Saturn as a metaphor for Higher Intellectual Center. Several confirmatory reasons follow:

The 'chief', or Harahrahroohry, of Saturn, was one of the beings who performed the sacred "Vznooshlitzval"[14] at the beginning of Beelzebub's exile. He is referred to as an "essence-friend." There is the implication that he knew Beelzebub *before* he came to visit Saturn after his exile. Beelzebub resides in his palace whenever he visits Saturn.

Gornahoor Harharkh, a subject of the chief, became afterwards the essence-friend of Beelzebub and was considered one of the foremost scientists among the ordinary three-brained beings of the whole Universe. His intellectual capacities were formidable.

The Teskooano, used by Beelzebub on Mars, was the result of the learning of Gornahoor Harharkh.

It is Gornahoor Harharkh who investigates the peculiarities of the Omnipresent-World-substance-Okidanokh. This is an extraordinary achievement, as Okidanokh is the Omnipresent-Active-Element that:

"… takes part in the formation of all both great and small arisings, and is, in general, the fundamental cause of most of the cosmic phenomena and, in particular, of the phenomena proceeding in the atmospheres."[15]

The experiments Gornahoor carries out are with the Anodnatious and Cathodnatious aspects of Okidanokh and there does not appear to be an inquiry into the nature of the third, Reconciling-force (named "Parijrahatnatioose"). This lack of recognizing the profound significance of the third force of Okidanokh is the primary reason why Gornahoor Harharkh concludes, during Beelzebub's final visit,

---

[14] Ibid., p 149.
[15] Gurdjieff, *Beelzebub's Tales*, p 138.

The Dilemma of the Toof-Nef-Tef

"'I am now in full agreement with the opinion of the *"result-of-my-all,"* that it was the greatest misfortune for me to have been occupied so long with this, in the objective sense, absolutely *"unredeemable sin."*'[16]

Gornahoor Rakhoorkh, a young *conscious* individual, is the *"son,"* the *"result of my all,"* the *"heir"* of Gornahoor Harharkh and the godson of Beelzebub (the 'Kesdjanian-result-outside-of-me.')[17] He *"smelled-out-its-very-essence"* (in regard to Okidanokh). To emphasize - while Gornahoor Harharkh carried out his experiments on *two* of the forces of Okidanokh (Anodnatious and Cathodnatious), he says very little about the third force (Parijrahatnatioose) and it is this omission that we feel represents the reason for the prior quote.

It is Gornahoor Rakhoorkh who notices that his effort to actively mentate (which is a three-brained reconciling function) is interfered with when the dynamo is on, (which utilizes only *two* of the three forces of Okidanokh). He recognized the *imbalance* which is the inevitable result when only the Anodnatious and Cathodnatious forces are utilized. They are *unreconciled* and produce a *"non-law conformable"* result.

It is Gornahoor Rakhoorkh who speaks out his 'discovery' concerning Okidanokh and its distribution within a solar system.

"'Upon my further experimental elucidations I also became aware, beyond all doubt, that although our solar system like all the other solar systems of the Great Universe has its own Ansanbaluiazar, and each planet with its atmosphere is a special place of concentration of one or another class of cosmic substances of the given *"Systematic-Ansanbaluiazar,"* yet nevertheless the cosmic-substance Okidanokh is an indispensable and predominant part of the presence of each planet.

"'And later, also thanks to my experiments, it became clear to me that this cosmic substance is, owing to the common universal equilibrium, concentrated in every system in a strictly corresponding proportion and is distributed also in a strictly definite proportion between the atmosphere of each planet of the given solar system, and that when this universal substance is used up by accident or design in any one place of atmospheric space, it must without fail be replenished for the equilibrium of its common proportionalness in the atmosphere, and this proceeds by its flowing in from other places, and thereby this balancing transposition of Okidanokh must proceed not only from one space to another in the atmosphere of any planet, but also from the atmosphere of one planet to the atmosphere of another planet, if in this other planet for some reason or other more than its established norm is used up.[18]

Beelzebub immediately sees the application of this principle to the dilemma of the Toof-Nef-Tef and presumably informs him as he promised that he would.

---

[16] Ibid., p 1153.
[17] Ibid., pp 1152-53.
[18] Gurdjieff, *Beelzebub's Tales*, p 1157.

The inquiry and exploration of the detailed manifestations of Okidanokh are clearly *intellectual* pursuits, pursued over a very long period of time and, most essentially, resulting in the recognition of the primary role that must be played by the Reconciling-force within Okidanokh (Parijrahatnatioose) if imbalance between centers (allegorically identified as *planets*) is to be corrected. *All* of these considerations are expressions of Higher Intellectual Center and concern the coating process of Higher Being-body.

The father-son relationship of Gornahoor Harharkh and Gornahoor Rakhoorkh is interesting to explore (given their assignation as expressions of Higher Intellectual Center). We have concluded that Gornahoor Harharkh is an *initial* expression of Higher Intellectual Center function which *matures*, under the influence of Beelzebub, and becomes or 'results' in, over time, Gornahoor Rakhoorkh (the Kesdjanian-result-outside-of-Beelzebub). These are important hints that Gurdjieff has set down in allegorical form concerning the possibilities of *our* Higher Intellectual Center.

It is notable in this context that Gornahoor Harharkh is a participant in the studies of the 'apes';[19] being responsible for the construction of the special section of the ship Occasion that made it possible for the apes to be brought *up* to Mars and then to Saturn.

The 'Omnipresent', (the transspace *communication* 'ship' on which Beelzebub returns to Karatas), is able to 'land' on Saturn (but not Mars). In our scenario, Beelzebub leaves our solar system *via* Higher Intellectual Center; a resonant image of this Cosmic Individual who leaves his mark on Earth (third brain), Mars (Higher Feeling Center) and Saturn (Higher Thinking Center). A portent of our possible future?

We understand Parijrahatnatioose, the third or Reconciling-force of Okidanokh, to be that force carried by emotional (feeling) center, primarily because of Beelzebub's role as the Kesdjanian 'godfather' of the maturing Higher Intellectual Center. It is the *blending* of the 'force' of Kesdjan with Higher Being-body that leads to the further perfection of this Body and to Higher Reason.

All of the images put forward by Gurdjieff concern the present circumstances (Earth or third brain) and the proper functioning and possibilities of the Higher Centers (Mars and Saturn) in each of *us*.

The *electricity* referred to has to do with the electromagnetic phenomena taking place in *our* brains-unbalanced when only the positive and negative forces are active and unreconciled. The entire psychological aspect of Gurdjieff's teaching concerns the recognition of this imbalance and the lawful struggle to reconcile these forces.

The mythic images of the solar system Ors and its planets (states of brained function) are a powerful Podobnisirnian (allegorical) teaching, with a host of inferences and questions for us to struggle to understand.

---

[19] Gurdjieff, *Beelzebub's Tales*, *"*Fourth Descent,*"* p 314.

The Conclusion

We return to our opening question concerning the dilemma of the Toof-Nef-Tef: Gurdjieff appears to be implying that our Higher Emotional Center is in real jeopardy as a result of the pursuit of *"naïvely egoistic aims"*[20] by our third brain. The Higher Emotional Center itself cannot understand the reason for this and it is only through the understanding provided by the Higher Intellectual Center that comprehension of the dilemma takes place. Emphasis here is placed on the limitation of the degree of Reason of Higher Emotional Center. It is the power of a *reconciled* Okidanokh from Higher Intellectual Center that can *rebalance* the misuse of Okidanokh by our third brain, bringing the proper integration of Higher Emotional Center (Kesdjanian influence) to bear on the *"naïvely egoistic aims"* of the third brain.

The Work brings the methods and understanding that make this rebalancing, this *reconciliation*, possible. In this Work, the power of *attention* (the photonic reconciling power of Parijrahatnatiooose[21]) is of premier importance.

As recorded by Madame de Hartmann:

From the very beginning the conversations related to attention. Mr Gurdjieff told us very seriously that attention is absolutely indispensible for any work we wished to do with him. If we did not understand that, nothing could bring us to the aim for which we came to him. All of us there already felt that we were more than just a body. We knew that 'something else' was in us, and we wished to know: what is that? What have we to do with that? How can we call to it? How can we bring it out? How can we rely on it and not depend only on the body? All this was really a burning question for us, and Mr Gurdjieff made it clear that if we didn't study attention - not study in the ordinary way, but putting all our attention on developing that attention - we would arrive nowhere.[22]

© Copyright 2012 - Keith Buzzell - All Rights Reserved

---

[20] Gurdjieff, *Beelzebub's Tales*, p 1159.
[21] Refer to chapter in this volume *"Okidanokh."*
[22] de Hartmann, Thomas and Olga, *Our Life with Mr. Gurdjieff,* Definitive Edition (London: Arkana), 1983, p 45.

The Dilemma of the Toof-Nef-Tef - Questions & Answers

Question: Thank you, Keith. I think those are profound insights. I really appreciate that. I just have a point about being a biologist like you and a physician like you about the thin covering of the frogs and the rabbits of their brain. I just had this insight that *"Oh my God"* that's what happens to people when they allow somebody else to dictate what they believe. Like for example, the solders going into the Army they get indoctrinated. They have let that cortex of theirs be governed by somebody else which prevents them from having any individuality. It's not only military indoctrination but you can think of a hundred ways in which we give up our ability to think for ourselves to some authority.

Beliefs and views that have coalesce inside of us for many, many centuries and Gurdjieff says right at the outset that that's what he's out to destroy.

Keith Buzzell: That really is a wonderful insight. And also I just read in scientific research that when the thalamus is removed say from a person that has a tumor or something or they had an accident where their thalamus gets diseased or something, they totally lose consciousness all together. They go into a coma. And the thalamus is the connection between the 3 brains. It processes information from the body to take it up to the cortex to the 3rd brain and it also processes information from the 2nd brain. When you remove central server, then you have not consciousness at all. You're totally in a coma.

Well it goes further than that, if I could remind you, that most of you, you can visualize the side view of a human brain and in the medulla and the pons, that's the lowest part of the brain itself, inside the skull, that is in direct continuity with the spinal cord. The cord comes out the lower end of the medulla, so we have the medulla and pons. In the medulla, starting in the medulla and extending up into the pons, right in the core of this early brain, is instinctive center; this is instinctive moving center. Moving center when you include the spinal cord but instinctive center when you're speaking specifically about the brained portion of this 1st brain. Now if you have an injury there, a tumor, a stroke or auto accident or whatever and you cut off this in the core in the medulla is what is called the RAS, that stands for reticular activating system, forget the name it doesn't matter, the important thing is that these are a bunch of little centers, neural centers, that provide attending the energies of *"plural attentions"* to the whole rest of the brain. And if you chop that right where we have mentioned so that the thalamus does not get this information and none of this division out into the 2nd and 3rd brain can take place, then you end up in a vegetative state, in a coma and nothing happens. The upper brains may be perfectly normal, I mean in so far as they have blood supply and so forth and so on, they have no neural interconnection with what, the lifeline, with hydrogen 12. In all of the, think back on the food illustrations in *In Search* and so forth and so on you end up with 12's in the lower story all over the place, all 3 end up here. That's what I am referring to. All those 12's are here, in the medulla and the pons in the in this reticular

The Dilemma of the Toof-Nef-Tef - Questions & Answers

activating system. Chop that and nothing goes further. If it's allowed to go further, then real possibilities of human experience begin to emerge.

Question: Askokin is sent to the moon. So in your image there, and Anulios, right, what is death? In your scheme there how do you viewing the death part?

Keith Buzzell: I don't know if I understand your question. I mean, the death part is the death part.......Well he says that through the deaths of the beings it sent in order to maintain....oh I see... the system so how are you viewing that metaphor?

Question: Well, we get conjectural and I think everybody has perhaps their own perspective on this, some people claim and it's there in the psychology literature pretty liberally that the most intense experiences occur at the moment of death. The most intense experiences, it's when the brain goes POW, ok? That's one way of looking at it. Just leave it at that.

Question: I have one question and two comments. My first question is this, if Mars represents a metaphor of the Higher feeling center, and Saturn is a metaphor of the Higher thinking center, then I totally agree with that. What is earth?

Keith Buzzell: Earth is the 3rd brain. The 2nd brain is Anulios, this little tiny tiny brain and that's the feeling brain in our lower parts that we've lost contact with. Nobody knows where it is any more. Grandmothers don't even tell stories about it anymore. Moon, Gurdjieff speaks about this so often, again metaphorically, and really the moon is what conditions our movements -- Motions, moving center. So the moon is, in this analogy, I believe, a very good metaphor for the 1st brain, for moving center.

Question: Mars is what? Higher emotion center. OK.

Question: So Keith, I always wondered in that exchange between Beelzebub and Toof-Nef-Tef. You remember that there are 2 parts to the exchange, first one there was a note that was passed to Beelzebub and it was translated by whom. Then there is a conversation in the palace, it is not clear at whom was the translator but the implication is that he was there as a translator. Do you see any significance in that?

Keith Buzzell: No. My comment on that is that I would have to go back and reread that section. Because I don't remember, just don't recall it.

Question: I can read it right now.

Keith Buzzell: Fine

Question: It's very short. *"This request of the honorable Toof-Nef-Tef was translated to me through our Ahoon by means of what is there called Kelli-E-Ofoo."* This is essentially a note. So

I think there is some significance there. It's not that Ahoon spoke Martian better he lived there longer than Beelzebub did so there's something there, who knows.

Keith Buzzell: Yeah…. One road that we may see to go down is the question who in the world is Ahoon?

Question: Yes

Keith Buzzell: That's a big deal. However we understand that then that might give us some hint as to why he is the translator here. I think it is also interesting it's Ahoon who brings up the question of art. It's Ahoon. He reminds Beelzebub *"You haven't talked about this" "you haven't talked about this yet"* and I just find that interesting that that should come from Ahoon and here this première opening into Art, the whole chapter that comes as a result. Beelzebub admitting to Ahoon, *"Yeah, you are right. I haven't taken that up. And this is an appropriate time to take it up.* So how we see Ahoon, that's a big deal too.

Question: I was wondering if Higher emotional and intellectual centers -- if you feel that that is a proper functioning of emotional and intellectual centers and also another question is, how does the difficult structure of *The Tales*, the use of hints and all these pieces we have to collect together bring us to a functioning Higher emotional and intellectual centers? And also third would be, what do you think the relation of *The Tales* and its structure is to the Movements? Or if you have an opinion on that.

Keith Buzzell: The third question is a real zinger. There are some folks who feel that in the end Gurdjieff preferred to be known as a teacher of dancing. So I think we have to have some very very long thought, I think right here the most able person the most able person to comment on that would be Toddy because her life work has been with the Movements and especially with her recent connectivity's with the inner meaning of Movements. She could far better answer your question on that score. It's a very good question. And one that I think any of us who have pursued Movements over the years which for us is 30-35 years, we know because we have felt, because we have experienced energies and forms and insights that could come in no other way. So it is enormously potent. Is it everything? No, I couldn't say that because I don't know. But it certainly is a magnificent structure that contains in it in its form but most especially much more important form the inner attitude. Where are we, where are each of us in our inner effort during movements. That's the key. Not the outer movement and whether we're doing everything precisely correct, so much of the emphasis on the last bunch of years has been on the form, and I think one of the things that Toddy has made increasingly clear to all of us is that it ain't the form. The form is the form, but inside of this there is a teaching, there is something that can open up parts of our life, parts of our inner worlds that almost nothing else can. You know I think it's remarkable that when you think of just in the last 15 years, what has happened to movements around the world. It's an astonishing growth, it's gone all over the place, and I mean outside of traditional Work circumstances as well as all kinds of groups that are working on Movements. They are attracted to it; they are influenced by it in a positive way. There is something here and much that isn't understood. The potency and the power of it, the future of it, especially among young people - especially among young people. I remember when I was young; I just fell in love with Movements. The first time I was in line I was stuck. That was it. So when you are young and you're more facile, you learn more quickly in moving center, then you can begin to experience things that are way beyond your intellect and your emotional development. You begin to have experiences that are so pure and that are so right in that moment. It may only be a fraction of a second, but it's real and it's there and you keep chasing it for years.

Question: Also the first and second questions.

Keith Buzzell: Yeah. Go over them again.

Question: I was curious because my experience has been with the sittings has been a sort of descent into myself. To formulate the question correctly, I was curious how the structure of *The Tales* and how difficult it is to unwind and the kind of effort that takes. How is that related to the proper development of the emotional center, the intellectual center? How does that assist that because that seems to be kind of the purpose, I if I understand your paper correctly.

Yeah, well in the early chapters, in fact, in 'The Arousing of Thought' Gurdjieff emphasizes how he is intent on speaking to the subconscious through the waking consciousness. I don't think we take this seriously enough because what we miss is the fact that everything here is going be Podobnisirnian, Allegorical, it's all going to be allegory. Don't take anything here, literally, if you do your just going to drive yourself nuts, because it all has to do with in here. It all has to do with there. So that's the first thing. To see that everything that you read in here when he starts talking about civilizations and so forth and so on, it's interesting, maybe it's historically true, maybe it wasn't. That's not the point. The point is that he is saying something about us and about how we have accumulated over time many of the deficits that now we have to deal with. I thinks it's astonishing how we're beginning to see in many many studies today, especially anthropological, archeological studies that the pattern of errors that began to appear thousands of years ago. I just finished reading a book that Harry Bennett loaned to me, called the *"Neolithic Mind"* written by two South African anthropologists and boy they raise so many interesting and important issues. They notice and they really pay attention to the fact that the Neolithic man/women, had a different view of what and how the world was put together and how human relationships were put together. It is so resonant with so much of what Gurdjieff says about Atlantian times, I believe - or I have felt this way for a whole bunch of years - that Gurdjieff is really talking about the time of Atlantis is late Neolithic times when in so many of the digs, for instance, that they made through the Middle East and now in South Eastern Europe, so many digs of Neolithic villages of so forth and so on, they can't find any fortifications; they didn't build walls. It's the community of people... and you ask, how can that be? Essentially, its saying is that they didn't go to war. What is Gurdjieff implying when he is talking about Atlantian and pre-Atlantian times? Before the city/state, before master/slave appears - he's talking about a time when man was more normal. And I think that we can read much into his, when he's talking about Tikliamish and when he's talking about the rise of things, when he's talking about Ashiata and Ashiata's effort, all of that has to be seen in the context that man was a more whole human being in the past. More whole in the sense that Anulios was not some tiny little speck out there - Anulios was real. And these Neolithic people in this book talk about it. They talk about how these people and how they manifested in their architecture, in their carvings, in the figurines that they made, in the symbolizations that they put onto stone and so forth and so on, that they were reflecting how they saw their inner world out there. Not the outer world that was there, but their inner world as experientially it was manifested out here. This includes the time of Stonehenge and all the henges throughout England and Ireland, France and so forth. It's a marvelous journey if you just find the book.

Question: The first question actually was, "Is Higher emotional and intellectual center simply properly functioning emotional and intellectual center"?

Keith Buzzell: Well I think here, we have to take, there is a very commonsense-view that I think we have to remind ourselves of that when Gurdjieff says that Higher emotional and higher intellectual centers are in us and functional. We should not be so naive as to think that they are any more than a child's brain, when the child first wakes up and begins to struggle to walk, that brain is fully functional but is it matured? Has it reached it's real capacity? No. Why should higher emotional and intellectual center be any different? They have their early immature manifestations, I believe this is what Gornahoor represents that early tremendously insightful and tremendously energetic but he misses something. He's not as mature as he becomes when he becomes, from my way of looking at it, when he becomes Gornahoor Rakhoorkh, he has matured. He's seen into things that he did not see before. So higher emotional and higher intellectual centers, sure they are functional, but they're only functional as parts of our brain that are not mature. They are not experienced. They have capacity. But we have to feed them correctly. All of what Gurdjieff says about Hasnamuss needs to be addressed - remember that a 3rd and 4th degree Hasnamuss has a completed Higher being body. That's no small thing. That involves Higher intellectual center. So a lot to consider in that.

Question: I will try speaking without standing up. Thank you very much for your statements and I was very much struck by a couple of them. One having to do when you were speaking with Irv here about the part of the brain, the RAS, this activating system, and this is going to make sense as I carry it forward, and how that is cut or severed, there are certain things that do not move the brain itself or we are interested in and what's interesting to me about it is that it represents a type of blocking, in other words, if when a severing is made of that. Just as Kundabuffer in a certain way blocked us and here's the connection: The concept of that you're bringing in around the 3rd force that takes place, in other words, why Gornahoor Harharkh and the son? There's such a difference there because, let's see if I can finally put this together... if we are using basically the intellect that we have or the attention that we have, our ability to be attentive is basically a plus/minus, plus/minus, plus/minus, always hooking onto something. What Gurdjieff is directing us to in that little section that you read is the study of attention and I looked over the literature in terms of the study of attention, there's not very much in the study of attention or about attention. And what I have noticed in my study in myself and of other people, is it's a hooking on all the time and to me this is what's stops the integration of what could take place if 3rd force were to be brought in. And I would guess, just a hypothesis, and I just wanted your opinion on it, that Kundabuffer or the change that was made is when we were cut off from 3rd force, meaning we were cut off and we were left with a certain type of attention that it's on/off, on/off, on/off and we keep fostering that kind of attention throughout our lives and the only time I have ever seen this addressed is a woman named Simone Wile, where she is in a nunnery I believe at the time and working with children on mathematics and she is watching them pay attention and then she says, "No, you cannot pay attention that way. Attention you looking at is a narrowing, instead of attention opening. Which is the type of attention necessary when we do the movements. So I'm saying a bunch of things here but it has to do with this 3rd force and how it relates to human attention at the present time and how it disharmonizes us, in other words, it's actually the function of attention itself and the way it moves that is in itself disharmonizing. I just wanted your opinion on that.

Keith Buzzell: For everybody here the most important emphasis that I think could be made on attention is that we have got to give up this notion of speaking about a singularity. It's not attention, it's attentions - pleural. We have many levels of, keep in mind, if attention is associated with somehow or other with hydrogen 12, which I think it is, every hydrogen category is enormous. Just think, hydrogen 768, food, food for man, what is food for man? Thousands and thousands and thousands of things. It's the same thing with every single hydrogen category. This is a marvelous insight on Gurdjieff part to put it this way because he organizes the whole of the forms and the energies of the universe around this principle of what it is that holds them together. What are the bonding energies at this level, at this level. What happens when the transition away from mass occurs and you're no longer dealing with mass but you're dealing with impulses and with electromagnetic phenomena with fields, with photons, and so forth. What does this mean so far as what is holding it but there is an attention that is appropriate for each one of those levels. If we didn't have this, how would we digest our food? How would we keep everything straight inside of us? This doesn't happen mechanically, alone, of course it needs lots of chemicals and lots of mixings and lots of time and so forth and so on and it also needs something in us elementally from our instinctive center that deals with holding all of this together in a pattern. Moving it here or there when it has to get moved from here to there. There's only one thing that will do that and that's photons. Nothing else will do this. Nothing. So for me, attention first of all, is pleural. There are lots and lots of attentions just like there are lots and lots of levels of photons of electromagnetic wave forms. A nearly infinite number of them. And they are all photonic in the sense that they all carry certain characteristic possibilities. Those possibilities are what on the surface we assign to attention. For instance, we start to talk about attention as a focus, the ability to focus. But if you now, in this moment, focus on something you won't stay focused for very long. That focus will lead to what I chose to call differentiation. You see multiples. All of a sudden you're looking at somebody's nose and you become aware of that nose is on a face. It's got things around it and then that's what I call making 2's. Making 1's is focusing but if we hold our focus on that it becomes in the nature of the photon it becomes differentiated, making 2's. Making more than 1's. And then the marvelous the absolutely miraculous power of attention is if you keep it, keep your attention on that and it makes 3's. Makes 3's. What's that? The pattern, the pattern - what is the pattern? Whatever the pattern happens to be, every 'aha' moment all of us have ever had... When you were in school and you were struggling with Algebra or formula or what this means or studying a foreign language and you had an 'aha' moment. Ah… that's what it means. That's what I'm talking about. That's when you saw the pattern, that's a 3, making 3's. Did it ever come from being inattentive? No. It came as a power. A power... one of the expressed powers of attention. So we've got these attentions, many many many attentions and every single one of them has all three powers. Never loses that power. As weak as that photonic energy may be in terms of pushing things around if you get high enough photons and they push everything around. You get up to gamma waves and they tear everything apart. But get down into what runs your brain into what are called elf waves, these are so tiny in terms of the energy that they have that they can't move anything. Anything. They can't move an atom, they can't move an electron, they can't move anything. But they can see patterns. They can provide information. Information...that's what runs the brain. It is the information. The building of images, the building of memory, the building of judgment, comparison all of our intellectual activity when we try to understand something better. What are we trying to do? Making 3's. Making 3's. Seeing patterns. Seeing what is the ultimate pattern. What is Law? What is the study of Law? It's the study of the pattern. How does it work out? All the study energy that we put in to the Enneagram, what is it that we are trying to really discover? What is the pattern? What is the pattern? How's the pattern held together, what is it that relates this to this, to this and then suddenly and many people here, Irv, well many people have written books, very interesting things that have elaborated on aspects of the Enneagram. And they're all true. Quantity varying. Because something has been seen in a pattern. You've seen something that makes sense. When we say something that makes sense, when we have those kinds of discoveries, that's the power of attention. The 3rd power of attention. It has seen something and given it a form. A 3. What I call a 3. Because it's a way of looking at the law of 3. We are making 3's and those 3's become 1's. You see that as soon as you see the pattern you say, "AH" now I have it. You've learned something. Now you don't take all 3 of those things into the next event, you take the result. You take the 3. Which becomes a 1, into the next event.

Question: I thought I'd heard its Russell right? I thought I heard Russell ask a question which I wish you would address a little bit more about attention. Is it possible that there is a kind of corrupted attention that is the result of Kundabuffer, however you see that, that could be expressed as an attention which is tightly or inwardly focused or hypnotic as opposed to the kind of attention that is necessary, say, in doing Movements but was observed by this Nun in teaching these kids. Is it possible that you could speak about, stick with your physical explanation of the photon and attention and is there a way to talk about Kundabuffer and also does it relate then to this story of Gornahoor and the lack of the 3rd force? Is that related to this…?

Keith Buzzell: The lack of the 3rd force is 3, seeing the pattern and this is what Gornahoor Rakhoorkh saw. He saw the pattern. He saw why he wasn't able to actively mentate, which is what, trying to come into a singular state and he saw that he couldn't do it, because he was getting screwed up by the dynamo, which is only 2's. And that was diverting his attention so that he couldn't bring the power, OK, that is built into attention, to come to 3's. The relationship to

The Dilemma of the Toof-Nef-Tef - Questions & Answers

Kundabuffer I think is a really good one but the road that I've tried to explore has to do more with image. Our brains, we have no, we really don't have anywhere near sufficient appreciation for how miraculous the images are that our brain creates. I'm not talking about visual images only, visual images is one part of it, but there are auditory images, all the images of sounds that are recognizable that have patterns, that have form that inform us. All of our external senses have those including balance, our sixth sense. Our inner organ functions also produce images. What do you think hunger is? Hunger is an image. It's the stomach in a certain state of metabolic activity that we see and objectively experience as hunger, fatigue, alertness, or vitality - any one of the many states that we experience. Each of those is an image. In other words, it is something that the brain has, through evolution, through hundreds of millions of years ,brought to a pattern - a '3'. And we experience that and that's great. Great. Except that it is not true. It is true in the elemental world in the digestion of food and of physiologic functions of the body. Of eliminations, so forth and so on. And of the immune system and what not. But how about the images that we create when somebody insults you, when somebody picks on you, when somebody accuses you of being stupid or whatever. That's an image. I have an image of my emotional states, I am offended, I feel fearful, I feel anxious. Kundabuffer gets related to this because unfortunately we must believe, I mean in the final living sense, we must believe the images that the brain produces. If you didn't believe that you were hungry, if you didn't believe you were scared whit less because this creature came around the corner when you were walking through the jungle, you better believe it! Because it's real. It's real, OK? Now go into an insult, go into a feeling of fear because this guy is your boss. Is that real? It's an image. Your brain produced the image. If you give that image the same reality that you give to hunger, you're in real trouble. You're being lead around by the nose the whole of your life. By the images that other people and other circumstances are creating in your emotional and intellectual world. That for me is Kundabuffer. That's Kundabuffer. Yes and Itoklanoz just feeds that. One of the first things that Gurdjieff reminds us of at the very beginning of *The Tales* is in affect really says *"Don't believe all these images that keep coming up inside of you. Don't believe that when you think you are angry that that's real. Don't believe that when you feel people are picking on you, that you have some insight into their world. Don't believe that, that's no so."* What is he saying? He's saying the image is not real. At that level it is not real. The end result of the image is the state of Kundabuffer. See, living under the consequences of it. The consequences for me here being the fact that we have this miraculous image building capacity in every human being and up to a point it is enormously useful. It keeps us alive. Beyond a certain point when it comes to sharing human relationships to Anulios to the whole world of feeling, of our relationship to one another, so forth and so on. That's when it gets into trouble. And if we believe it, we're sunk. We're just lead around by the nose by life out there. That's Kundabuffer.

Seminar 1: Chapter 34 - Beelzebub's Tales

Russia

Facilitator: Paul Bakker

Introduction

Facilitator: Let's take a few moments to collect ourselves in silence, and gather our wits.

I wasn't sure how to do this, the moderation of this chapter, so what I came up with as a scaffold to have our discussions around is that I identified a couple of sections in this chapter that are somewhat isolated from each other in the sense that they seem to be about a specific topic. So I will read out the list that I put up.

The first section that I identified is the meeting with the important power-possessing Russian. The second one being the talk with Mullah Nassr-Eddin. The third Beelzebub's struggle to get a permit for a laboratory. The fourth the intrigues that he sees within the Trusteeship. Then, the audience he has with the Czar. Then there are two that are related somehow, but one of them is about Solioonensius connected with Bolshevism and after that I saw a section about Egypt and how somehow there was a sort of Egyptian Bolshevism going on at that time. Then the section after that is about the question that Hassein asks of Beelzebub and the answer. And finally the two good customs that are discussed.

Those are sections I could identify. Maybe we could somehow treat them sequentially.

I noticed that there's been an interest in reading actually from *The Tales*, so at certain points I will be asking persons to read aloud a couple of paragraphs that I thought were interesting, so don't think that strange; I will just mention somebody's name and then they will read it. So here's the first one, Bonnie will you start? This is on the first page of the chapter.

(reading): "All the further events, during this last sojourn of mine on the surface of the planet Earth, connected with the abnormal form of the usual being-existence of those three-brained beings who please you, and, at the same time, many trifling incidents of all kinds which elucidated the characteristic details of their peculiar psyche, began from the following:

"Once, walking one morning by the said Pyramids, a certain elderly being, a stranger, and in exterior appearance not a native, approached me, and greeting me in the manner customary there, addressed me with the following words:

Seminar 1: Chapter 34 - Beelzebub's Tales

"'Doctor! You will perhaps do me the kindness to allow me to be your companion on your morning walks? I have noticed that you always walk in this neighborhood alone. I am also very fond of walking here of a morning and as I, too, am quite alone here in Egypt, I venture to propose to you that I should accompany you on these walks of yours.'

"Since the vibrations of his radiations in relation to mine appeared not acutely 'Otkalooparnian,' or, as your favorites in such a case would say, 'since he appeared to be sympathetic,' and furthermore because I myself had already thought of establishing here also corresponding mutual relations with someone, in order as a rest from active mentation to converse sometimes by following only the course of freely flowing associations, I at once agreed to his proposition and from that day forth began to spend the time of my morning strolls with him."

It is an ever occurring theme throughout these *Tales* of our abnormal form of being-existence and with this last descent of Beelzebub in his pursuit of really understanding that, this chapter, as I think Paul was beginning to talk about the different stories, we're part of that story, we're the characters and we can learn so much with just experiencing this book, so, one more thing: the story of the Toof-Nef-Tef, when I first read Beelzebub a few times, I felt quite distant from this funny name, beginning as a Plef-Perf-Noof, getting on to a Toof-Nef-Tef. But later readings I really began to emotionally really feel this gentle creature, wanting - like all of us - wanting to help, and that's when I began to experience emotionally what it is that we get to see about ourselves as we study and share this book.

Facilitator: So this is an open discussion of this chapter, so anybody...

Discussion

Questioner 3: I was just going to mention that in the last part of what Bonnie read is one of my many favourite little lines in this book, about *"for a rest"* from his active mentation. Beelzebub has decided to engage in this standard associative thought, for taking a rest. I just like that. That's all.

Questioner 4: Just listening to you I remembered.. He told Ouspensky: *"The problem with you, Ouspensky, is you're always thinking. I think only from time to time."*

Facilitator: Just to be sure, the idea is that everybody who wants to say something speaks out so please participate and feel free to take the mike. Maybe I should ask the next person to read a bit. It's a bit further on in this chapter.

Questioner 4: This is page 598 and this is Mullah Nassr-Eddin speaking and they are together in Persia and then Mullah says this:

" 'Just now, in the company of a large number of *"well-bred-turkeys,"* a *"crow"* of this country passed by, who although one of the chiefs and of high rank, was yet nevertheless rumpled and badly molting.

" 'During recent times, I don't know why, *"high-rank-crows"* of this country no longer in general take a single step without these *"well-bred-turkeys"*; they evidently do this in the hope that maybe, perhaps, the pitiable remains of the feathers would, owing to their being constantly within the powerful radiations of these turkeys, become a little stronger and cease to fall out.'

"Although I understood positively nothing about what he had just said, yet already well knowing his habit of expressing himself first of all allegorically, I was not at all surprised and did not question him, but patiently awaited his further explanations.

"And indeed, when after he had pronounced the tirade and had thoroughly finished 'hubble-bubbling' the water in his 'Kalyan,' he - while giving in his subsequent speech with the 'subtle venom' which is proper to him, a definition of the whole presence and general essence of the beings of the contemporary community 'Persia' - explained to me that he compared the beings of this same community 'Persia to the birds, crows, while the beings of the large community 'Russia' who formed just that cortege which had galloped along the street, he compared to the birds, turkeys.

So now we have Mr. Gurdjieff comparing nationalities to animals, you see? America, burros and English, sheep. He was always comparing these Russian turkeys and Persian crows. Now what is the idea?

Questioner 5: What were the Americans again?

Questioner 4: Burros. Donkeys. They work like burros. They work, I don't know what they work for. So you know, when I read this some time ago, I was reminded that they said that Gurdjieff left fifty commandments to the daughter of Jodorowsky, the guy from Chile who made movies in France, The Topo, the best movie, about the teaching of Gurdjieff. If you have never seen that movie, see it. It's called The Topo, it's about the teaching. And has a daughter, Eugenie. Well he left fifty commandments to her. Now people say that it's not true, that he never left those commandments. But I read the fifty of them and the one that caught most my attention was one that says *"Never take a photograph with an important person"*. Never photograph yourself with an important person. And here he's telling that the crow is the in the company of a general, you know, so, I don't know, but anyhow I'll talk more about this chapter later. (A question is asked about the film.) El Topo, yes this guy from Chile. I met him in Paris. The movie came out in 1977, it's called El Topo. It's the teaching of Gurdjieff as he saw it. He's Chilean. You go to YouTube and you find the video of the interview he gave, very smart guy. He still lives, in Paris.

Questioner 6: One quick observation I had was the word radiation which seems to have been used in both of these excerpts, that were read. It seems that the elderly Russian and Beelzebub had,.. their radiations were somehow compatible, maybe? And here, with these two beings, one is

Seminar 1: Chapter 34 - Beelzebub's Tales

hoping to benefit from the radiations of the other. I don't know what this all means but this notion of radiations between people and their linkages, I don't know whether they are real or allegorical.

Questioner 7: It's not in relation to that paragraph, but it's interesting to me that in this section of this descent, that he is talking about, he's choosing really the period of time in which Gurdjieff himself just lived through the Bolshevik revolution and he's choosing this as an example for something that has literally been going on for all the people that he's writing to at this time, for his groups, and then he's going to be bringing out, or focusing on two issues here. One is our lack of conscience and the other is this law of Solioonensius. And I just think it's interesting, because this is something that's happening - he's commenting on the present that he's living in or that he just lived through. And he's about to see World War II, it's about to start. I think it's just an interesting framework that he's writing in, right here.

Facilitator: I noticed that by asking Will to read this section which is already a bit further on, we totally skipped what the Trusteeship is all about and I wonder if people have views on the Trusteeship and on the problem with drinking. Is there anybody who would like to shed a light on that?

Questioner 8: This section with the Trusteeship seems to be one of many examples of posing a problem without a solution. And it certainly resonates for me regarding all organizations I've ever been associated with or know about. On the one hand as individuals there are problems that an individual cannot really address. It needs to be a larger group of people with more resources and talents. And yet inevitably as the group grows different divisions appear, ego's appear. If the group has any success whatsoever, other people who then want the glory jump on to the band wagon, plus out of the window the original people who started it. It seems insoluble. Any movement towards a larger group effort to solve problems seems to lead inevitable to this kind of chaos and falling out the MI-FA into a different octave. So I'm wondering if anybody has a solution this problem. (Laughter.) I mean, what do we do in the face of that? I get the feeling that something must be done. I suppose this is not a reflection of the kind of dilemma that the Toof-Nef-Tef felt and even it's there at the very end of the book when ENDLESSNESS poses this question to Beelzebub, what has to be done.

Questioner 9: This is just kind of off the top of my head, to respond to your question, but I think the hope is in raising the consciousness of the planet as a whole, the collective consciousness, and so we have to keep trying. I mean the League of Nations was the first stab at a multinational organization to solve problems and the League of Nations failed miserably, but then we tried again and now this is the United Nations which came about after World War II, which had its problems but it maybe was a step up from League of Nations and obviously it's not doing a very good job either, but little by little as our consciousness as a whole increases, then the possibilities for these bureaucratic organizations maybe increases a tiny bit. That's all I can say about it.

Questioner 10: It think it's also maybe helpful to recall the reason for the sixth descent, the whole of the sixth descent, is when - you remember - Beelzebub on Mars looking through his Teskooano sees this person holding a stick with a puff of smoke coming out of it and somebody at some distance falling over dead, and he decides that this new representation of warfare, which he has not seen before, is extremely important for him to get to the bottom of. This was his primary motivation as I remember for the whole of his sixth descent. So I think keeping that in mind Russia is one step in his effort to get to the bottom of war. So I think everything that Gurdjieff describes throughout these chapters, throughout Russia, can be beneficially seen in that context. What is he telling us about war, about the causes of war. There is something about his presentation to the Czar that has to do with war. There is something that has to do with his application for his investigative laboratory that has to do with war. It all has to do with war. Many, many steps, enormously complex as has been mentioned already, but I think it is important to remind ourselves throughout in all of our discussions: What is he up to here? Because he is trying to get to the bottom of war. And that means ultimately, it's in us, the causes of war in us. So how do we see what he's talking about in terms of us?

Facilitator: Keith, in terms of what you were speaking about with the Toof-Nef-Tef and the two parts of Okidanokh, relative to this question of war, it seems to me this other point that he brings up, on 595:

"Well, it was then that I constated, among other things, that in the presences of the beings belonging to just this contemporary community, their, as it is called, 'Ego-Individuality' began during the recent centuries to form itself particularly sharply dual."
"After I had constated this and began specially to investigate this question there, I finally elucidated that this dual individuality obtained in their common presences, chiefly owing to a non-correspondence between what is called the 'tempo-of-the-place-of-their-arising-and-existence' and the 'form-of-their-being-mentation.'

He seems to say that this sharp duality of being is elaborated by the talk he with Mullah Nassr-Eddin about the turkeys and the crows etcetera. So I'm trying to fit that into subconscious, waking consciousness, two-natured. I think it has a place but I'm not exactly sure, I don't think it's exactly the same. Especially with his examples it is more based on culture, a conflict of cultures, but again this has to do very much with war, again this duality, this something that cannot be reconciled. I'm curious what others thought about it.

Questioner 4: Well, Keith says something very important here, and it's the fact of the sixth descent. Now you know that the book opens with the Karnak moving to the planet Revozvradendr, for a conference. He's telling Hassein about all that. But if you look very carefully, you'll see the that the first five descents, the Karnak is moving towards this planet and the sixth descent, it's moving away from this planet, back to Karatas. So, what happened at the conference? I ask myself always. What happened at this conference that made Beelzebub change his mind? What happened there? I don't know, because he never tells us. But the sixth descent is to go into why war occurs on Earth. And Timothy Leary, the father of LSD, maybe not a good person to quote, but I respect him - the way he died. You know how he died? All his life he said *"Why not?"*, and then one minute before he died he said *"Why not?"* and died. So this is a truly remarkable man. And you know what he said? This book is the best book of the 20th century because it is the only book that tells us how to end war. And that is the sixth descent: How to end war. And where does it begin? The chapter *"Hypnotism"*. Right up to his sixth descent, the first chapter is *"Hypnotism"*. That's an odd something. Maybe Keith can say something about that.

Questioner 12: I guess I take some exception to purpose of the sixth descent being just about war. I think the observation of the war was the impetus. But he goes on to say a few times, and even in this chapter, I'll read it:

"When this sympathetic elderly Russian finished speaking, I, having thought a little, replied that I might very possibly consent to his proposal to go to Russia, since that country might perhaps be very suitable also for my chief aim.

"Further I said to him: 'At the present time I have but one aim, namely, specifically to clear up for myself all the details of the manifestations of the human psyche of individuals existing separately as well as in groups."

I think that's it.

Questioner 4: But you know, he says that the main property of Kundabuffer is suggestibility. Among all the properties of Kundabuffer, suggestibility is the worst one. And now he begins with hypnotism.

Questioner 13: I had an insight here. What I noticed for myself is I'm always at war. You know, most of the time, with short breaks when I go to sleep at night. So, I'm at war with my wife, I'm at war with people in my past, in my head, conversations about that. I'm at war with my body, which isn't the way I want my body to be. So I have the solution. If everything else would just change I would be just fine. I see that in war. If they would change, then we wouldn't have to kill them. We wouldn't have to attack them. We wouldn't have to do what we do. It's always them. We're always at war with them because they do not fit our beliefs, our preconceived notions of how they should be etc. etc. You know, I've worked on myself a long time, but I've never really seen in that way, that I am at war, in a way, with the world. From the point of view of Kundabuffer, of vanity, pride, self-love, conceit, my way or the highway, I'm right, you're wrong all dominate. That's a pretty violent stance to life, a very violent stance. So looking outside at what we can do to change, I'm not sure what I can do except work on myself.

Questioner 4: But that's only one aspect. The other is cosmic. War occurs because of cosmic laws, not only your personal problems, or my personal problems. They are cosmic laws and that's what we have missed. That's why the book tells us what wars are.

Questioner 13: Well, some archangel, was it Looisos who put Kundabuffer in us? Well that's quite a cosmic influence, a guy out there coming and putting an organ in my ancestors, that has followed us for many millennia and yet I can blame that. You know, that's created my psyche, right? So, that's all I can know in my experience.

My experience is at war with the world, with life, with the Republicans, I mean, that's a just thing, you know, with the Republicans, or with whatever, whatever your particular cause is. This year for many of us, we're at war with the 1%. Those greedy bastards. They want to pay less taxes. It's an endless stream of things we can find to be at war with.

Questioner 4: Well, I don't want to have an exchange with you...

Questioner 13: You ARE having an exchange with me.

Questioner 4: ... but my point is that all you bring here is psychological. But there is a cosmology. We need a psycho-cosmology. That is why I criticize the *Commentaries* by Nicoll. Because it's all psychological and most books are psychological. What about the cosmology? That is very important. And here in the case of *"War"* the cosmology is the law of the equilibration of vibrations. This fundamental cosmic law that we have to understand and Beelzebub did not understand until he got to the sixth descent.

Questioner 13: Yeah. Sorry, that was my point of view. Anybody else want to comment on that?

Questioner 14: I'm going to throw in a totally different element here in this discussion of war. It's a sociological element that's not psychological nor cosmic, but this is from a book I read recently called *"The end of war"*, by a sociologist from some college back east - I forget his name or where he's from - but the book left a strong impression on me. And he noted that there are several countries in the world that just made the choice not ever to have war anymore. These include Costa Rica, which after a bloody civil war in the 1940's just disbanded their army and said, *"we're not ever going to do this again"*. And they've never done it again, since the 1940's they've never had an army. Switzerland has decided the same thing in the 19th century and they've never had any war since the 19th century. The Scandinavian countries, Iceland, there are several countries in the world that just made the decision: *"We aren't doing this anymore."* So that was a sociological decision, even though we still have violence in ourselves and we always will have violence in ourselves, collectively, we can make the choice not to have war. He's proving that with these examples. So I wanted to throw that in there.

Questioner 15: A comment I have about the Solioonensius is that - I don't remember where in the book it is but Hassein points out at some point that they take it for a time that God needs help; that Askokin is required, it makes them feel religious. It makes us go to war. Because we don't know how to make this stuff. But apparently with the normal state of things it should make you feel religious and make you feel remorse.

Questioner 16: Please forgive me, I feel hugely intimidated speaking publicly and I always hesitate to share my personal opinion on things. I'd like to just quickly re-iterate the framework I

Seminar 1: Chapter 34 - Beelzebub's Tales

stated last night and then lead into my understanding of this chapter on Russia. In *Life is real only then when I am* Gurdjieff has now finally boiled down to the very essence with the whole of his teaching which is simply that we're triune beings comprised of three diverse, independent, autonomous, separate, co-equal, heterogeneous forces. Okidanokh as it says here:

"You should also know that only one cosmic crystallization, known as the 'Omnipresent Okidanokh,' although also crystallized from etherokrilno, has its prime arising from the three holy sources of the sacred 'Theomertmalogos,' that is, from the emanations of the Most Holy Sun Absolute. "Everywhere in the Universe this Omnipresent Okidanokh, or 'omnipresent active element,' takes part in the formation of all arisings.

So within ourselves, one of these forces which is intended to handle the multiplicity and diversity of the life that we're a part of, represents one of the forces. It's a denying force. At the other end of the spectrum is the second force, the affirming force of our essential non-phenomenal self, that is the animating life force of the physical body. It only experiences one condition: The unity of everything existing without exception and in this way, Keith, I often think of Mars and Saturn representing - it would be easier to say that rather than higher emotional and higher intellectual to simply say the essential self, that second force within ourselves which experiences, has big eyes, big wings and strong feet. It is anchored always in everything in an ocean of white light in infinite extension and we fail to educate our children of that possibility, that potential that's available within them. As Gurdjieff continues the third force is when we by intentional contemplation blend our full possession of our essential self together with our historical personality to create a third force of personal being-ness. So that's in sum Gurdjieff's ideas regarding self-perfecting. One reason it's important to understand this principle relates to Gurdjieff's explanation to his grandson of the difference between the reason of knowing and the reason of understanding. In the reason of knowing all we are doing is using our historical personality to respond to whatever circumstances happen to appear before us at any given moment in time. But in the reason of understanding we are blending either the essential self with our historical personality or our historical personality with the perceptions of our essential self in order to arrive at a just comprehension of the totality of which we are a part. I'll just move on quickly to this chapter on Russia. The way I read this chapter within this context, this old Russian that Beelzebub meets is really none other than prince Lubovedksy from *Meetings with Remarkable Men*. It's on possible way of tying *Beelzebub's Tales* into *Meetings with Remarkable Men* which was written specifically to educate our essential self, once we understand that. But in the meantime, what Gurdjieff is now doing is using Russia as a metaphorical example of some the issues that we have to deal with in self-perfecting. As we know Russia is characterized by alcohol. All of us are drunk in our historical personality, we're just like drunk sailors. We just go from conception to our last breath in a state of complete and perpetual conflict. And so each of these particular segments of this particular chapter represents metaphorically, allegorically, aspects of self-perfecting. So when we read about this general, whether he's a crow mixed in with a peacock and openly being a turkey, this is just our higher aspirations to be great people blended with our heredity and our unfortunate childhood experiencings that leave us less that perfect. And then just finally, in terms of self-perfecting, if we look at this United Nations, this collective effort to do something, Gurdjieff is again simply pointing out to us the difficulties we have within ourselves, imagining that within ourselves are all these different people, you know, it's Ouspensky's multiplicity of men within one. So, anyway, I read each one of these different aspects of the chapter on Russia as aspects of self-perfecting and things that we need to educate in our historical personality about what our challenges are in order to facilitate the emergence of our essential self as the affirming force in our personal law of three.

Questioner 7: I think there's something very important here in what Will said and I want to come back to it and that is, you were making a distinction between Nicoll's work and All and Everything in terms of Nicoll's work being psychological and I'm not going to disagree with you at all, not a disagreement, but this particular book, in fact all of Gurdjieff's books, are about, I think as was mentioned earlier, they're about our inner life. So in fact, as much as we might like to get away from it, we're not going to get away from the fact that these are completely psychological and Gurdjieff is the first person truly to lay down the fact that war is not sociological, not economics, in other words not even for a specific territory, but it's a psychological disease which is - and here's your point so importantly - which not only is a function of the psychology that's going on in each of us individually, but is also affected by our place in the cosmic scheme, the Solioonensius he's talking about. I think that's the dilemma he puts in front of us here: that we're responsible and yet, it started much earlier than us and you've got Solioonensius going on and so you need to be aware of at least those three factors: something happened to you early on, something's off here, something is happening cosmically and you've got a lot of psychological predispositions that you have to become knowledgeable about - understanding-wise - you have to be able to understand them. So I see it very much as, no matter what we're doing, we're talking about the psychology of our inner life. Anyway, I just wanted to come back to that, because I think that this chapter is about Solioonensius, conscience...

Questioner 4: There is a difference between Solioonensius and war. Solioonensius are revolutions, like the Bolshevik revolution, the Cuban revolution. They are Solioonensius. But war is not Solioonensius alone. It's part of it but it's not that alone.

Questioner 7: They're the human reaction, the unconscious reaction, the hypnotized reaction - we're in a hypnotized reality - to the effect of tension, or stress, caused by large planets, just as we get angry, I get angry at your wife when you're stressed. Here humanity doesn't know what to do with the stress and they're not able to religiously perfect themselves so they release, psychologically release the stress, so it's not Solioonensius, but it's connected and it's in reaction to Solioonensius.

Questioner 4: Yes, I agree with you, but Atarnakh made one big mistake. Atarnakh was the one who wrote "Why war occurs on earth". The self-loving, self-proud Atarnakh, you know what that means. And he made one big mistake. He did not go deep enough into the study of war, like we do. We don't go deep enough into what we do. And he was able to relate wars to a law that requires quantity, so we die in war because the moon or nature requires large quantities of vibrations coming from us. But what Atarnakh forgot was the quality of vibrations. It's not the quantity that is important, it's the quality of the vibrations that's important. And this is the law of

Seminar 1: Chapter 34 - Beelzebub's Tales

equilibration of vibrations that Atarnakh never took into consideration and Beelzebub learned during the sixth descent. Because when he, do you remember the chapter about the second descent to the planet Earth, for sacrificial offerings?, he didn't know the law of equilibration of vibrations yet. That's why it's very important that we understand the law. And here we go back to the third striving. You know it's funny, he says *"more and ever more"*. I asked one guy *"why ever more, why not just more?"*. He said *"No no no, because every time we have to go back and study the details of the law"*. And it's true what you say. It's ultimately psychological, but with a cosmology. I've seen many books that only take care of the essence, personality and the body in the context of the psychology, but they miss the laws. We have to study the laws. In us, of course, in us, not in everybody, but in us

Facilitator: I would like to ask if maybe we could move on to the section which is all about requiring a permit for his laboratory. That's one point and another point is, on this side of the room, I've not heard many people talking so can I somehow ask you to consider expressing your views? Is there anybody who has anything to say about this whole dealing with the permit? It's all so strange to me that he's so elaborate about his failure to get a permit for setting up a laboratory. What does it all mean?

Questioner 6: A question, is there something similar to this permit story - he's going to get a permit, he goes everywhere, he can't get the permit because he's not aware of the customs there. Well he's trying to follow the rules, but he doesn't realize the custom is different. And eventually everything works out fine. There's a similar story somewhere else where he's trying to find a doctor, or Ahoon is trying to find a doctor. He doesn't know the custom that, you know, anybody with a Ph.D. could be called a doctor and again he goes around houses and tries everything and then comes home and the baby's delivered, everything's nice. There seems to be a big similarity between these stories. Perhaps this is a pattern, we could think of other stories where the characters are different, situations are different, but there's a form that is invariant between these. It seems to be a style, an approach to the Legominism.

Questioner 17: I don't know what the connection is with this, but there's the portion where the Commission has to go back to ENDLESSNESS to get his - basically a permit - to do the Ilnosoparnian process. That might be something to consider as well.

Questioner 18: Also, I don't know what the meaning of this is but, he tries to get a chemical factory and that, to me, makes my associative mind think of the food diagram and trying to teach that in Russia and what kind of resistance he found, because he understood a lot more than he was able to immediately transfer to everybody. And of course it takes years for the transfer to take place, so for some years he must have been wondering and looking and watching to see if this growth would occur with the words and ideas he was putting forth. So maybe this chemical factory and the struggle to create it might relate to that.

Questioner 15: One perspective on this incident is - I think it's related to Gurdjieff actually setting up the Institute in Russia, he was not successful and it wasn't really because he couldn't get a permit or didn't know the customs, but the political situation was impossible for him - and I think the chemical laboratory is an analogy for the Institute that he started.

Questioner 4: ...seven aspects. Each one is correct. For me, it is how difficult it is to get something on Earth. Have you tried to get a driver's license in Florida? I did, a month ago and it's a mess. These people ask for so many stupid things, and it goes back to the instinctive sensing of reality. I can see you in front of me and I can have an idea or instinct of who you are, without all these bureaucratic things. And it's going to get worse and worse with the internet and Google. You should come to Salt Lake City and find a restaurant by instinct. You don't have to go to any cell phone.

Questioner 1: There's an app for that. (Laughter.)

Questioner 19: I'm thinking about if me and myself are the warring parties, it can be quite difficult to get a permit for trying to end this internal war. I think about myself and my inner enemy. I think there is an enemy inside - my worst enemy is inside me - and I don't get the permit to try to solve this situation.

Questioner 20: It's often the little things that stop us. I coach self-employed people to market themselves to get clients and I've noticed time and time again that the thing that stops them is seemingly very small. I worked with a guy years ago and he wanted to do mailings, he wanted to get out, he wanted to do all the stuff, but he couldn't get his database program together and he had to do it himself. And it's like, *"I'm trying to get a permit and it's stop for this and stop for that"* there is always some reason that we're always stopped. I don't have a big conclusion but I see that kind of thing in my clients and in me all the time. There's so many things that are stopping us. And I remember the thing that ultimately stops him in that is he has to go to a doctor and he can't go to the doctor because the doctor will discover his tail and that's the end of the story, until he goes to the Czar and all of a sudden he's given the permit because he's an known entity or something. But it doesn't sound too unlike my life in trying to make things happen, and continually, continually there's stops. But these stops are only superficially external, because sometimes it's just a believe stopping us from doing something, like I can't do it because of this, because I have to do it by myself, because I don't have enough time, because bla, bla, bla, etcetera, etcetera. So I'm not sure that's what he's talking about but that's what came up.

Questioner 21: Having spent 35 years as building inspector, as a local power-possessing being in a small community (laughter), and everybody had to come through me, I was the only inspector and building official, and the reason I took the job is to be close to Annie Lou Staveley and the Farm where I was. It was the closest throughout the country and it was the closest I could practise my skill, but anyway, the picture here is that he goes to all the wrong places for the permit. He has to go to the midwife, to all these things, and the result of it is, as soon as he touches what is apparently higher, then he gets the permit. Then how does that correspond inside us? We're going to the wrong places for permission. We're asking all the wrong parts of us for permission to do

Seminar 1: Chapter 34 - Beelzebub's Tales

what we wish to do and we're being stopped because we haven't accessed the higher part that will give that permission.

Questioner 10: One curious part, just to finish this story up there, is he finally after his presentation to the Czar, he gets the permit and then he just like crazy does everything he can to get the hell out of Russia as soon as he can. That's another question: What is Gurdjieff trying to tell us there? He's got the permit and he's got the permit for a certain kind of reason that has to do with this abnormal respect, this abnormal place that he begins to occupy among all the people around in the neighbourhood that he was in, who suddenly look upon him as a.. Why is that connected up to his leaving Russia right away? What's going on there? I find that part of it interesting too. He has to get a permit, but then all of a sudden doesn't want the permit anymore.

Questioner 7: It's an interesting thing you bring that up because that's a theme running around in Meetings With Remarkable Men also. We're going to look at that chapter, Ekim Bey. In other words, he looks at a personality there where that comes up again and my sense is part of it has to do with what was... He's telling us something again about our psyche, how we respect and we're hypnotized, so here are all these people, they're looking at him as if he's really important. They're not really sure why, but he wants to get away from the vibrations. That's what comes up for me in that particular example.

Questioner 10: If you take that back to what your neighbour raised as a possible way of looking at this, I think it takes on even more significance. Is this a reflection to some degree of the early days in St. Petersburg and what he began to run up against? He finally gets the permit, he's able to trick his way around all kinds of things, but he doesn't stay. He sees that the future of the school, the future of his work is not here. It cannot be here. So then all of a sudden he begins to trek across Russia and finally down into Essentuki and from there to Constantinople and so forth. But I think it adds right on to see a kind of an echo of St Petersburg in the early manifestations of Gurdjieff.

Questioner 22: Now the question arises for me, this seems to be very much related to the peacocks and the turkeys and the crows, you know, the Cossacks who go riding by and the Mullah sitting on the roof, and he looks down at them and goes *"Ekh"* or whatever and this whole of class. And the power possessing beings have all of this control over the crows, you know, the crows in each of us. I'm sure there's a peacock in each of us and the turkey as well. It all seems to tie together.

Questioner 23: I don't know if it's appropriate to raise the question of ego in this, whatever anyone has to say on that.

Questioner 1: What about you?

Questioner 23: I'm just raising a question, I haven't a clue how it fits into... I'm inquiring.

Questioner 7: With your question I would add to it, just as a question: He's directing us to the fact that a lot of these wars are due to individuals who, at some moment, decide they need to be free. They need to be free, they have to have freedom.

Coffee Break.

Facilitator: I'd like to begin by expressing that I would really like to hear more of those people who haven't spoken yet, so if you feel inclined to say something, please do. So let's start again where we left off and this is where Will wanted to say something about the chapter.

Questioner 4: Ok, about a year ago I asked myself is there any other way to study this book, *Beelzebub's Tales*, because I go tired of reading the book from the beginning to the end. I've read it already seven times. So then I made a discovery which is my own discovery, which is to read the book in terms of triads, that is, take three chapters, as a triad. And then I began to identify triads in the book. For instance, arch-absurd, arch-preposterous and the extraction of electricity are one triad. The organization of Ashiata, the destruction of Ashiata and the fruits of former civilizations are another triad. And, you know, I began to read it that way, which makes it more exciting for me. And then, one of the most important triads that I found is Russia, France and America. These are the only three chapters on nationalities except the little bit about Germany, which has a very important meaning. When I go to a triad, I see the holy denying, the holy affirming and the holy reconciling. We always begin with the holy denying, always, always. I learned this from Sophia Wellbeloved, when she gave an interview in the Stopinder and she said Beelzebub's triad is the holy denying, of the series, of the three books. And that makes sense to me because then I realized that we always have to go with the holy denying first because that's the only force that crystallizes in us, because of our abnormal life. So we have to begin there. So Russia is the holy denying for Mr. Gurdjieff. He went there, he studied there and he left Russia, for France. And France became his holy affirming, the accident, everything that happened. And then he came to America, and America became the holy reconciling, for him and for Beelzebub. Both of them, because they are the same anyhow.

Inaudible question

Questioner 4: Yeah, you can find triads all over the book, and read them in that order, but of course you have to read the book from the beginning to t the end. I did it seven times. Don't go into this the first time.

Questioner 24: We'd like a list of your triads.

Questioner 4: No, no. they are personal, like a said. I don't want to influence other people.

Questioner 24: Yeah right. (Laughter.)

Questioner 4: He's sarcastic. Now, the thing is this, he left Russia and he went to France, but he went to America nine times. Just before his departure from the solar system Ors, he went to

Seminar 1: Chapter 34 - Beelzebub's Tales

America and America became for him the place of rest. The chapter America is the longest chapter in the book, you all know that, and in that chapter he finds the reconciling force for him. This is a personal note. I've lived in New York for 26 years and moved to Florida now, because I've retired, but I used to teach a graduate course in electo-engineering at the campus in Manhattan university. Now the building is right on top of the Childs cafe where Mr. Gurdjieff used to go with Orage and his friends, while writing Beelzebub. So every time a give a class I'm on top of the cafe, you know, and that's a good experience, but not only that, Mr. Gurdjieff always went to the hotel on 7th avenue and 53rd, the Wellington, and he stayed there. So most times, I go to my quarter and I go to the hotel, I sit down in the lobby for a while and then I walk to my building, to the university to give my class, so I walk the steps that he walked almost everyday in the morning, which is seven blocks, exactly seven blocks, or seven alleys. The seventh stopinder, you know, that's my mind working. So why is the holy reconciling America, this is from page 1051, from the chapter Beelzebub in America: *"And you, just you, my heir, to whom has already been transmitted and will be transmitted by inheritance everything acquired by me during my long existence - of course only in so far as you yourself will deserve it by your own conscientious being-existence and honorable service to the ALL-COMMON FATHER MAINTAINER, our ENDLESSNESS - I command you,"* - this is the first, second time that Beelzebub commands Hassein to do something for him - *"I command you, if you happen for some reason or other to be on the planet Earth, to visit without fail the city of New York, or if by that time this city should no longer exist, then at least stop at that place where it was situated and to utter aloud: "'In this place my beloved grandfather, my just Teacher Beelzebub, pleasantly passed a few moments of his existence.'"* Why was America the best place for Mr. Gurdjieff? He said it in the book. Because the people who came to America from Europe were very common people. They were not from the nobility and with these people you can be in good contact, because their radiations are different from the people of the nobility. So he loved America and this continent, this America is the place where the teaching probably will be brought to life. That's what I think anyhow.

Facilitator: Russell, would you please read?

Questioner 7: This is page 621: *"After this unforgettable 'supreme presentation' of mine, I very soon left St. Petersburg for other parts of the continent of Europe and began to have as the chief places of my existence various cities of the countries which were situated both on that same continent Europe as well as on other continents. I was again later, many times, but for other affairs, in the same community Russia, where during that period of the flow of time their great process there of reciprocal-destruction took place and the destruction of everything already attained by them, which this time, as I have already told you, was called by them 'Bolshevism.'"*

"You remember I promised to relate to you about the fundamental real causes of this archphenomenal process."

"Well, it is necessary to tell you that this grievous phenomenon arises there thanks to two independent factors, the first of which is the cosmic law Solioonensius, and the second is always

99

the same abnormal conditions of ordinary being-existence established by them themselves." p.621-2.

The thing that gets me in that section again is that he is bringing our attention again to the two factors. One is the cosmic, and then the other is the fact that we are, for the lack of a better term, abnormal. Our psyche is abnormal. Those two things together lead to this terrible reciprocal destruction.

Questioner 2: I would like to understand from you Russell and maybe you Will, and anyone else that would like to help me with this: Solioonensius is as I understand it a bit of a tension that goes on cosmically, and cosmically within us. Now the way in which three-brained beings in our first and second brain react to that tension - we go to war with ourselves or war with everything in the world. So then how do we bring in this reconciling, this something higher, that when we are aware of this tension within us, how do we work with it?

Questioner 7: What comes up for me in very simple terms is, if I have something very difficult going on inside me, then I have a couple of choices: I can distract myself, I can take it out on someone near to me, or in a relationship of some sort, I can in some way numb around it. The most difficult thing is to, say it's sadness, to use something very simple, something that's painful - which I guess, I wouldn't say that Solioonensius is painful, but that type of stress could be painful, difficult to bear - the hardest thing is to remain in touch with it, both in my feelings and in my body, and to bear it and not to distract but in fact to will-fully be present with it. And the analogy that always comes up for me is when I look at the beasts of burden, like a horse, or I've seen them ploughing in Africa with camels, and even goats, I go: What must it be like to begin to plough for that animal? They have to get used to the harness, they have to get used to the irritation, they have to get used to the weight, and you can either do that mechanically and be negative about it or you can do that will-fully. So for me it's being able to be present with it and to tolerate it. Then it becomes useful, it's transformational. At a personal level that's how I work with it. And that's what I see we can't do. Since 9.11 we had an opportunity as a country here to hold the sadness, to hold the tension, to hold the grief. We couldn't do it for more than a couple of months. So we had to react rather than to learn to respond. If I can hold that pain then I can respond to what's needed rather than, safe to say, most of the time I'm in reaction.

Questioner 25: I noticed with myself back in the late 60's in San Francisco where it seemed like there was a lot of Solioonensius with people wanting to be free, the Vietnam war and everything, and it seems to me that Gurdjieff talks about how it also increases your need or your wish for self-perfection. So I always felt that that's a proper reaction to the war in the fact that if you can find that within you then it can lead you to work is what I think happened to me. I think I'm here because of Solioonensius.

Facilitator: So what I read after where Solioonensius is introduced that we as human beings on this planet the way that it acts on us is that we see whatever results from it as a disease. And then our

Seminar 1: Chapter 34 - Beelzebub's Tales

inner god self-calming comes in to somehow deal with it, and it always results in what it results in, namely, war. That's just something that I would like to share.

Questioner 4: A disciple asked Mr. Gurdjieff: How can I become detached? Because in the final analysis we are all attached to something. And this is what Bonnie says about being attached to my emotions, my body, my everything. And the answer he gave was so simple: Find an ideal. Only if you find yourself an ideal you will be able to detach yourself.

Now I found my ideal and it works. Because I get attached, and very strongly sometimes you know, my emotional centre goes crazy, my horse begins to kick very easily you know. So my ideal is very simple, and I got it from *Beelzebub's Tales* for myself. I'm here to serve three things in life: one is Nature - I have to serve Nature, no matter what, that is serving the moment, I think that's what it means, I have to serve Nature, this is beyond anything. I'm here to serve God, because God is not Nature, Nature is created by God. So this is the service to our COMMON FATHER that is again and again in the book. And the third is I am here to serve my own soul, my individuality. I cannot escape from that. I have to build my higher being-body, and you know I have to get a soul. Now by serving God I serve humanity also, because God is everything.

So find an ideal in your life and you will be detached. Because you will never be detached, you will be attached. And Mr. Gurdjieff says the more you go into this way you're going to go into the other way. See, the more your being becomes higher, the more your darkness is going to be, because they go parallel with each other. This is the problem for me that this was the main mistake Ouspensky made: he wanted the light of the teaching and he forgot about the darkness. There is darkness in all of us. And we cannot avoid it. So find the ideal, that's my answer.

Questioner 2: There's something I've been trying to understand is how do you detach from this darkness? In other words, I'm always noticing that happening within myself, and at the same I'm trying to put my attention on the part of me that's noticing it, so that I can be present to it. But it's still there. So you have to learn to live with it, is that what you're saying?

Questioner 4: You have to live with it. I spent three months from December to March in a deep, deep depression. I lost contact with the whole world. Only my wife and my children. I moved from New York to Florida in February, and I had to ask my son to drive from Florida to New York to pick me up because I couldn't drive. I was in a very deep, deep depression. Now what did I do? Go to bed and live with it. What else can I do? Just live with the depression. And that's my darkness. It's going to be there always, but you're going to come out, one day. You won't be attached to it.

Questioner 7: This is a very big question because it brings up the study and trying to understand negative emotions, whether it's depression or anger or whatever you consider to be a quote unquote negative emotion. And I've been looking at this for years, this issue, and I've found a paradox. And the paradox is, let's just say that I am depressed and I have a bunch of depressive thoughts going on, hopelessness, whatever it may be, and I notice this. I can try and stop it, I can try and stuff it, and it has an opposite effect, it actually increases what's going on. An alternative, and it's used psychologically quite a bit, and it makes sense when one thinks about it, is, if you want to understand about identification or attachment, be attached intentionally. A simple example with depression would be to amplify it inwardly, to say it, to verbalise it. 'This is hopeless; I can't do anything about it; there no way I'm ever going to find another job.' Whatever it may be. And what happens is, and this is the paradox, what happens is you have detachment, in other words, if you take on something and do something intentionally. You're angry at someone, not that you go and hit them, so I could be angry at you and if I were intentionally, inwardly, to verbalise that, the part of me that steps back is where I really have detachment. It's a paradox. If I go the other way, and I try not to think about something, if someone says, don't think about a pink elephant, this is Ouspensky - don't think, stop thoughts - I don't believe it can work. And he had to drink more and more, my guess is, to try and do that. Anyway, that's what I've found. So it has to do with tolerating, being with it, but intentionalising it. Being identified I recognise I am identified, okay I'm identified with what I'm saying, now I'm going to be present and I'm going to be here identified, okay, then something is separate then. But if I try not to be identified, good luck. I'm always identified with something or the other.

Questioner 4: I felt so bad my wife got tired of me. She said, I don't want to hear you any more. But I told everybody, I feel bad. And when I'm happy I don't tell anybody, I just leave it. But you know something, I'm Catholic, I was brought up in the Catholic religion, I did all the sacraments of the church, even marrying, everything but death! And as a Catholic the person who most influenced me was St. Augustine, doctor of the Church, first doctor of the Church, brilliant man, and he wrote a treatise called Treatise on Grace, I read it. And St. Augustine says that there is no work that we can do, salvation comes only from God. I believe in that deeply deeply, and I found it in *Beelzebub's Tales*. All we can do with the work we do is to go to Holy Purgatory. But from Holy Purgatory to the Holy Sun Absolute there is absolutely nothing we can do. Only God can do it for us. Beelzebub was pardoned twice, first for his posterity, that the sins that he committed in his youth will not be transmitted to his posterity. And the second was return to Karatas, and be crowned. Now the funny thing, and this goes to Catholic teaching, and I tell you something, they asked Mr. Gurdjieff, What do you think about Catholicism? He said, The best religion that ever existed on Earth. This I can quote you if you want, he said it. But it was corrupted later by the fathers of the church.

But you cannot do anything about being in a cave in Holy Purgatory. To be in a deep depression is to be in a cave in Holy Purgatory. And that's why our ENDLESSNESS comes to that planet, to give some grace. And this is deep into the Catholic teaching. The second prayer of the Catholic teaching is the Hail Mary, and it says there, Holy Mary, mother of God, pray for us sinners now and at the time of our death, Amen. You have to have somebody to intervene for you. And for Beelzebub it was first Angel Looisos, who went to our ENDLESSNESS and he asked him to pardon Beelzebub. And the second was who? Ashiata. Ashiata went to our ENDLESSNESS and said pardon Beelzebub, he did a great work for me. So not only God gives the salvation but somebody has to intervene for you.

Seminar 1: Chapter 34 - Beelzebub's Tales

Questioner 22: I guess that I would just like to say that I appreciate what Russell had to say because, for me, and I appreciate what you say also Will, but Beelzebub for me is very very far off, very high up, not that I don't aspire to that, but where I find myself now is aligned with what Russell is speaking about. And I seem to remember, and correct me if I'm wrong, that Gurdjieff was writing about his writing, and that in his deepest hour of suffering, I think this was after his wife died, he said he really put himself into his writing, and that he found that he did his best writing, and it was very, very intense. And what I understand from that is his counsel to us about suffering intentionally, because we're going to suffer anyway, as you say Will, and we can suffer mechanically and feed the Moon, or we can do our best to suffer intentionally through being-Partkdolg-duty, and serve ENDLESSNESS.

Questioner 26: Something I noticed for myself is that I'm always lying to myself. But I don't think it's useful to talk about these things in general ways. So if I say I'm lying to myself, what is the lie at any given time that I'm telling myself? So one lie might be when something doesn't work, for instance. So when something doesn't work, something in me says, it should work, it should work. That is a lie. So in the face of everything happening in life, there's something coming up in lying about it. It's like, that should be this way, they should be that way, I should be more able, but if I really look at it that is a lie. It's not true, because in that moment I'm just not succeeding at that thing or doing what I want to do, so when I put a should on it, it's a lie. So I've noticed big insights and realisations and breakthroughs when I'm willing to tell the truth about that lie. Is it true that I can't do this? Is it true that this is hopeless? Is it true that I should be able to do this? And the answer is inevitably that it's not true, that I should be able to do that, I should be happy. So if you're depressed what are we going to think? I should be happy. I should be happy. And that just makes us unhappier. But when I uncover the lie that seems to always pop up, what's possible then is for me to really observe what's happening in the wake of that lie. So what's happening in the wake of that lie is, I should do this, and I feel bad, and then I mope around, and I beat myself up, and I compare myself to others etc, etc.

So the transforming question for me is, who would I be if I couldn't lie? If I couldn't say that? If I couldn't believe that any more? Who would I be if I couldn't believe I should be better? Do you get what I'm saying? If I could say that. So, I've gone through this many times, so I don't want to give you a lot of examples, but I see that something opens up, and what opens up is just being myself, because the lie has been uncovered. It's like that lie is just bogus, it's just bogus. And I'm just left with myself, observing myself, being with myself, then things open up. So I'm always looking for lies. What am I telling myself? What would I have to believe to feel that way. What would I have to believe to keep saying that over and over again. And it's a very cleansing thing, you know, telling the truth to ourselves. And we're not doing that, or at least I notice for myself, most of the time I am lying to myself in some way.

Questioner 27: I'd like to go back a little bit in the discussion, not to respond directly to this, and say something about what I understand to be appreciation of tension. Solioonensius was mentioned, and depression was mentioned. I'm going to add another example - I always say my two greatest teachers were my first wife and Pierre Elliot. Now what my first wife did for me is she presented me with a lot of injustice, I find, saying, Why are you treating me so badly? So I perceived that as very unjust, and the reaction that I got inside was a very furious one. So in tension there is an immense amount of energy. And a lot of times I made the mistake of reacting or explaining or justifying, as we probably all do, but at other times I was holding that, like Russell was describing it, or that's the way I understood your example. So I think for those of us who see how little we change in life really, and how much of our changes are imagination, we come to appreciate the negative form, we come to appreciate the tensions that life throws us, presents to us, and we come to appreciate the efforts and opportunities that we have, and the efforts that we can make in those situations, only in those situations when the fire is there can there be cooking. And what we're doing here is just getting ready, just reading recipes. But when the fire is actually there and the cooking can take place, that's when we need to awaken, that's when we need to become present. And those things happen for all of us, I know that. I know we do that. And we recognise those things, and we appreciate their value, And they're small things in our lives. And yet, that's where hope comes from, they're the only things that we actually do. And everything else is preparation and talking about stuff.

Questioner 22: I just wanted to respond to that, because you said that so beautifully and I think that that's so true, and associatively it just reminded me of Mrs. P and when she said to us, the two best triads of the six triads are when second force enters first, because one is the triad of transformation, and the other is the triad of digestion. Dave could you go into the six triads a bit?

Questioner 28: I remember somebody mentioned George Cornelius yesterday. And I was visiting with George, and it was in the process when Mary was dying, and I took a walk with him round his property in Cave Junction. And he said, I don't know what I'm going to do when she goes. And I didn't say anything, I just walked with him. And then he turned his attention to me, and our situation at the farm, and he said - and this is the connection with the triads - he said, You know Mrs. Staveley isn't going to live for ever either, and you people up there at Two Rivers Farm haven't done enough work in understanding octaves and triads, so if you don't get busy and do it, you're going to be up shit creek without a paddle. That's my comment about triads.

Questioner 29: To speak a little bit more about the dark side of things. Gurdjieff himself obviously experienced a lot of that. Many times in his writings he'll talk about that he had black thoughts, he was depressed. He had his ups and downs too. It's not like you just turn on higher emotional and higher intellectual and oh, you're free! And in fact he has to take a rest from active mentation. It's not something you can do all the time. And that would be appropriate. And then there are times when he does become very depressed, and a great example of it is in *Life is Real* when he's around the spring there. He says, I can't remember myself any more. It's gone, what's happened? That has to be a very depressing moment. But rather than numb it, or stop it, or run away from it, he starts actively mentating and confronts it, and dives into it and says how do I resolve this? I think that that is a great example for us, like you said of staying with it, you can be in the dark, it has value, it's a good shock, it's a way to regeneration.

Questioner 25: That was the morning of November 6th 1927. [sic]

Seminar 1: Chapter 34 - Beelzebub's Tales

Questioner 21: This will be p.642. Leading up to this, he had described the Egyptian beings skewering the ruling class of Egypt and throwing them into the Nile river, and he compared them to the Bolsheviks and their method of killing numbers of people, and he commented that the Bolsheviks should be commended because at least you could recognise the dead when they'd finished with them. Then Beelzebub was silent.

A little later Hassein, having first made quite an unintelligible grimace, and then with a voice expressing pained tenderness, turned to Beelzebub who was still continuing to think.

"Grandfather! Dear Grandfather! Manifest please aloud those informations which you have in your common presence particularly dear to me, and which you have learned during your long existence and which may serve me as material for the elucidation of that question which has just arisen in my essence, and even for the approximate representation of which I have as yet positively no data for a logical confrontation in any of the spiritualized parts of my common presence.

"This question arising in my essence, the answer to which has already become necessary to the whole of my presence, consists in this: To inquire about the reasons why, namely, if these unfortunate three-brained beings who breed on the planet Earth do not have the possibility, owing to reasons not depending on themselves, of acquiring and having in the period of their responsible existence Divine Objective Reason, why since they arose so long ago and their species has continued to exist such a long time, could not those customs have been gradually formed by now, only thanks to the flow of time, in the process of their ordinary existence even under those abnormal conditions, and those proper 'instinctive-automatic-habits' have been acquired in the presences of every being in general, thanks to which their ordinary existence, both 'egoistically personal' as well as 'collectively general,' might flow more or less tolerably in the sense of objective reality?"

Having said this, our poor Hassein began questioningly to gaze at the Cause of the Cause of his arising.

At the question of his favorite grandson, Beelzebub began to relate the following:

Why of course... my dear boy. In the course of long centuries of their existence, and among them as every- where on planets where beings arise who spend likewise part of the time of their existence simply in the ordinary process, many customs and also what are called 'moral habits,' at times very good and useful for their ordinary existence, were also gradually formed, and even at the present time are sometimes formed among several of their groupings; but herein lies the evil, that such a being- welfare as becomes fixed in the process of ordinary existence from the flow of time alone, and which improves thanks to transmission from generation to generation, also soon either entirely disappears or is changed to such a direction that these happy achievements of theirs are transformed of their own accord into 'unhappy' ones and increase the number of those small factors maleficent for them, the totality of which year by year 'dilutes,' more and more, both their psyche as well as their very essence.

"If they were even to possess and were to use at least those 'trifles' worthy of the three-brained beings, then this would already be to the good for them, or as they themselves would say, 'would-in-any-case-be-better-than- nothing.' p.642-3.

Questioner 25: Something that comes to mind in regard to that is when Ouspensky was talking about octaves he would always talk about how there was a shock, and if there wasn't a shock it would go in the opposite direction. So maybe the solution to the problem is being-Partkdolg-duty, it might just be that simple. I mean not easy, but simple, in the fact that just by remembering ourselves we keep the octave going in the correct direction, rather than it just mechanically happening, and going in the wrong direction. So by being present and paying attention to what's happening we keep the octave going in the right direction. I don't know how clearly I'm saying this, but by being aware of the problem, that's actually the solution, is what I'm saying, I think. Because in a sense it's conscious labour that's leading us in that direction, because we're aware of ourselves being aware, and so the octave doesn't go in the opposite direction, it keeps going straight because we're doing the right thing more or less. I don't know how I am, but right now, coming to myself, I'm trying to be present, so I stay on track. If I'm not present I'm going to be knocked off by whatever happens, by the external vibrations that are in the room. But if I'm present then I can keep staying on the point, and maybe I'll get clear eventually, and I'll make some sense. But I think the point is that if we work then we solve this problem because we're taking an advantage of what's inside us that's correct rather than being knocked all over the place.

Questioner 19: The thing seems to me to be, what is this awareness? Because I feel that okay Gurdjieff tells us that we are third force blind. That is absolutely correct ninety nine percent of the time. But there is a possibility of letting the third force operate, as I would call it. In my experience it was connected. I felt a need. Now I need the third force. And it was formed in me as this I need the third force. So this is awareness. But it is a very seldom awareness for me.

Questioner 30: One image that we were talking about in the break is, it sort of builds on something that Will said and something that we've just been discussing now, and for me to think about the reconciling force as an ideal, as some destination that you're heading for, being aware of the dark side or whatever we're going to call it as being, a current or a tide or a wind or whatever, and then our work and our intent as sailing a ship that way, and so accounting for the tide and the wind, with a destination, with your intention of setting the sail and the rudder, to account for those other forces, whether it's the denying force, so that you wind up where you're heading, towards that reconciled state.

Questioner 25: It just seems to me that if you can notice that that's happening, if you can notice that you're doing it, and then you can be aware of yourself noticing it, then you have the three forces, you have the positive and the negative and you're aware of yourself being aware of those two forces simultaneously. So you've got your three forces going. And that would be the third

Seminar 1: Chapter 34 - Beelzebub's Tales

force, I think. And then of course if you could become aware of the fact that that's happening then you can become aware of the fact that you're aware of the fact....

Questioner 31: What you said makes me think of a feedback loop and a homeostatic system.

Questioner 25: That was good because my speciality in engineering was control systems. So, feedback control theory. But you see this thing is the mystery of the Holy Trinity. We will never understand that. No matter how much we try. And here is the story of St. Augustine I love to say. St. Augustine went to the beach and solved the mystery of the Holy Trinity for ever, for once and for all. He was there thinking and thinking and thinking, and then he saw a little boy with a bucket going into the sea. He filled the bucket and then brought it back to the beach, to the sand. So he went back a hundred times. And St. Augustine woke up and he asked the boy, What are you doing? And the boy said, I am trying to empty the sea into the beach. And St. Augustine said, That's impossible. And the boy replied, So it is what you are trying to do!

Facilitator: So before we stop, I have just one question myself. From this part that was read by Bob, it seems that by moral habits alone, if they would survive, we would be able to have a state of being-welfare that would allow us to evolve more desirably. And then later on he goes on to describe how these moral habits become degenerated. So he mentions a lot of factors that are responsible for this, if I'm not mistaken, schooling and suggestibility are among those. Is this a correct understanding? That's what I'm wondering.

Questioner 7: I've just been reading this part, the thing about suggestibility and falling under the influence of someone else's direction. So the question is, what's that in me? It's like, I'm always passive in terms of influence, not proactive. Whatever is trying to influence me I go with it. I am easily suggestible. And it goes down very dark paths and incorrect paths and bad decisions and that kind of thing. So that's what I'm getting out of it.

It relates to your point about, you were trying to say, what happens if you keep this triangle going, and you mentioned that was homeostatic, and it seems to relate to what you were mentioning about, let me see if I can lock the triangle with these three forces inside me. If I could do that, well, in relation to your question Paul, the difficulty is homeostasis. Gurdjieff is describing a homeostatic environment where homeostasis means there's a resistance to change. That's what a system is, it resists being changed. And so just as we might learn to be more present, that that would be a different octave or a different system. The system that's been established by hundreds and hundreds and hundreds of negative things is homeostatic and it's going to resist change.

Questioner 25: They said that the teaching of Mr. Gurdjieff is Samkhya. The teaching of Samkhya is the Prakriti is going to always resist. And the nature of the Prakriti, which is Nature is always to resist.

End of Session

Gurdjieff and Steve Jobs

John Amaral

Abstract

George Ivanovich Gurdjieff's whim *"to live and teach so that there should be a new conception of God in the world"* invited us to understand and reconcile Okidanokh, known to us as the Great Ray of Creation', 'the Emanation from the Sun Absolute', the "'hydrogen' Table," the 'Big Bang', or the entire EM spectrum of photonic emanation, whose 'heavenly' province began to be spirited away from the Church and scientifically imaged in the collective Western mind by James Clerk Maxwell's equations; first published in 1861 and promoted by Heaviside in 1884, approximately coinciding with the time of Gurdjieff's childhood. The publication was followed in a very short time (as little as 15 years) by two-way radio telegraphy and telephony, followed by radio broadcasting, electrical generators and motors, DC and AC artificial light, spark coils and plugs, transformers, mechanized factories and mass production assembly lines, relativity theory, particle physics, atomic energy and weapons, x-ray photography, satellites, moon landers, personal computers, cell phones, radios and bankcards, and so on. One particular inventive use of Okidanokh-dependent technology, arguably the largest construction ever by Man, which has the potential to reconcile, in a very big way, his second functional brain (the 'brain' which Gurdjieff observed as atrophied and a cause of lopsided 'topsy-turvy' imaging and unbalanced mentation), is... the internet. There has been no greater perfected use of this invention than in the products offered by Apple Inc., conceived, nurtured, selected, marketed and delivered in 'differently thought-out' ways by Steve Jobs. The subject of this program is to place those products and Mr. Jobs' handiwork in the perspective of Mr. Gurdjieff's ideas. In this light, we can consider Beelzebub's statement to Hassein at the end of *The Tales*: *"The sole means now for the saving of the beings of the planet Earth would be to implant again into their presences a new organ... of such properties that every one of these unfortunates during the process of existence should constantly sense and be cognizant of the inevitability of his own death as well as the death of everyone upon whom his eyes or attention rests. Only such a sensation and such a cognizance can now destroy the egoism completely crystallized in them."*

Perhaps there is no more striking and apropos statement by Steve Jobs than: *"Remembering that I'll be dead soon is the most important tool I've ever encountered to help me make the big choices in life. Because almost everything - all external expectations, all pride, all fear of embarrassment or failure - these things just fall away in the face of death, leaving only what is truly important. Remembering that you are going to die is the best way I know to avoid the trap of thinking you have something to lose. You are already naked. There is no reason not to follow your heart."* (Stanford Commencement 2005)

Gurdjieff and Steve Jobs

INTRODUCTION

INVITATION TO PREPARE FOR A&E PRESENTATION APRIL 25-29, 2012
"Gurdjieff and Steve Jobs (Apple)" by John Amaral

APPENDIX 3
Please view and ponder the following media (3.5 hr; possibly view shorter ones first and have fun):
RICHARD FEYNMANN
Richard Feynman re Gurdjieff's Third Striving 54:38:
http://www.youtube.com/watch?v=Mn4_40hAAr0&feature=related
Richard Feynman re Gurdjieff's Okidanokh, Maxwell, etc. 9:45:
http://www.youtube.com/watch?v=LPDP_8X5Hug

ESSENTIAL STEVE JOBS
Steve Jobs' neXt strategy meeting, building consensus 21:16:
http://www.youtube.com/watch?v=sOlqqriBvUM
Steve Jobs' on Gurdjieff's answer to Hassein at Stanford 2005 Commencement 15:05:
http://www.youtube.com/watch?v=UF8uR6Z6KLc
Steve Jobs' iPhone unveiling 10:02: http://www.youtube.com/watch?v=JFUYQlk7AZg
Steve Jobs' iPhone 4 keynote 4:50: http://www.youtube.com/watch?v=wn3OCIcE8ds
PBS Retrospective: One Last Thing 56:26:
http://www.youtube.com/watch?v=SQr0HddYk94&feature=related

CLOSE ENCOUNTERS EVIDENCE
http://en.wikipedia.org/wiki/From_the_earth_to_the_moon
6:47: http://www.youtube.com/watch?v=01bY66rklwU&feature=related
9:59: http://www.youtube.com/watch?v=SF_gxlpVDaY
7:57: http://www.youtube.com/watch?v=gBVoIT3KRYI&feature=related

STEVE JOBS, BUILDING APPLE
Bicycles for the mind 1:39: http://www.youtube.com/watch?v=ob_GX50Za6c&feature=related
1980, the roadmap 23:00: http://www.youtube.com/watch?v=0lvMgMrNDlg&feature=related
Apple beginnings 10:38: http://www.youtube.com/watch?v=8LJRZ5CPuCY&feature=related

STEVE JOBS, THE MARKETER
Apple internal town hall pre-Macintosh release 6:40:
http://www.youtube.com/watch?v=lSiQA6KKyJo
Macintosh unveiling 4:48: http://www.youtube.com/watch?v=G0FtgZNOD44
Introducing the Apple store 4:15:
http://www.youtube.com/watch?v=IBMR3FUNsD4&feature=related

All & Everything Conference 2012

On music 2009 18:21: http://www.youtube.com/watch?v=15107GLdSy4&feature=related

JOBS' RETURN TO APPLE AFTER TEN YEARS IN EXILE (where he built neXt and PIXAR)
Intro to Think Different Campaign/Here's To the Crazy Ones 6:54:
http://www.youtube.com/watch?v=VCz_SiPD_X0&feature=related
Excerpt: on core values 1:08: http://www.youtube.com/watch?v=c2cDQw-Cmd4&feature=related
Excerpt: here's to the crazy ones 1:01: http://www.youtube.com/watch?v=8rwsuXHA7RA

STEVE JOBS, THE SEASONED MANAGER
Handling a non-expression of negative emotion in 1997 5:18:
http://www.youtube.com/watch?v=FF-tKLISfPE
On teamwork 0:25: http://www.youtube.com/watch?v=vVCB1vJWQIE&feature=related
On team management 2:28: http://www.youtube.com/watch?v=39mXMv8MyNI

RETROSPECTIVES
Retrospective 2:57: http://www.youtube.com/watch?v=PAkZz0mERNw&feature=fvsr
Retrospective: Apple gadget summary 1:30:
http://www.youtube.com/watch?v=wv6CPi-6S0Q&feature=relmfu
60 Minutes w/biographer Walter Isaacson 28:08:
http://www.youtube.com/watch?v=51J5K7VMsg4&feature=related
Kawasaki on Jobs 47:09: http://www.youtube.com/watch?v=DR_wX0EwOMM&feature=related

PROLOGUE
John Patrick McGree, my dear grandfather (my childhood *"Beelzebub"*), was not an unhappy man. But one day he said to me, *"Your childhood will be your happiest time."* What did he mean? Did it have something to do with responsibility? If true on some level, can we take this statement in a larger sense regarding 'humanity's childhood?' Arthur C. Clarke refers to *"Childhood's End,"* the day when Mankind realizes it is not alone and never has been. When it comes, what will our responsibility be?

"When I was a child, I spoke as a child I understood as a child, I thought as a child; but when I became a man I put away childish things." - Paul of Tarsus (58 CE)   We've heard St. Paul's advice before, but is it really a good idea to lose childlike understanding, wonder and love of learning? What about play? What about games? In childhood, particularly through games, we learn at a great rate. Learning makes us happy.

Gurdjieff urged us to strive to learn. He also says *"Wish effort be? Practice suffer do;"* and 'all is suffering.' Can we reconcile happiness and suffering? What in the world do high-tech products have to do with this?

Our theme is a big topic and will require several types of media, as well as your kind assistance to make sure we all have a familiarity with:

1.~ Gurdjieff's relevant ideas
2.~ the timing and significance of the publication of Maxwell's equations about electromagnetism, Gurdjieff's "Okidanokh"
3.~ the primary function of tools, dependent on electromagnetism, released by Apple over 34 years, particularly the last seven years before Steve Jobs died.

We would like to be on the same page with respect to what happened to the 'heaven' of the Church. Then we will have a better opportunity to grasp some of the most important topics of our time and a possible motive for Gurdjieff's whim to effect a change in the meaning of the word "God."

1.   MAXWELL'S INSIGHT

Maxwell's descriptions of the laws of electromagnetism were distributed in 1884 (150 years after Isaac Newton 1642-1727), well after the Renaissance, just after the beginning of the Industrial Age (that is, 50 years after Eli Whitney's cotton gin 1765-1825). Without Maxwell's insights regarding the electromagnetic nature of the 'invisible world' (formerly a part of the mysterious 'heavens'), we would have no internet, personal computers, cell phones, portable media players, not to mention electric clocks, indoor lighting, radio and television. The relatively long duration between Newton and Maxwell is significant and underscores that the rate of innovation accelerated after Maxwell. It is still accelerating and that is symptomatic of our times, a problem for mankind but perhaps a blessing in disguise if we can meet the challenge!

2.   ENDLESSNESS/GOD, Gurdjieff, circa 1924-1930 (italics added)
a)   THE PHYSICAL UNIVERSE

"And indeed, each of them is the 'image of God' - not of that 'God' they picture with their bob-tailed Reason, *but of the real God, as we sometimes call our common Megalocosmos.*" (BT 775)

"The third [striving]: the conscious striving *to know ever more and more concerning the laws of **World**-creation and **World**-maintenance.*" (BT 385)

"If we take Holy Sun Absolute to be **World** Three, it would seem consistent to also identify it as the Being of ENDLESSNESS - with World One referring to the Will of ENDLESSNESS. Thus, the expression *"I Am" becomes a compressed statement of the Will and Being of ENDLESSNESS. The existent Universe becomes, in this view, the creative expression or outflow from 'I Am'.* " Keith Buzzell, from Chapter 8 "Okidanokh" in *Gurdjieff's Whim*.

"And thereupon when OUR COMMON FATHER ENDLESSNESS ascertained this automatic moving of theirs, there then arose for the first time in HIM the Divine Idea of making use of it as a *help for HIMSELF in the administration of the enlarging **world**.*" (BT 762)

When we put together these ideas expressed by Gurdjieff - that the Being of ENDLESSNESS *is* The Great Megalocosmos (our Universe), that HE needs our help and that we are to strive to know HIS nature - the well-known Baltimore Catechism statement that we are to "know, love and serve

God" comes into an adult perspective which revises and clarifies our understanding of the nature of God and the purposes of our lives.

b) OKIDANOKH/ELECTROMAGNETISM

The Being of ENDLESSNESS is the Great Megalocosmos, which he expressed as OKIDANOKH and which we understand to be the full range of Electromagnetism. As Richard Feynman said in 1965, *"*Quantum Electrodynamics is nearly *all* of physics.*"*

(SEE APPENDIX 1 for supergraphics of the enlarging world.)

2d. THE *"*ENLARGING WORLD*"*

2d1. What *is* Gurdjieff's *"*enlarging **world**"? Is it Man's world or God's world? How do they differ?

As God's world, would it refer to a Universe with an <u>infinitely</u> increasing amount of mass, or to a <u>finite</u> Universe which is expanding ever larger in time and space?

We are familiar with Gurdjieff's ideas that we have three functional brains, that the functioning of our brains is not balanced and that this imbalance is most often manifested as an undeveloped or atrophied second brain (the brain of relationship criticized in the expression "we are third-force blind," the third force, the reconciling force, being expressed as the relationship between the first and second forces.

As Man's world, does the enlarging world refer to an expanding awareness of the world of the first brain (of mass-based digestive transformations and physical, chemical and electromagnetic phenomena) or to an expanding awareness of the world of the second brain (beyond play, respectful communication and cooperation to historical perspective, faith, hope, love and conscience) or does it perhaps refer to an expanding awareness of the world of the third brain (beyond ideas, abstractions, math, science, language, philosophy and culture to 'attending the planning of words', good judgement, character, leadership, principle, degrees of reason and wisdom?

Gurdjieff implies that it refers to all of the above taken together in harmonious proportion.

To cope with our exponentially 'enlarging world', special strategic tools, appropriate to our time and circumstance, which help develop and facilitate second-brain skills and second-brain digestion, would be especially useful to assist us in our striving to generally harmonize our emotional function. What should our attitude be toward such tools? Gurdjieff's student, JG Bennett, particularly encouraged his own students to use tools attentively; to keep them cleaned and ready.

2e2. WHY GURDJIEFF'S WHIM?

Today on this planet, while some of us are thinking parochially (and worriedly) about the implications of a world government leading to a homogeneous society, a 'New World Order,' others are busying themselves birthing new species: genetically engineered organisms, robots, androids and exploratory vehicles to and from alien worlds. Yet, others are living paleolithically in caves without running water but possibly detailed emotional lives. The range of the current composite human timeframe is thus very big, compared with the length of our individual lives. Historical perspective and unerring prediction of the operations of natural law are therefore of crucial importance for humanity's survival.

How will Man reconcile the challenges attending his own 'sorry-scientific' invention; that is invention of which the consequences are not sufficiently or reasonably considered? Gurdjieff, followed by JG Bennett, conceived Man's natural role to be as an energy transforming apparatus having a definite place in an automatic cosmic food-chain. Still, Mr. Gurdjieff had a *"Whim"*: to change, in our time, the very meaning of the word *"God."* BUT WHY? Could it be to prepare Man for an enlarged, less anthropocentric role in the Universe, as a 'help to ENDLESSNESS'? What would our role be?

With Gurdjieff's *"Whim"* in mind, I invite you to speculate about what would happen to the remnants of our limited conception of God if we were to have conclusive popular evidence that sentient life from other worlds is visiting earth. How would you prepare Man for that circumstance? Would you build a giant radio telescope to receive and broadcast extraterrestrial messages, or write and film science fiction? Perhaps you might wish write a book like *The Tales* - an unequalled allegorical space-opera with remarkable men, devils, archangels and a remote Father, fantastic means of interstellar locomotion, arcane atmospheric dangers, and so on. A book that metaphorically transmits natural and moral lawful lesson and method.

The idea that Man is not alone is not new, of course. Formerly, we read about the possibility in fairy tales and in science fiction, roughly beginning in 1620, with Edwin A. Abbot's *"Flatland,"* Jonathan Swift's 1726 *"Gulliver's Travels"* and more famously with Jules Verne's 1865 *"From the Earth to the Moon;"* the latter being, since 1969, fiction no more. In 1869, aficionados of Verne's story were called *"loonies"* or *"lunatics"* (*"luna"* is the Latin word for *"the moon"*), but we don't hear those expressions much today as we find the idea of interstellar travel familiar, at least conceptually. While moon-shooters were considered 'loonies' not so long ago, we've had over 100 years of sci-fi in print, movie, and broadcast. Recently, astronomers have found evidence that there are earth-like planets in the known universe. Gurdjieff hints that life there is likely, carbon-based or not, to be *"three-brained,"* like us. On the other hand, isn't it surprising that, given the long wavelength of thought energies, we aren't communicating directly with them? Perhaps some of us are, but we don't have much to share yet.

Semi-concretely, there is plenty of anecdotal evidence: myths and drawings of ancient astronauts, unusual maps and puzzling artefacts, as well as YouTube videos of perhaps the real thing. See, for example, what YouTube makes possible for us to share: SEE APPENDIX 3

It's interesting to ponder the effect that the first direct-to-the-public alien contact would have. Reflect on the newly-minted-shrinking-world instant immediacy of Twitter, cell phone GPS-cameras and 24-hour network news (whereby as shown by Orson Welles production of HG Wells' *"War of the Worlds"* in 1930, *"Chicken Little"* and the *"Boy Who Cried 'Wolf' "* can now, so to speak, more easily yell *"'Fire' in a crowded theatre..."*). But consider just one symptom of our times: would the vast wasteland of reality-television, X-Factor and talk-radio ever be the same?

Apple's new saucer-shaped office building on a 150 acre property in Cupertino will have a diameter of 1,615 feet; more than twice the base of the Great Pyramid (756 feet) and more than the diameter of the Pentagon (1,566 feet). It will be visible by telescope from other planets, and will join other such large structures (pyramids, earth-drawings, etc.) which have that beacon-like distinction. We can expect the Apple office's unitary glass-ring window construction will be quite a reflector of light; much more than the missing capstone of the Great Pyramid.

3.   DISRUPTION - a timeline of Steve Jobs' tools

Remarkable tools disrupt vulnerable industries and create new successful ones. Through Pixar, Jobs disrupted Animated Movies and became Disney's largest shareholder. Some of the industries that Apple has disrupted are: Typesetting, Publishing, Layout, Printing, Photography, Information Consumption, Music Recording, Entertainment Retailing, Information Retailing, Consumer Retailing, Cell phones, <u>Learning</u>. Soon to be added is Television Sets. Had Steve lived longer, with the influence of Apple, I'm convinced that he would have thoroughly disrupted and modernized the two biggest problem industries in the United States: Education and Healthcare. Let's hope that Apple management (or someone) is up to the task.

(THIS SECTION IS THE ONLY 'GEEKY' PART)
*Asterisks/italics indicate MAJOR product/process innovations, highlighted text means to pay special attention:

Year	Product	Description
1976	*Apple I*	juxtaposition of *"apple"* with *"computer"* to soften and paradox
1978	Apple *II, III*	*text-based: word processing/spreadsheet, primitive email, personal µ*
1981	*Lisa*	*graphics-based: mouse, desktop, folders, trash, menus, for consumers*
1984	*Macintosh	transportable, MacPaint, MacDraw
1984	*Mac production	robot factory
1985	*LaserWriter	**desktop publishing (Jobs saves Apple, boosts desktop sales)**
1986	**Macintosh+**	**Steve Jobs leaves Apple**
1986-1997		poor leadership and slow innovation at Apple (flops: Newton, Portable) email saves the computing industry; Apple 3 is months from bankruptcy
1989	Mac Portable	laptop, trackball, heavy clunky flop
1997		**Steve Jobs returns (and saves Apple by consolidating product lines and changing the company name "Apple Computer" to "Apple, Inc.")**
2001	*iPod	*Digital 'Walkman®' (Jobs' greatest genius move - music-driven - SoundJam + IBM miniature hard disk - vision of the 'digital hub')*

Year	Product	Description
2001	*iTunes	librarian, device manager, sales of music/movie/tv/books/news, etc. Jobs persuades Music, Movie, TV, Book, Newspaper Industries
2001	*Apple Store	flattened retailing/captive audience (Physical/Internet)(a la RadioShack)
2003	xCode	integrated rapid development platform for iOS and OSX
2005	iPod Shuffle	tiny solid-state iPod
2007	iPod Touch	iPhone without the phone (for music, video, games and apps)
2007	*iPhone	Phone + Email + Computing Apps and Games + iPod + GPS + cameras clock, compass, altimeter (time and space) AT&T is an important player here and Jobs persuaded them
2007	iTunes University	consortium of colleges giving away free courses through iTunes
2008	MacAir	light, thin, unibody, minimalist, portable Macintosh
2008	Unibody	carved solid aluminum chassis for portable computers
2008	Macbook Pro	Apple finally perfects the power portable, 10 years after the first portable
2010	Apple TV	couch-potato appliance for your LCD
2010	*iPad 1, 2, 3	larger iPhone/iPod Touch
2012	*?iTV	form-factor is unknown at this writing

(END OF THE GEEKY PART)

4. TOOLS FOR THE SECOND BRAIN

Apple's disruptive products make us generally smarter and more productive. As with paper and pen, the intelligence of the materials attracts the intelligence of the user; these products are intelligence amplifiers. They are especially useful for second-brain functions, such as:

> Seeing and hearing (they excel at imaging, which is essential for all the brains but is particularly valuable for second-brain function)
> Learning and play (e.g., games, music and art; also the form-factors of Apple products are artistically delightful and invite esthetic appreciation; they enhance the experience of information consumption and put one in the mood to create; they appeal to artists)
> Communication (e.g., visual teleconferencing and media production)
> Collaboration (they have a standardized user interface and are consistently easy to use which invites group play and fun.)
> Faith (upgrades produce increasingly faithful images; visual and aural, static and dynamic)
> Hope (we expect Apple products to be constantly updating and improving; we *hope* for them.)
> Love (like the products of careful craft, they are quintessential distillations of countless person-hours of intelligent attention and countless rounds of selection. The products that survive this process have a kind of character like a good basket. This is unusual for a mass-produced item.
> Conscience (they increase our capacity to efficiently perform obligatory tasks)

BENEFITS

All & Everything Conference 2012

The Apple product list includes many majorly disruptive, second-brain tools.

Year	Product	Description
1978	*Apple I, II, III	introduced the personal computer
1982	Lisa	introduced the desktop metaphor
1984	*Macintosh	packaged the desktop simply and affordably
1986	*LaserWriter	('Gutenberg in a box') beautiful typography and layout in the hands of all
2001	*iPod	can put a complete music library in your pocket, plus podcasts and videos
2001	*iTunes	intelligently manages media and devices; millions of downloads
2001	*Apple Store	allows Apple to improve retailing unimpeded by resellers
2003	xCode	over 500,000 apps are available in 2012. This is astounding!
2007	*iPhone	integrated pc, ipod and phone; lowered costs of apps/media/delivery restructuring software prices to $.99/FREE; streamed movies to $4
2007	iTunes University	"Learn anything anywhere anytime."
2010	Apple TV	Apple has accelerated the demise of television (result is pro-education)
2010	*iPad 1, 2, 3	(the internet in your hand) high-touch digital reader
2012		(Here things begin to get murky, because Jobs is gone)

Consider products which show attentive craft, particularly the craft of making artful tools.

"We have seen the enemy and it is us." - Pogo (by Walt Kelly)

Apple's tools are both disruptive and reconciliatory; they are responses to what is needed. They have become available exactly when we need them to digest the energies of our accelerating environment; a need made more urgent by the threat of nuclear weapons. In particular, Gurdjieff says that we are atrophied in our second-brain capacities - of relationship. *Second-brain tools can be seen as antidotal. They enhance and facilitate relationship:* The technologies invented by Steve Jobs & Company can be seen (in his words) as 'bicycles for the mind,' tools particularly designed to replace popular but inefficient tools for second-brain digestion and expression, which simultaneously disrupt the associated industrial institutions which market and deliver them.

"It's up to ourselves." - Dushka Howarth, Gurdjieff's daughter.

It is particularly important to note that the success of such inventions depends, to a large part, on the business survival of the companies producing them, in this case, Apple. To restate: no Apple, no *"insanely great,"* esthetically-pleasing tool-toys. While Apple is at the front of product development and selling, the effect over time has been to drive up the quality of competive products in the marketplace. If you are not using Apple products today, you are still receiving some benefits of those products in the competitive products you use. One effect of this innovation is that, despite the vast wasteland that television has become, the upper level of college students today is better informed about what is going on in the world than any generation ever has been. These are the children who will meet each other and the aliens.

SEE APPENDIX2: Preface to Gurdjieff's Whim

STEVE JOBS' WHIMS
I think Steve wanted to be a music star, but he didn't know where to begin or have time for it, so he patronized those he liked in a big way. The recent Grammies and Oscars acknowledged his contributions to the music and movie industries.

Among his aims were to revolutionize the way we learn and the educational system. Reforming healthcare was on his mind but that subject was unfortunately too complicated for his immediate moment.

At Mattel Toys in 1980, we had some sayings: *"A good education and a good time."* and *"Insidious education,"* This referred to the understanding that learning, music, fun, games and entertainment are inextricably related. But these categories alone cannot drive the computer industry which Steve found himself in.

Steve Jobs on education
He was not kidding; he believed a high-school teacher had saved him from a life of crime.
"Apple for the teacher."   Apple I and II   1976
"Bicycles for the Mind "   1980
"Why 1984 will not be like 1984"   referring to Orwell's novel
Gifts of computers to schools   "More than anyone." -SJ
Wheels for the Mind Magazine   for teachers
[Apple Global Education   teachers consortium   not started by Jobs]
Apple Classroom of the Future (ACOT)
Apple Education   iTunes U, ibooks Author, Textbook sales in iTunes, discounts
Apple Distinguished Educators (ADE) program for outstanding K-12 teachers
iTunes University Consortium   free courses
"Crazy Ones" promotional posters for educators

SJ on music:
Jack Tramiel, founder of Commodore Computer and another colorful character was also a marketing genius. In January 1982, he released his flagship C64, which emulated the Apple II and Atari computers but outsold them, partly because it was available through mass-market retail stores instead of computer dealers. It was cheaper but it also had something extra: the SID chip he had commissioned for making three-voice music. It's low manufacturing cost of $135 allowed it to be discounted and its wild success was not lost on Steve Jobs; he began building superior sound and music into Apple computers and putting attention on vertical integration of chip design and manufacturing. Later, he championed the purchase of what became the Apple Logic music recorder/editor and caused a simplified version to be tightly coupled with Mac Desktop Applications. He called it *"GarageBand,"* which revealed his intense interest in music performance and production.

For Macintosh, he invented Software Evangelists and he hired Music Software Evangelists
He hired Ella Fitzgerald for his 30th birthday party.
In *"Here's to the Crazy Ones,"* a short Apple mission video, he featured John Lennon, Bob Dylan, Miles Davis, Maria Callas, Frank Sinatra, Joan Baez and Pablo Casals along with Einstein, Edison, Feynman, MLK, Isadora Duncan, Mohammad Ali, Hitchcock, Ghandi, Martha Graham, Jim Henson, Richard Branson, Pablo Picasso, Jerry Seinfeld, Buckminster Fuller, Ted Turner, Amelia Earhart, Frank Lloyd Wright, Ansel Adams, Caesar Chavez, Jackie Robinson, Charlie Chaplin, Francis Ford Coppola, Orson Welles, Frank Capra, James Huston, Jane Goodall, James Watson, Jimmy Carter, Gregory Hines, Rosa Parks and Al Gore, (S Jobs).
He hired pop musicians for major Apple events and in advertisements (John Mayer, etc.)
He hired Tony Bennett to capstone the last Apple MacWorld Keynote.
Wikipedia lists nearly 450 pieces of popular music that have been used at Apple public events, reflecting, I think, Steve Jobs' eclectic tastes in music.

5. THE ADMINISTRATION OF THE *"ENLARGING WORLD"*

What do we need to do? How do we help ENDLESSNESS administrate the enlarging world? I refer you to authors such as Gurdjieff, Bennett and Buzzell. However we understand this, we need assistance to interface ourselves with the vast quantities of material generated by the enlarging world and it's ubiquitous reporting; for this we need great tools.

Image always precedes technical innovation; today's products are personal imaging tools to help us to keep up and hopefully make three-centered decisions, including about the products of our innovation. Once upon a time, the 'world' was imaged as flat and art was concerned with the physical: that is, present-tense. The introduction of perspective either caused or was a symptom of a very big idea: that we can leave behind Flatland and flat thinking and explore, at least intellectually, the dimensions of space, time and beyond, *if* we can efficiently *image* them first.

For example, a new idea was seen in Egyptian statues circa 2500 BCE, where one foot steps symbolically forward into the future. But the full penetration of this idea required four thousand years, until, shall we say, the end of the Renaissance. The penetration of popular invention today is obviously accelerating due to the Maxwell 'event' and the applications of electromagnetism.

In 1865, science fiction writer, Jules Verne, published *"From the Earth to the Moon."* From that time to 20Jul1969, the day Apollo 11 landed on the moon, was about 100 years. Verne published several similar stories around the birth date of Gurdjieff. From where did he get the ideas? From where did Gurdjieff, 50 years after Verne, get the idea of putting devils on spaceships?

The 100% penetration time of big inventions is diminishing:
    landline telephone (1877 - 1980) ~100 years
    penicillin (1875 - 1940) ~65 years
    television (1927 - 1970) ~40 years
    personal computers (1978 - 2000) ~20 years
    cell phones ~10 years

There are lots of examples of acceleration in many areas. Looking ahead, there will be challenges brought by technology in particular, which add to the already many challenges to the second brain of man:

genetically engineered organisms
robots
nanoparticles
androids

The Singularity: *"The year 2045, [when computers will supposedly become more intelligent than humans] (is) the expected moment when technological change becomes so rapid and profound, it represents a rupture in the fabric of human history"* (TIME Grossman, February 2, 2011, p. 43).

6.   STEVE JOBS, THE MAN

For a perspective on Steve Jobs the man - his vision, persuasive abilities and personal growth, I invite you to compare how he appears, progressively, in the following videos.

7.   WHAT I'M DOING PERSONALLY TO MEET THE CHALLENGE

Some of us will share Steve Jobs' vision and continue his work as part of our own whims. The critical mass of insights and methods brought by George Gurdjieff, together with Steve's tools, can create a 'tipping point' favoring our endeavor.

Along with many colleagues, at the 1984 Macintosh introduction, I instinctively saw that it was an instrument designed to make us smarter and more productive by bringing us distilled data in the sense of how the Sufi's put it: a beehive, where the honey gathered is quality information (literally *"intelligence"*), gathered by countless millions of people over milennia. I expected this information would put us in touch (as does music) with the creative souls of many minds, and it has. And so, I met Steve the first time and I was on my way as Mac Developer 1234 (and perennial consumer of things Mac).

Some years have passed and I am still at it for the same reasons. The road has been smoothed. I hope software I'm developing will disrupt and revolutionize music learning. Why this? Because I believe that even a small percentage change in the number of music makers could leverage a big negative change in the number of young men willing to be soldiers. The jury is out on my thesis. There is possibly even contrary evidence in my own family, but it's still a reasonable whim.

There are two threads to my work:

US School of Commercial Music: efficiently training professional musicians to have distinctive musical voices. (www.usschoolofmusic.com)

All & Everything Conference 2012

USSCM Software:

1   COLOR VISION AND COLOR HEARING
Some primates made a big leap 56 million years ago to color vision (http://www.sciencedaily.com/releases/1999/11/991109072142.htm), so what about color hearing? My team is producing software which we hope will increase the incidence of Absolute Pitch Recognition from 1 in 10,000 to 1 in 100. After 100 years, it would be cemented in the gene pool. (By the way, there is evidence that the planum temporale housing language and AP processes also hosts second-brain functions related to the communication of emotion in many cultures but not all.) A related aim is to produce game-like environments for acquiring music performance skills using actual human performances.

2   DESKTOP SOFTWARE
We are finishing up a long project of adapting two legendary Macintosh apps into one essential tool that runs and syncs on iPhone, iPad and OSX.

FINAL WORDS
Tying together the elements of this program, I want to point out that, despite 47,000 years of earthly cities, we have precious few physical artefacts of former civilizations. One of these is a 40,000 year old vulture-bone flute. We can logically ask *"Where did their stories go?"* We could use them now...

One sci-fi scenario has the aliens waiting on the fringe, more or less patiently, to see if self-destruction happens again this time around... If we reach the Singularity, things will change at any rate. In this short time-bubble we enjoy, tools have arisen which may make it possible to preserve more within humanity for future generations.

We don't have to think very much to see that Gurdjieff's answer to Hassein at the end of *The Tales* concerned his big question about the solution to war. His solution of an implanted reminding factor that we are going to die is related to his assessment that we have immature second brains. That is, if we were mature, we would not need such a factor. We don't have to look very far to notice that the most well-known business leader of our times, a man who was anti-war and pro-music gave a grandfatherly variation of the same advice. Can we point to any other highly-visible person outside of the entertainment industry who has articulated Gurdjieff's solution so intentionally? We should not be surprised. Gurdjieff is a grandfather of our time and, like us, Steve Jobs is a grandchild of it.

A CAUTION
Macintosh, started as a cult project within Apple and many people have compared it to a cult in recent times. It is a very competitive company with a strong secrecy policy, tightly-scripted events and salespeople. This is a finely-tuned, well-oiled machine. The dangers are that innovation will stop and that the innovation will not target the second brain. Here is what one observer, Rebecca Greenfield (The Atlantic Wire) said: *"Apple has created new industries with the iPhone, iPod and*

iPad. Maybe we'll see an exciting something in the TV department. But, beyond that, all we're seeing are battery and screen improvements on the same gadgets. And, as a result, we may see the end of Apple," according to Paul Graham (ycombinator.com): *"Apple's revenues may continue to rise for a long time, but as Microsoft shows, revenue is a lagging indicator in the technology business."*

Also: this presentation focuses only on the second-brain connection of key products. It is not an apology for wrongs people may or may not feel about how Apple products are manufactured.

All & Everything Conference 2012

APPENDIX 1: SUPERGRAPHICS OF THE ENLARGING WORLD

1. unfolding geometry
2. spiral emanation
3. ladder map ray of creation
4. breakout
5. typical em spectrum

These illustrations from Keith Buzzell's books involve simple geometry to help us begin to visualize very big concepts in a simple way. They are not the whole concept but representative of it. They have their origins with Gurdjieff as told by Ouspensky. This introduction is simplified.

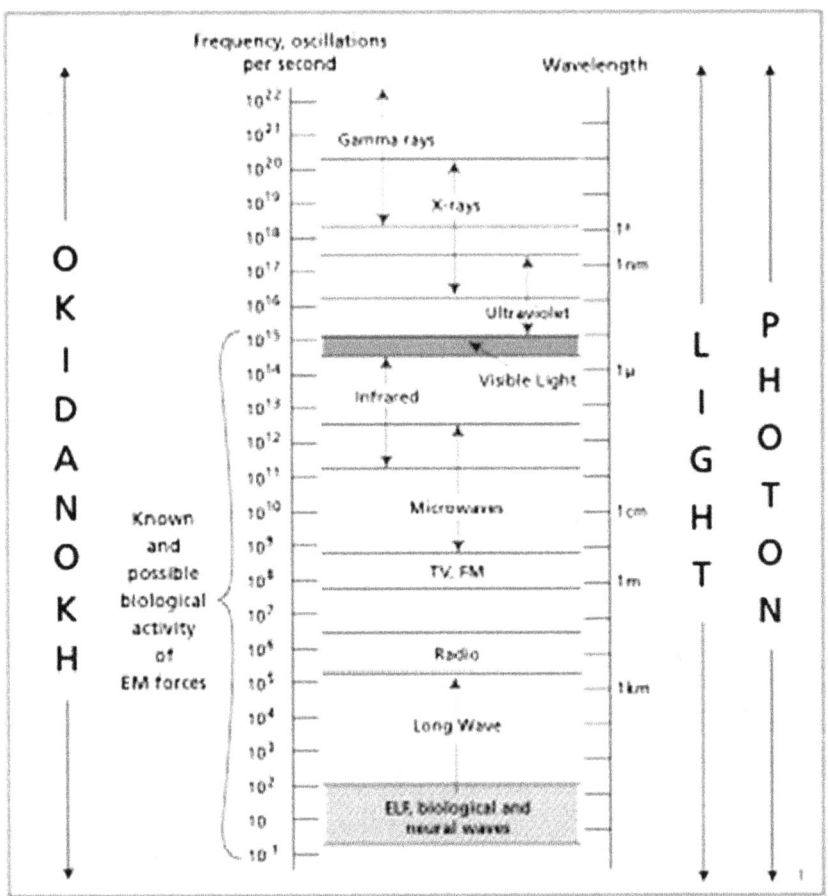

5   Here is a typical scientific electromagnetic spectrum chart which reminds us that the photon (light) is the carrier of electromagnetic force and that all of it is Okidanokh. *"Fiat Lux. Fiat Erat Lux."*

Gurdjieff and Steve Jobs

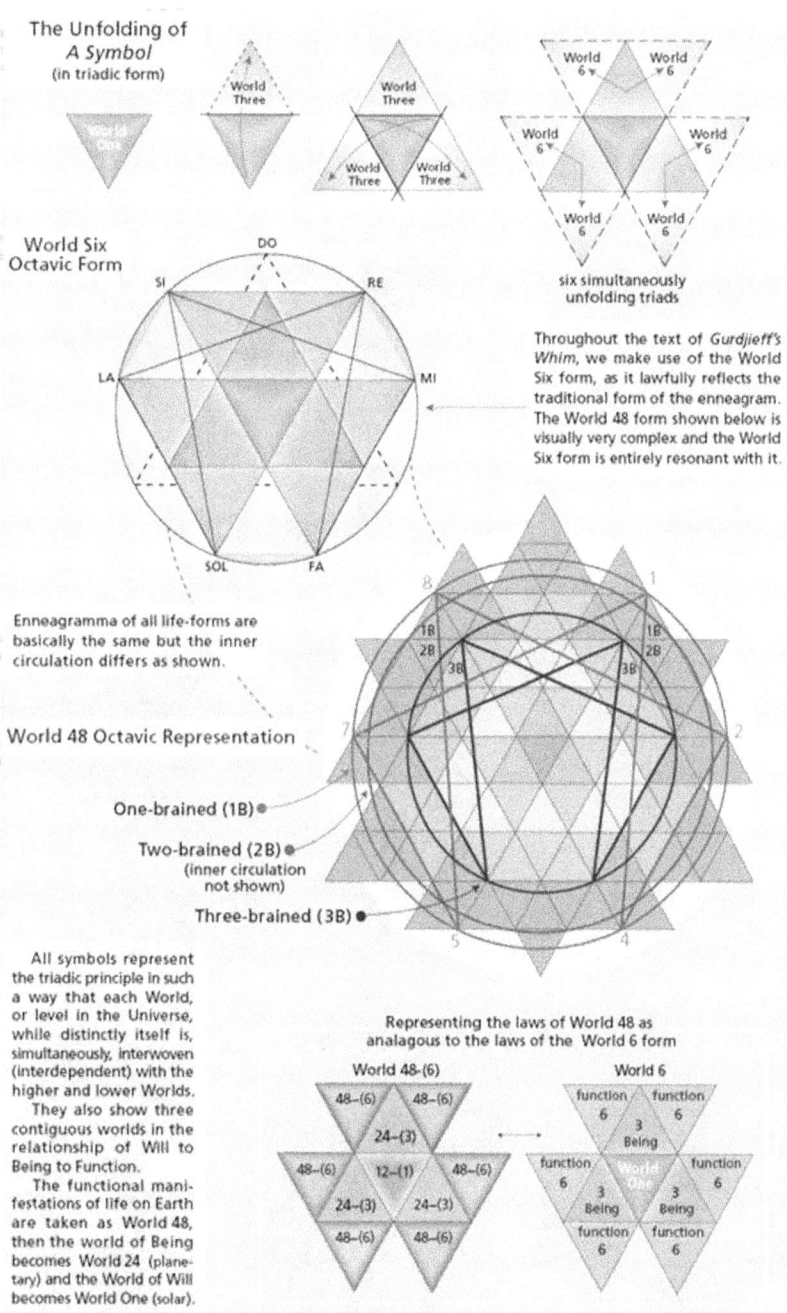

PANEL 1b

1   We begin with a triangle which can represent ENDLESSNESS prior to creation. The first unfolding yields a form which can represent World Three, the Holy Sun Absolute (the abode of ENDLESSNESS) and the second unfolding can represent World Six, having six principles or laws and six the points of a rudimentary enneagram.

123

All & Everything Conference 2012

PANEL 2b

A Symbol of the Cosmos and Its Laws in Triadic Form

The Emanation

LA — H6 Will

World Six — Okidanokh appears outside of Holy Sun Absolute — *Djartklom*

SI — World Three — Being

Enneagram of the "Forced Need" of ENDLESSNESS

SOL — H12 Attention — Photonic Actions

"First concentrations" lead to World 12 Suns

Divine Attention, Will, Love

DO — World One

Great Ray: do, si, la, sol, fa, mi, re

Lateral Octave: do, si, la sol fa, mi, re

Organic Life On Earth

FA — H24 Images — Field Phenomena

Planetary World — World 24

MI — Earth World 48

H48 Impulsakri — Electromagnetic Impulses

Lateral Octave: fa, sol, la, fa (one-brained, two-brained), si, do, FA, sol, la (three-brained), do, SOL, si (Kesdjan Body), SOL, Higher Being-body

By ordering worlds into higher and lower levels of unfolding, and by connecting these worlds in such a way as to make the entirety of Creation an interdependent *one* or *whole*, Gurdjieff united the seemingly disparate manifestations of humanity with higher world laws. The Law of Three Principles/Forces provides the relational scaffold for this unification.

World 96 Crystalline 'Moon'

RE — H96 Moon

2   Here is depicted the moment of Creation (the "Big Bang") and subsequent material Worlds Okidanokh appears as a unifying substance throughout the entire Creation.

PANEL 3b

Beelzebub's Tales and *In Search*
~ Megalacosmos ~

Ray of Creation		'Hydrogen' Table	Modern Science	Three Foods of Man
DO	World One — Absolute	do + ⎫	Prior Universe	Higher Degrees of Reason
		si − ⎬		
SI	World Three — Holy Sun Absolute	la ± ⎫ +	Multiverse?/ Alternative Universes	
		sol − ⎭		
	Entry into			
	World Six	fa + ⎫ ±	Initial Moment	
LA	Okidanokh — All Suns	— − ⎬ ···· H6	Big Bang, Great Photon, Highest of Gamma waves	
		mi ± ⎭ +		
	Djarklom	re − ⎫ H12	Appearance of mass, confinement of high energies	
		do + ⎬ ±		
SOL	Sun — World 12	si − ⎭ ···· H24	Nuclear fusion, creation of the Periodic Table of the Elements, atoms, ions and simple molecules	
	First generation of Suns – early galactic forms	la ± ⎫ +		
		sol − ⎬ H48		* DO — Impressions Octave
		fa + ⎭ ±		
FA	All Planets — World 24	— − ⎫ ···· H96		
		mi ± ⎬ +	~ Life Appears ~ as a case of persistent molecular forms (water, atmosphere and rocks) plus resonant energies	
		re − ⎭ H192		
MI	Earth — World 48	do + ⎫ ±		* DO — Air Octave
		si − ⎬ ···· H384		
		la ± ⎭ +		
		sol − ⎫ H768		
		fa + ⎬ ±		* DO — Food Octave
		— − ⎭ ···· H1536	Crystal molecular forms, no intrinsic energies of transformation (aside from radioactivity)	
		mi ± ⎫ +		
		re − ⎬ H3072		
RE	Moon — World 96	do ± ⎭		

Left vertical labels: Common-cosmic Sacred Heptaparaparshinokh; Ray of Sacred Creation

3   Here, from left to right vertically, is the Great Ray of Creation in descent, correlated with the 'hydrogen' table, the scientific terms for materials and Man's possibilities for the octavic digestion of physical food, air and impressions.

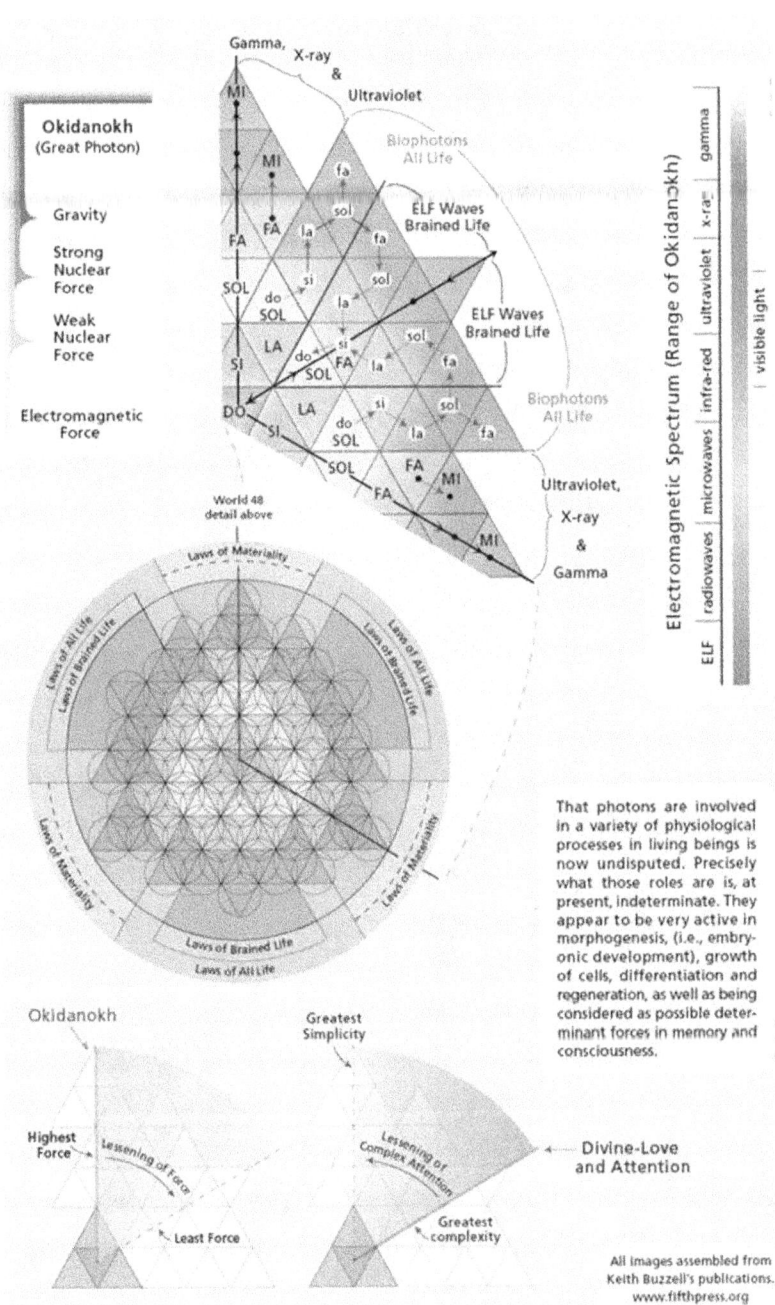

4 At top left is a depiction of the development of the four forces known to physics after the Big Bang. At top center is two of the six lateral octaves possible on the Symbol unfolded to World 48, where we live, showing the spectrum of electromagnetic radiation. At top right is the frequency spectrum of electromagnetic radiation spread as a vertical ladder.

Gurdjieff and Steve Jobs

APPENDIX 2: My editorial preface to *Gurdjieff's Whim* by Dr. Keith Buzzell

"...with God on our side..." [1]
"Imagine there's no heaven, It's easy if you try, No hell below us, Above us only sky... Imagine there's no countries, It isn't hard to do, Nothing to kill or die for, And no religion too... Imagine no possessions, I wonder if you can, No need for greed or hunger, A brotherhood of man..." [2]
"...the real God, as we sometimes call our Great Megalocosmos" [3]

When we take a broad historical view of Mankind's conceptions of God, as far as the political animations known to us as organized religions have gone, we can see that, while at their origin they were focused on Man's inner world and the possibilities of real transformation, they have for most epochs been inextricably bound up with war. Perhaps since the beginning of human culture, shamans, soothsayers and priests have been embroiled in and enlisted to calm the minds of soldiers of all stripes into thinking that God has given them an edge in their military endeavors or at least assures them that their cause is 'just', 'right', 'conscientious', 'propitious' and so on, while in reality, the primary result has been generally that a lot of people have died and someone has gotten rich.

In the recent epoch, essentially 'our time', particularly in the West and now spreading Eastward, a new force, *Science*, has entered the food octave of 'religious' politics. It contains 'digestive enzymes' and carries 'higher hydrogens' in the form of quantifiable observations and ideas concerning the 'Great Megalocosmos'. For the last 100 years, Gurdjieff's ideas, among others, have been 'greasing the wheels' of this process.

Thus, our former views of God have clashed with Science and have to be reconciled anew. And, once they have been reconciled, it may prove difficult to organize a religion around them or to succeed for very long in holding forth the conviction that 'science' can be used to prove that 'inferior' beings must be obliterated or conquered or systemized into castes.

Before Science was taught routinely to schoolchildren, in order to explain and model the obviously superintelligent origin of Nature, Man endowed his god(s) with features that seemed more easily comprehensible and Natural, beginning with his own. Gradually, as Nature has become better understood scientifically (abstractly) and predictably ('lawfully'), it has become increasingly difficult to explain the micro-actions of Nature as individually willed by anthropomorphic higher intelligences which can be 'prayed to' and supplicated for exception, so much so, that, in our time, we have seen the asymptotic merge of Science and religious creation myth (the metaphorical seeds of a theory of 'Natural Law'). Those who attempt to understand and

---

[1] Bob Dylan 1963
[2] John Lennon 1971
[3] George Gurdjieff 1930 (BT p775)

reconcile God with Natural Science have therefore developed new creation myths more congruent with scientific observation - Gurdjieff's myth having rather advanced features, as is discussed in this book about Gurdjieff's Whim.

One can imagine how Gurdjieff must have reasoned to consider all known creation myths and modern science before presenting his solution in *The Tales*. Along the way, to facilitate our understanding, he describes a higher science he calls *"Objective Science,"* so that he can ask us to personally take up his questions and guide us to find 'answers' which we can personally 'make our own'. One of the features of Dr. Buzzell's books has been and is to help us reconcile these two Sciences.

- *What is the purpose of life on earth?*
- *What is the solution to war?*

Gurdjieff's questions are familiar to us. His great written *"ten-volume"* work, *All & Everything*, can be understood as containing metaphorical answers to the first question. Any reader of Gurdjieff's *"First Series,"* *The Tales*, knows that he was also very concerned about the second question, which he called *"reciprocal destruction"* (contrast that conception with his other term *"reciprocal maintenance"*), and his criticism therein of our imbalanced centers, a cause of our inability to actively digest our experience, which primarily manifests as an immature second brain and a misused third brain, is foundational to answering the second question, about which he encourages us too... to care.

Auxiliary to these questions, his lesser-known 'Whim', *"to effect a change in the very meaning of the word 'God,'"* can be seen as an essential part of his solution for the cause and abolition of war. By his 'Whim', Gurdjieff couples his fundamental questions with implicit ones which can only be answered in the context of Objective Science:

- *What is the nature of God?*
- *Is there individual life after the death of the body and what is its relation to God?*

In *The Tales*, Gurdjieff describes two other related disablements for us to ponder:

- *our externalization of good and evil outside ourselves*
- *our elevation of military men as 'heroes'*

In his Second Series, in the essay *"The Material Question,"* Gurdjieff explores a further war-related disablement:

- *our problem of acquiring necessary money "without resorting to any means which could one day give rise to remorse of conscience"*

Gurdjieff warns us that the abolition of war may take a very long time and not to be overly ambitious. Beelzebub answers Hassein's question of what can be done by suggesting that there be implanted in men a new organ *"like Kundabuffer,"* whereby each of us would become consciously aware of the inevitability of our own death and the death of everyone upon whom our eyes rest. Regarding *"like Kundabuffer,"* an understanding of what Gurdjieff meant by *"implanted"* might be related, on the one hand, to empathetic ideas but on the other, to an increased sensitivity of our second brains with respect to what are called *"mirror neurons,'* so as to more fully cognize and digest the loss of people close to us due to death.

Interestingly, after all this, it must be admitted that Gurdjieff's ENDLESSNESS cares about us and has Hope for us.

In the current volume before you, Dr. Buzzell explores the reasons for and implications of Gurdjieff's Whim.

***

Will these questions be answered in our lifetime?: What architecture has mother earth (intentionally?) buried (Atlantis?) under the sands of the Sahara Desert **and the waters of the mythic 'debunked' Bermuda Triangle?** How were the big stones of the Temple of the Sphinx put into place? What are the true ages of the Great Sphinx, Egyptian culture and the pyramids? Why is the first pyramid, the largest? Why did Egyptian civilization seem to appear suddenly full-blown?

(I had an exchange with a colleague who pointed out to me that the exercise of relationship is not the same thing as social behavior which I found useful to ponder.)

Dogon creation myth, the 'face' on mars, crop circles
http://en.wikipedia.org/wiki/Bermuda_triangle
http://en.wikipedia.org/wiki/Great_pyramid

All & Everything Conference 2012

2b. ACTIVE MENTATION

But wait…

One More Thing…

This would not be a fitting discussion about Steve Jobs without One More Thing…

And there is one more thing:

An early close friend of Steve's, who hung out with him and traveled with him to India, worked on the Apple I, II and Macintosh. He sent me the following note on 15 Apr 2012, because he had been sent a notice of this program:

Hi John,

I remember your name from MacWorld a year or two ago… cool to see this topic, you know Steve was really into Gurdjieff and had a copy of *Beelzebub's Tales* by 1975, also *Meetings with Remarkable Men* which I also read and the subsequent film we watched together and really liked it…

Cheers, Daniel

© Copyright 2012 - John Amaral - All Rights Reserved

Gurdjieff and Steve Jobs - Questions & Answers

"Gurdjieff and Steve Jobs", the video, was posted at YouTube in four parts: http://www.youtube.com/user/macmidi

Post-Video Discussion:

None of this video would have been possible without a foundation of Keith Buzzell's insights and latest book *Reflections on Gurdjieff's Whim, Part One*.

This sheet tries to summarize what I feel are important points. The video covers a lot of points, so I thank you for your attention.

The reason that I circulated a list of links prior to presentation of the video was to give the opportunity to prepare for it; to become familiar with where it would be going and what the history of Steve Jobs was. This is not about Steve Jobs; not really. Of course he did amazing things. In the last 7 years of his life to disrupt so many industries and come out with these amazing products…

I went to Dr. Buzzell one day and said look, I think there's an idea here but I'm not sure how to articulate it. He suggested that we could see Apple's tools as second-brain enablers. That's how I've come to think of this and I can frame Apple's work as filling the gap of the second-brain disablement with tools which help us absorb second brain information and think better, as is presented in the video.

The summary listed here: war, 'sorry' science, health, education, the increasing rate of absorption of innovation (which, giving us less time to react, is an echo of *The Children of Cyclops*, Dr. Buzzell's book about the subliminal effects of television: that images go so quickly that you don't have time to consciously digest them, so they get in 'under the radar' and fill up the unconscious in a way that is fundamentally manipulative.)

Regarding imaging, my point is that tools that Apple produces are increasingly better at imaging; at giving us increasingly faithful resonant representations so that we can get closer to reality. The example I like to give is that a telephone call to China, contrasting 20 years ago with today where you can use Skype and talk face-to-face. Imaging products are getting better and better. They are also making it easier to manipulate images, and therefore to make our judgement about what is fantasy more difficult. However, they also help us report and collaborate (saving money by avoiding travel). As an example, Apple is designing products in California but not building them there, so they have to have good communication with the people who do build them, mostly far away in China.

All & Everything Conference 2012

Some things I would ask you to ponder as take-aways are: Could we see accelerating innovation as part of a large plan on the part of the Earth or 'higher powers' to encourage us to harmonize our second brains? ENDLESSNESS needs our help but we need the help of these tools to reconcile our society.

Another point is that if you don't use an Apple product, you still benefit because Apple features get copied in other products you may use. That may seem like a fan-boy approach to high-tech but Apple is the most successful company in this space for a reason. They were a very different company with Steve and will try somehow to preserve that: they do no market research or asking of people what they want. Steve would tell us *"This is what you want."*

Q: Could you give a short definition of second-brain tools?

A: A brain is something that takes in information, process it and expresses. I see the second brain as the brain of reconciliation, relationship, emotion and feeling. The point that we are disabled in the second brain is that we fail in these areas. This leads to all kinds of problems, including war. Second-brain tools help us by imaging the world more and more faithfully. One example is to compare the telephone with Skype. Televisions have improved resolution so much that you can almost imagine being present on and in the scene. Increasing resolution increases the Faith or faithfulness of the image. All of these tools are increasingly good at imaging.

They are good at other aspects, too, such as the ipod with the potential for immense libraries of music in your pocket. That is also a kind of 'imaging'; it's staggering the amount of music you can carry around now. This means that you can get almost whatever music you want at any time. Steve tapped into this desire on the part of humanity to have as much convenient portable access to the music of our cultures as possible. It also makes the world smaller because we can in a moment download music from, say, Indonesia. We can go in many more directions; we have more degrees of freedom now [and become more facile participants, at our level, in helping ENDLESSNESS reconcile an aspect of HEROPASS: the capacity for all possible motions.] The internet puts us in touch with so much, including the expression of other cultures. For example to produce this video, I went on Google and did lots of searches to find the necessary images in a relatively short time. Do you see what I mean?

Q: As a follow up to tools and technologies, could you help me understand or give impressions about face-to-face communications? For example, this entire All and Everything Conference probably could be delivered over the internet without any of us traveling and coming to sit here in the room together and yet I suspect that it would be an entirely different experience. So how do we reconcile our love and fascination with technology with the influence we have in each other's presence?

A: One way of speaking to that is that we all have reactions and opinions about this subject. We know that in-person is very different than watching someone on a television screen and we get 'sucked-in' to the screen, which is an exploitation of our hypnotic function: which facilitates learning, discussion, you and I talking while tuning out the rest of the room, and so on... It's always going to be better in-person. It's always going to be richer but technology is approaching a very rich simulation of reality and we have to become more and more discriminatory to know the difference. One example of this is that it's possible to alter pictures with PhotoShop. Formerly, we could trust that an image is a picture and now we can't, so we have to become less vulnerable to suggestion. But we can't ignore that it's expensive to be here in several ways. There are people who would like to be her but can't for whatever reason. When we get a number of people in a room such as this, a synergy is more easily created; it's kind of a 'brain' or 'mind'. We have to learn to be communicative eloquently; I personally think I'm a better communicator for having worked with the tools in the real world.

In 1984, when we saw the Macintosh, we realized there was something special there. We didn't have the details at that time of how it was created: Partly because Steve had been ostracized from Apple management, he took over a small project and molded it to the vision that had been inspired when he visited Xerox PARC (Palo Alto Research Group). But one innovation he added was that he insisted on having great looking fonts. It was the fonts, also included in the LaserWriter, that established the Macintosh and saved Apple from bankruptcy with the LaserWriter. Jobs had learned at Reed College that fonts are a distillation of thousands of years of art and communication with the written word.

To get back to your point: whether it's better to be together as in this Conference, or better to be online, there is no question that when we narrow our attention there are disablements. Using Skype, for example, involves a narrowing of attention; the trouble is getting stuck there, stuck in the 'Skype world' and stuck with online games. New kinds of social relationships are being created that we have to learn to reconcile. A big example that everybody knows about is FaceBook. Looked at it from one point of view, FaceBook is a reflection of a personality who is not 100% comfortable with being with people. On the other hand, it reinforces existing social relationships and makes it possible for us to communicate in new ways.

Q: It seems to be that regardless of how we feel about technological development we are going to have to learn to use it. All that aside, doesn't technology pollute the environment? It requires rare-earth minerals that are difficult to extract.

A: Yes. High-tech companies have a responsibility to help recycle their obsolete products. Yes, it's sustainable but there are a lot of other things of greater concern: advances in genetic medicine, nanoparticles and androids are all scary topics.

Q: I found your talk really stimulating and it's hard to know where to begin with some of the questions that are raised in my mind, but first off, the All and Everything Conference is based on a 'book,' one of the first technologies that broke down the barriers of communication, and you could have a big conversation about the pros and cons: about the benefits and deficits of literacy on memory, and the spread of the written word; this is a really old conversation that is brought into this really amplified environment through converging technologies and all of this accelerated stuff that you're talking about. OK, I'm just going to put that out there as one thing. I just keep thinking that we're all here because of a book.

The other thing I'm thinking about is that I have a love-hate relationship with Apple. I've got a Macintosh and I really enjoy using that platform, etc. etc., and who cares? My hate part with the whole thing is that in some ways, I think of Steve Jobs as a commercial terrorist, in having introduced this mania of style which has, by coupling itself with technology is insidious. Was it Gurdjieff who said *"Don't have yourself photographed with a famous person."*? The Macintosh has become identified with famous people and the users are encouraged to identify themselves with famous people. I, iBook, iMac, iPod, iDunno. The amplification of ego in relationship to the technology is, for me, really huge, as well as the loss of the self in the technology. A book can be terribly distracting… it is not intrinsically a terribly liberating or mind-expanding technology. You can get yourself lost in Zane Grey or whatever. The other thing I'm thinking about is this: Gurdjieff experienced near-death. I wonder about the power of that statement of the value of knowing one's mortality and what kind of experience he had; when and how did that inform him of his own sensibility, his own coming to understand the real world? But not always does it happen that one can have a near-death experience and have one's being expanded as a result of it: Baba Ram Dass was amazed to find that, when he had a stroke, he didn't have a spiritual experience. Your talk stimulates many questions in my mind.

A: I don't think I need to say anything at all; I think that was great.

C: (follow-up comment): I was with Dushka many times and she affirmed that Gurdjieff, if he were alive, would be using the internet to achieve his aims.

Q: I'm wondering why you're putting an emphasis on Absolute Pitch? Does this relate to the *"Nirioonassian world sound"*?

A: My observation is that people with AP have an extra tool: the color discrimination associate with AP helps a musician react faster and more sensitively to music. There are also arguments in the other direction. But think about only being able to see in black and white; AP is a tool. My experience is that people with really good ears MAY be extraordinarily emotionally sensitive (or disordered).

Q: Thank you very much. I found this to be very interesting and I'm glad I watched it before I came. There are three things I would like to say. One of these is that I was reading an article in the Atlantic Monthly about loneliness; but I don't want to go into that because I realize there are two ends to every stick. And so there are many many aspects you brought out that are very positive. We are who we are; we each have our Itoklanoz, vulnerabilities and suggestibilities and through our own work we have to overcome our own suggestibility; so I don't really see that as being the issue. Everything we've ever done has to be inevitably reconciled: the use of electricity, nuclear power plants and on and on. One of the things you said that interested me that was very small and may have gone by a lot of people is that you mentioned war and that there might come a time when young men might not want to go to war. So, I'd like you to speak a little to that, but I also have a note to read here: *"Gurdjieff loved automobiles right up to the end of his life. He was enthused and interested in wire recordings and other inventions."*

A: Steve Jobs was anti-war. He thought about it a lot. He came out of that culture: the hippy/LSD culture at the time of the Vietnam War and I trust that that is pervasive (at least for now) in the Apple culture. In fact, he was very upset that the US Government was using Apple IIs to calculate missile trajectories. When I was a kid there was a play on television called *"The Bad Seed,"* which explored the idea that there might be kids who were really bad; evil. This got me thinking at a pretty early age whether that's true. Do we believe that humanity, people, are basically good? Do we believe that Faith, Hope and Love come from above and are part of the substrate of the universe? I believe that it is true and I believe it more having studying Keith Buzzell's material. I would suggest that this might be useful to people: the idea that there is a cosmic Faith, Hope and Love that gets divided down into our world. My thesis is that if we are able to become more in touch with the world of the second brain, however that happens, but particularly through reconciliation of the things that are coming at us from outside, all of this technology coming down in the future and the tremendous amount of information because everybody has a cell phone with a camera; the internet is being sliced and diced in various ways by people who want to make money, and we are riding the Devil's back if you want to put it that way, we can send an email to China in seconds; it's making the world 'smaller' and that's helping us reconcile relationship.

I'm watching my nephew who is at Annapolis getting a 'free' engineering degree; he played a little bit of keyboard and guitar and I'm wondering if he can morally survive the indoctrination. But that's Annapolis and it's the government and they have a very good indoctrination. The rest of us might be a little bit less likely to get mad at somebody that we know a little bit better. The externalization of evil is harder to do in a world that has good imaging and communication. That's hopeful.

Q: I'd like to thank John for all his work in bringing a very controversial topic to this conference and forgive me from being cheeky. When I bought an iphone several years ago, a friend said to me *"It will change your very being."* (laughter) A thing I value most about the iphone is that I can read *Beelzebub's Tales* wherever I may be. I have to admit that I watched your material, a lot of it, before coming here and discovered again while watching your documentary and discovered again the negativity brewing in me, but with my iphone, I could stop watching it and read *Beelzebub's Tales* and got many new insights during your presentation (sound of laughter).

Q: Loved this. Thank you John. So, Steve Jobs… he made people love their device, by putting a lot of feeling into it, so that the user touches and feels connected with their ability to use this new technology. And that's why his products are so great because you feel so great using them; you feel connected to the use of them. And it doesn't help train attention, to use all this stuff. We have to make sure that that's the prime training of our kids and all people. And that science of attention is the key to transformation. And these tools ruin that in many mechanical beings, of course; they make it harder and harder to train; they take the attention training away; the attention span is less.

In the '80's I did shows and for 40 minutes I had perfect attention; now it's really tough; I have to work hard in schools. These tools are fantastic for exactly what you're saying and can help us to do something great and we can use them, but there's no *"i"*; there's no use of the imaging that the second brain creates; it's 'it' rather than *"i"*; so that's the key: *"I"* and attention.

A: Computers are largely untapped in education; one of the best (nearly unavailable) applications is one-on-one skills training. One of the things I'm interested in is music performance, which is a place where you have to be there (mentally) as a preparation for playing with other people. We have not yet used computers in an interactive way; they have not yet become good teachers for us; at some point, that's going to change and they are going to become more and more helpful. We're starting to see that in small ways. The other side is that we can get trapped in playing video games and other disablements. We can do a lot more with computers that would be good for us.

Q: It's an amazing topic that brings up so many questions about our relationship to organic life and the universe. The question I have is that I have difficulty reconciling the harm that comes to our organic life through the production of our technologies. Can you address that for me?

A: Well, I didn't say it before, but we don't know what happens when you start pushing a lot of electrical energy into the atmosphere of the earth. (the work of Wilhelm Reich is one place to start). We do know that there are increases in leukemia from large flows of electrons such as under power lines and above underground rivers with electrolytes in them. There are other instances of electromagnetic pollution that are largely not understood, such as cell phones. The internet is one of the largest things that man has ever done. It by and large was conceived so that it could not be censored, although some agencies are doing that somewhat. (The potential for human connectivity of the internet is very great and we have to develop antidotes to the risks it may bring.) I don't know if this is an answer to your question but there have to be things introduced into the environment that might have toxic costs and we have to weigh such costs - each and every one of us; perhaps to examine our own life and to see what's useful to us in our life. I don't know if that begins to answer your question; it's a big question.

Q: I also have grappled with the question of technology, blessing or curse. I'd like to say something about Steffan's presentation when he raised the question of productivity and discipline: I have found, in using computers, and I've wasted many hours, that there comes a point when a voice within you says *"you're wasting your time,"* which is in our understanding is a 'sin' because we have a limited time every day when we can make good use of our time, so I think there's a function of conscience that tells us at some point *"you should be stopping; you're on the wrong track; stop here and stand back."* So I think that to me is my personal answer to the question of whether technology is a blessing or a curse. You have to listen to your inner voice. We could have a discussion for another week obviously about this topic. But you have to find that point in yourself when you should stop.

Moderator: Thank you, I'm very grateful for that comment and we have to stop now.

Gurdjieff, Plato & Pythagoras: Roman Coins & Planetary Connection

George Beke

Abstract

In February 2002, Dushka Howarth brought a very special audio recording to a celebratory meeting at Lillian Firestone's apartment on the upper West Side of Manhattan. It was a recording of the talk that her father, George Ivanovich Gurdjieff, had given at Christmas time many years earlier, in a hotel suite when he was visiting New York. Hearing Gurdjieff's own voice was mesmerizing and galvanizing.

In broken English, he gave the people assembled there a Christmas cadeau, a special holiday gift. There is a *"point"* in the heavens, Gurdjieff said, to which universal prayers were addressed, where the collective efforts of countless saints and sages were stored over the eons. From this special location in the heavens, a striving person could *"suck, borrow, or steal"* a finer substance, and with it coat one's inner bodies through the *"I Am"* exercise, through self-remembering.

Where could this point in the heavens possibly be located? That is a most absorbing journey from Pythagoras himself, to Plato, thence to Cicero, and finally arriving at Macrobius, who reveals that the Gates of Heaven lie at the intersections of the path of the Planets (along the Zodiac) and the Milky Way, which was seen as the heavenly abode of souls.

Have you seen the Milky Way recently? Have you seen the Zodiacal Light along which the Planets construct the stairs to the heavenly abode (Parabola Fall 2011, p. 74), and which intersects the Via Galactica at the celestial gates?

It's quite a thrill, which reveals Gurdjieff's connection to Plato's X (Chi) in the sky, and through Plato to Pythagoras himself, who paved this ancient road.

And the coins of Roman emperors bear witness to Plato's celestial intersections over hundreds of years, from Domitian to Antoninus Pius, to Marcus Aurelius, to Licinius and Constantine, etc.

Gurdjieff, Plato & Pythagoras: Roman Coins & Planetary Connection

> *"Everything Christian came from old Greek, then they spoil. All, all comes from Greek."* - G. I. Gurdjieff (*Ladies of the Rope*, William Patrick Patterson)

In this explosive statement, Gurdjieff reveals the source of his esoteric ideas: not the Sufis of the Muslim world, nor the Lamas of Tibet, but his own homeboys, the Greeks who laid the foundations of Western civilization more than two and a half thousand years ago.

At the beginning of *Beelzebub's Tales*, Gurdjieff demurely refers to himself as a mere Teacher of Dances. But buried in the pages of his hefty tome, we find that the Sacred Dances that he teaches originated in ancient Babylon where a club of the 'Adherents-of-Legominism' had long ago been formed. Who were the founders of this esoteric sect?

> *"As I learned later, this uniting of theirs had been brought about by two learned beings who were initiates of the first degree... One of these two initiated learned beings of the Earth who had his arising among, as they are called, the Moors, was named Kanil-El-Norkel. The other learned initiated being was named Pythagoras, and arose from among,*

Gurdjieff, Plato & Pythagoras: Roman Coins & Planetary Connection

as they are called, the Hellenes..." - G.I. Gurdjieff, All And Everything (Harcourt, Brace and Company, 1950), p. 455.

Here Gurdjieff traces a clear line between himself as Teacher of Dances and Pythagoras who helped start a club in Babylon that passed on esoteric knowledge through arts such as acting, painting, and dancing. Each art was performed on a different day of the week for the edification of the populace at large but, according to Beelzebub, sadly only one form has managed to survive in its esoteric aspect to modern times. Can you guess what the surviving art form is?

What was Pythagoras doing in Babylon anyway? Supposedly he had been studying in Egyptian temples when the Persians invaded, and he ended up captive in Babylonia according to neo-Platonist street talk. Gurdjieff not only demonstrates his familiarity with the myth but also his engagement with the journey of Pythagoras to discover ancient knowledge across the continents, a journey he would repeat himself.

After his detainment in Babylon, Pythagoras traveled to Magna Graecia, the Italian peninsula, where several Greek colonies were seeking a solid foothold. At Croton, he started an esoteric school that would profoundly influence Western thought. What did Pythagoras teach? That's hard to say, since students had to take a vow of silence. Anyone who revealed the secret teachings to the uninitiated masses was ostracized and declared dead to the community.

Moreover, the Pythagoreans preferred a cryptic method of communication that Gurdjieff would practice, a method he referred to as *"burying the dog."*

> *"Their writings were not composed in popular or vulgar diction, or in a manner usual to all other writers, so as to be immediately understood, but in a way not to be easily apprehended by their readers. For they adopted Pythagoras' law of reserve, in an arcane manner concealing mysteries from the uninitiated, obscuring their writings and mutual conversations."* - Iamblichus, *The Life of Pythagoras*

Anyone who has read *Beelzebub's Tales* should recognize the Pythagorean effort to not be *"easily apprehended"* by the reader. Most illustrative of this method is Chapter 17, whose title states its subject matter: 'The Arch-absurd: According to the Assertion of Beelzebub, Our Sun Neither Lights nor Heats.' In order to dig up the dog buried here, one must avoid the trap that's been set and resist the bait of useless cogitation. It matters little whether the Sun lights or heats. Instead the meta-question is: What does this point to?

The answer is that this chapter points to the Pythagoreans.

> *"The Pythagorean Philolaus says that the sun is a vitrescent body which receives the light reflected by the fire of the Cosmos, and sends it back to us."* - Stobaeus, *Eclogues*

All & Everything Conference 2012

That the *"Sun neither lights nor heats"* of its own power proves to be a tenet held by certain Pythagoreans, and Gurdjieff merely uses that as a pointer to the Pythagoreans themselves. Care to test your understanding of the Pythagorean method of *"burying the dog?"* Read the next chapter, 'The Arch-preposterous,' and see if you can guess who Gurdjieff is pointing to there.

So what about those Pythagoreans? What made them so important anyway? Pardon my sanguine opinion, but I'd say they were the godfathers of Western civilization. Arguably the greatest of Greek philosophers, Plato himself was greatly influenced by the Pythagoreans, who he met on his voyages to Magna Graecia. When the Spartan ambassador sold Plato into slavery at the urging of the tyrant of Syracuse, the Pythagoreans ransomed Plato, a debt he would repay with gratitude over many years.

Plato's most valuable gifts to us are his Pythagorean texts, where he uses myth and allegory to weave a picture of what his oath of reserve only lets him reveal *"through a glass dimly."* A charge leveled later was that *"Plato Pythagorizes,"* an accusation not only correct, but a fact that we should celebrate, as it gives us a glimpse into Pythagorean thought through the curtain of one of the greatest Greek minds.

Plato's most Pythagorean work is commonly held to be Timaeus. Rafael's masterpiece in the Vatican, the 'School of Athens' fresco, depicts Plato holding this book while pointing upward to the heavens. That is fitting because in this text Plato describes how the Creator modeled the cosmos out of primal material that he shaped and molded into two intersecting celestial circles. One of these circles, our author reveals, is the course of the Wanderers in the sky, the ecliptic along which the Planets delineate the constellations of the Zodiac.

The Pythagorean 'law of reserve' would not let Plato divulge the whole enchilada but, if we dig carefully, we can confidently discover the identity of the other celestial circle, whose intersection with the Zodiac takes the form of an X in the night sky.

How can we be sure that Plato's X in the sky was popularly known in the Hellenistic world? From the testimony of one of the earliest Christian apologists, Justin Martyr, whose harangues at the emperors of Rome eventually earned him his nickname. In one of these public letters, Justin argued that Plato's celestial X was in fact a foreshadowing of the Christian cross.

> "And the physiological discussion concerning the Son of God in the *Timaeus* of Plato, where he says, 'He placed him crosswise in the universe…'" - Justin Martyr, *First Apology*

So what does Plato's cosmic X, which the Christians sought to appropriate, actually represent? According to the Roman writer Macrobius, the intersection of the Zodiac (the path of the Planets) and the Milky Way indicates the very Gates of Heaven. Since Macrobius is commenting on Cicero's *Dream of Scipio*, we should find similar elements in Cicero's work, which of course we do, and we find these as well in Manilius' *Astronomica*, an astrological handbook from the time of

Gurdjieff, Plato & Pythagoras: Roman Coins & Planetary Connection

Augustus.

Cicero translated Plato's *Timaeus* into Latin, dedicating it to his neo-Pythagorean mentor, Nigidius Figulus. He paid homage to Plato's *Republic* with his own *On The Republic*, and he reworked the *Myth of Er* at the end of *Republic* into the *Dream of Scipio* at the end of his own book, the coda that Macrobius would use to frame his exposition of the neo-Platonist worldview. In other words, there's a direct line from Macrobius to Cicero, and then to Plato, a tradition that extended over 700 years.

The Milky Way was the abode of souls, and these spiritual entities descended along the path of the Planets, a golden chain in the night sky, and they would return along the same route at the end of their stay on earth. Souls who had lived impure or criminal lives could not rise to the highest heavens, but floated around in the ether's lowest regions. Amazingly, this exact explanation of the soul's journey is given in *Beelzebub's Tales*.

> *"As soon as the body Kesdjan of the being is separated from the planetary body of the being, it at once rises according to the cosmic law called 'Tenikdoa,' or as it is sometimes called the 'law of gravity,' to that sphere in which it finds the weight proper to it equally balanced and which is therefore the corresponding place of such cosmic arisings..."* - All and Everything (1950), p. 728.

By 'sphere,' Beelzebub obviously means a planetary sphere, and such planetary spheres can already be found in Plato's *Myth of Er*. Moreover, Plato places a Siren atop each planetary orbit, embedding the Pythagorean Music of the Spheres into his story.

> *"And up above each of the rims of the circles stood a Siren, who accompanied its revolution, uttering a single sound, one single note. And the concord of the eight notes produced a single harmony."* - Plato, Republic

Can we find this Harmony of the Spheres, the Pythagorean connection between the musical scale and the Planets, buried in Gurdjieff's book? Yes, we can, in the description of the Nirioonossian-World-Sound:

> *"It was first discovered by that learned member of the society Akhaldan... At that time, this learned member during his observations of different cosmic phenomena... constated that in a definite locality... the same definite sound always arose and was heard for a fairly long time... And therefore he then on the spot constructed an elevation such as he required for the observation of 'heavenly bodies'; and he constructed this required elevation on this spot because he wished during these observations of his at the same time to observe and investigate also this 'cosmic result' at first entirely incomprehensible to him."* - A&E, p. 868.

Gurdjieff's Nirioonossian-World-Sound is in fact the *"single harmony"* of Plato's *Myth of Er*, the Pythagorean Music of the Planetary Spheres. Where can we find the ascension to the heavens linked to the Harmony of the Spheres? The Roman jurist Martianus Capella describes such a planetary ascent through musical intervals in his *Marriage of Philology and Mercury*, while hundreds of years earlier Cicero already attests to such a journey in his 'Dream of Scipio.'

The ascent of the soul through the Planets would be invoked on Roman standards carried at the forefront of Roman legions ('Celestial Symbols on Roman Standards,' *The Celator* numismatic magazine, June 2011), while the intersection in the sky that indicates the Gates of Heaven would appear on Imperial coins over hundreds of years ('Plato's X on Roman Coins,' *Coin News*, January 2012).

Gurdjieff's links to this ancient tradition are evident in his writings: the Nirioonossian-World-Sound is the Pythagorean Music of the Spheres, the body-Kesdjan rises to an appropriate planetary level following Pythagorean soteriology, and Pythagoras was the co-founder of the 'Adherents-of-Legominism' in Babylon whose sole surviving art form Gurdjieff teaches.

Those points paint a direct path between Gurdjieff and the ancient Greek cosmology of Plato and his spiritual forefather Pythagoras.

© Copyright 2012 - George Beke - All Rights Reserved

Gurdjieff, Plato & Pythagoras - Questions & Answers

Question: Thank you, George. I have a few comments, very short. The first is that there are other connections between Beelzebub and Pythagoras. One is that the planet Karatas has two suns: one is called Samos, the city where Pythagoras was born. Another thing Mr. Gurdjieff told Solita is that seven times seven is you, but then he told her *"That's too advanced for you."* Another thing that he told in a Paris meeting to a bunch of disciples is that if you connect to that point up in the sky, you can materialize a saint on Earth. And then one guy asks him, *"Can I do that?"* And he says, *"No, no, this is not good for you, you better do the stretching arms exercise… For somebody else…"* [Much laughter…] But I have one question for you: The chapter of Ashiata, the chapter of Lentrohamsanin, and the chapter that follows that is the fruit of ancient civilizations, of former civilizations. Now in that chapter, we know that Ashiata taught objective conscience. We know that Lentrohamsanin destroyed that seven centuries after. All this is allegorical of course. But then come the Greeks… The Greeks are destroyers of objective reason and the Romans are destroyers of objective morality. How did the Greeks destroy objective reason? They did it because they were bored. They were fishermen by the sea and they didn't have anything to do, so they invented a game. And this game is called *"pouring from the empty into the void."* They were expert at that, and because of this game they destroyed objective reason. Now the Romans did it by having sexual orgies, like Caligula, the emperor. So what do you think is the Greek that Mr. Gurdjieff is referring to when he said that *"Everything comes from the Greek?"*

Answer: It's called Burying the Dog: I say one thing, I mean something else. And if you just listen to what I say, you go right ahead, you can believe whatever you want. But if you dig deep, if you dig up the dog, you will know the truth.

Question: When you talked about the enneagram… The Greeks didn't have any idea of decimal representation of numbers.

Answer: They didn't use the decimal point, per se. What they would do is they would take a thousand and divide it by two, you'd have five hundred. Divide it by three, you'd have three, three, three… They didn't have the decimal point but they could generate the numbers. If you take ten thousand and divide it by seven, you will get one, four, two, eight, etc.

Question: We do experience that he buried the dog, and we do experience the great gift that we get to dig. In your own digging, what do you feel or think that Gurdjieff was trying to tell us when he did speak about the Greeks. He spoke about Pythagoras in one way… What do you feel he was trying to tell us with his representation of the Greeks?

Answer: Look at the story of Pythagoras, the history of Pythagoras. He comes to Croton, he starts schools in Croton, Tarentum, several other places, and what happens? People turn on him. For a short while, it's going great. The Pythagoreans are actually governing the different city states, and then other people say *"No! We want to have democracy. We want to have the people decide what they want to do."* And what do they do? They hunt down the Pythagoreans and chased them out of the country. That's why Pythagoreanism after that went underground. You don't see it much every day, and even Gurdjieff doesn't come out and say *"I'm a Pythagorean."* He buries the dog very deeply.

Question: Did the Pythagoreans organize their hierarchies by Being, rather than by democratic vote?

Answer: I don't know. I wasn't there, at least not that I remember.

Question: In the Bible, in the *New Testament*, Jesus performs the miracle of the loaves and the fishes. He sits down five thousand people... and divides two fishes amongst them all. That is a geometric diagram of the Golden Mean. And the disciples are always asking him *"What's going on here?"*

Answer: There's a lot of connections to the Pythagoreans in the *Bible*. Every time that you hear numbers of that sort - granted it's been corrupted through the centuries - but the basic thing of numbers, that's Pythagorean. As a matter of fact, Gurdjieff mentions the Essenes in his book. The Essenes have supposedly kept uncorrupted the ancient teachings of Jesus and, according to Josephus, the Essenes were very much like the Pythagoreans.

Question: Pythagoras is one of the great beings in *Beelzebub's Tales*. He founded the club of the Adherents of Legominism with the Moor guy, and this is the only club that Beelzebub would join on Earth. He never joined any other club, and he became a member. That's how important Pythagoras is.

Answer: Thank you.

Question: I was interested in that quote from Gurdjieff, where he said *"concentrate on a point in the sky."* He didn't say it was that intersection between the planets and the Milky Way. Do you have any independent evidence that's what he was referring to?

Answer: It's called inductive reasoning.

Question: My first question is if you have related the comma to the inexactitude?

Answer: Yes, that's exactly it.

Question: My second question arose in the quote where Gurdjieff used the word *"invented"* when he referred to reincarnation. Is he bringing this notion of reincarnation into question?

Gurdjieff, Plato & Pythagoras - Questions & Answers

Answer: At some point somebody invented this. Somebody had to formulate that maybe there's a cyclical rebirth, and actually it's very much in the Eleusinian Mysteries. Persephone is taken to Hades, and then she comes back in the spring, as new foliage in a continual cycle.

Question: Gurdjieff writes a very complex book, yet he also said, I'm not sure where, that you need to know really very little, but to know that very little requires a tremendous amount of work. In his statement, which I never heard, where he says the *"point in the sky,"* if you go back and I'm not sure where you will find this quote either, where he talks about that there is no need to go to the stars to study the stars. There's no need to go to the solar system to study the solar system, because those materials actually are right here on this planet at every moment.

Answer: Some people say you can read this book and you don't have to worry about anything else, you don't have to know anything else. And that is a bunch of malarkey, because what Gurdjieff was saying was *"These are pointers"* to all and everything. There's a very good reason why he called it that. When you read the chapter on *"The Sun neither lights nor heats,"* he's pointing to the Pythagoreans, because there were Pythagoreans who wrote that the Sun reflects the heat from the cosmos, and does not give heat by itself. Gurdjieff doesn't mean that. He's saying *"Look at the Pythagoreans."* He's pointing to the Pythagoreans. The next chapter is about Alchemy. Beelzebub goes to the planet Saturn, there's a big bird there, a crow, a scientist who sees things turn into gold under an apparatus. Gurdjieff is talking about Alchemists! He's pointing to different things, and if you just read things the way they are written, you'll never understand that. You need to open your mind and get everything else that he's talking about. He's referring to things… He's not telling you everything.

Question: I wonder if you've come across information about objective music that you could share?

Answer: Pythagoras was supposedly able to take different scales, modes, and he could calm people down, or he could get them all excited. He could manipulate people's emotions through music. People still do that today. Popular music is all about that.

Question: Quick question: You obviously went to Pythagoras, following the pointers. Can you tell us what we would find if we also went there?

Answer: In my opinion, Pythagoras was the godfather of Western civilization.

Question: He went to Egypt…?

Answer: He went to Babylonia… He went to Las Vegas…

Question: Las Vegas…??!

The First Page of Beelzebub's Tales

Irv Givot

Abstract

This paper is a commentary on the first page of *Beelzebub's Tales*, and it is an attempt to uncover the deeper significance of what is hidden in that page. But rather than simply elucidating the meaning the three remarkable paragraphs on this initial page, I try to take the reader though my own process of coming to a totally new understanding of what is buried between the lines, and also through my process of searching for those *"entirely new principles of logical reasoning"* that Gurdjieff affirms is necessary to *"fathom the gist"* of his writing.

The themes that are woven through this first page concern the reliability of *"indubitable convictions,"* the nature of belief, the law of three, and of course the sacred invocation: *"In the name of the father, and of the son, and in the name of the holy ghost, Amen."*

This latter *"definite utterance"* itself is an expression of Triamazikamno, which I discuss, and also has practical implications for one's own inner Work. There are clues that the first page sounds the note *"Do"* not only for *Beelzebub's Tales*, but for the 2nd and 3rd series of his writings as well.

The First Page of Beelzebub's Tales

"In the name of the father, and of the son, and in the name of the holy ghost, Amen."

Now that I've spoken those words, upon beginning this commentary on the first page of Chapter One, *"The Arousing of Thought,"* I begin from a different place in myself: more open, more grounded, more in touch with my aim and myself.

It was because of my reading of Keith Buzzell's book, *Perspectives on Beelzebub's Tales*, by the way, that this writing came about. In the chapter titled *"Conviction,"* which I just finished, Dr. Buzzell gives many examples from throughout *Beelzebub's Tales* showing the emphasis Gurdjieff placed upon convictions in general, especially those derived from one's own reasoned deliberations, as opposed to those acquired from outer influences and conditioning.

The example that drives home Dr. Buzzell's point is that a reference to this appears in the very first sentence of the first page of *Beelzebub's Tales*, which starts thus:

The First Page of Beelzebub's Tales

"Among other convictions formed in my common presence during my peculiarly composed life, there is one such also - an indubitable conviction - that always and everywhere on the earth, among people of every degree of development of understanding, and of every form of manifestation of the factors which engender in their individuality all kinds of ideals, there is acquired the tendency when beginning anything new, unfailingly to pronounce aloud, or if not aloud at least mentally, that definite utterance understandable to every even quite illiterate person which in different epochs has been formulated variously, and in our day is formulated in the following words:

"In the name of the father, and of the son, and in the name of the Holy Ghost, Amen."

So, after reading Buzzell's chapter on convictions, I was moved to reread the first page of *"The Arousing of Thought,"* the first paragraph of which I quoted above. Later, I was dozing off to sleep in my outdoor bed under a brilliant canopy of stars on a warm August night. For some reason that might be attributed to Grace, or maybe planetary alignment, I found myself in a state where more sincere self-reflection became possible.

I began to peer into my own past experience in terms of the question, *"How many times in my life have I begun new projects, or 'anything new' for that matter by saying the words, or even having the thought: 'In the name of the father..?'* Certainly not even once before I first read *Beelzebub's Tales*, and pitifully few times since then. In fact I could only remember a small number of times in connection with group work of various kinds.

The problem, as I began to see it that night, was that one would need to wake up just at the moment of starting something new - which is precisely the point in time, for me anyway - when my head has been filled with a hundred different considerations, not to mention distractions, preoccupations and/or fixations on some aspect of the new project. And not only to wake up at that moment, which I know for myself takes many years of practice, but also to remember at that same moment to *"intone"* as Gurdjieff describes in paragraph two of that first page, this universal formulation. Without a specific aim to work in this way, it became obvious to me that it just wouldn't happen.

As I lie there under the stars, memories of the way I have started new ventures came back to me, and these ways could not even politely be called *"consciously,"* but would better be characterized by words or phrases starting with H, as in

    Hit-or-miss
    Haphazard
    Helter-skelter
    Half-assed, or
    Haltingly.

The humor here somehow allowed me to stay in touch with the twinge of remorse I was feeling, and enlarged the scale of my pondering. I thought to myself, "If there's one thing I've learned by this time, it's that I'm not unique or special, and if I don't remember to say this or any other particular invocation upon starting something new, probably very few other people do either.

I then asked myself, " how many people do I know that 'unfailingly pronounce aloud, or if not aloud, at least mentally,' this invocation to the holy trinity when starting something new?" I couldn't think of anybody that I was certain could remember to do it *"unfailingly."* The next question: *"Have I ever known anyone in my entire life capable of always remembering to intone these words at the appropriate moment?"* Maybe a small handful of people. A very small handful.

But he said with such force: " An indubitable conviction - that always and everywhere on the earth.. there is acquired the tendency.. unfailingly to pronounce.. that definite utterance.."
Here is where I began to smell a rat. Here is when I first suspected that maybe I couldn't just literally accept what he wrote in that first paragraph as I had always done before. From this suspicion, a new understanding began to dawn on me.

As an aside, I have to say that I love the metaphor of the *"dawning of a new understanding."* Because it is as if I've been in the darkness, stuck with a passively acquired belief for many years, and now, slowly, inexorably, a new light comes in that allows me to see what I've accepted as fact in a new and different way. And once that light enters, it is never again the same.

My first reaction - after my pondering in the starlight - was that I'd been tricked. His conviction was that there are people everywhere in all times who always invoke the holy trinity, upon starting something new, and I believed him. So much for *"indubitable convictions."* I must have read those opening paragraphs at least twenty times (it could have been more) and I never before suspected anything amiss. I never questioned his conviction. My reaction now seemed analogous to a baseball batter expecting a fastball from the pitcher and being fooled by a curve. Even worse, a batter not even suspecting he'd been fooled. It was a feeling of suddenly realizing that I'd been outsmarted by someone far more clever than me. But these analogies are not quite an exact representation; it's more like, here in the first sentence of the entire book there is already a teaching, but it requires thinking out of the box to grasp it, and I've been too oblivious to notice it all these years.

What could this teaching be?

First, I will confess that I've had a lifelong habit - a trait I suppose I could blame on my ancestors - of being quick to jump to conclusions. Fortunately my son, who has suffered by acquiring this unbecoming habit, and my wife, who lives with it every day, have joined forces to gently persuade me to undermine my habit by always considering other possibilities besides my initial conclusion. Thus I've learned from them to question, and in this case I remembered to ask, "what are all the possibilities I can think of for why there should be this glaring discrepancy between my own experience - after decades of Work - and Gurdjieff's *"indubitable conviction?"*

The First Page of Beelzebub's Tales

So I will list and discuss some of the more plausible possibilities for his clearly intentional either deception, exaggeration, metaphor, joke, symbolic truth disguised by seemingly untrue assertions, or whatever is going on in that first sentence of *Beelzebub's Tales*.

One possibility is that this is the first example in a theme that recurs throughout *Beelzebub's Tales*, of how contemporary people have a degenerate psyche, and some efforts that have always been possible for humans are no longer possible. In other words, in past epochs when people had a higher degree of individuality, his conviction would have been true. But for us *"men"* in quotation marks born in the twentieth century, who in general are not even remotely in touch with genuine being impulses, the *"tendency"* to utter those words upon starting something new has never been acquired.

The practical value of interpreting his conviction in this way is that it can lead to a feeling of remorse, as it did for me (after the twentieth or so reading) when I finally began to question the hidden intent of that first sentence.

But there is also something unsatisfying about this latter interpretation, because 1) he said that people *"always and everywhere on the earth"* utter those words upon starting something new - always and everywhere includes the present time also, and 2) *"civilized"* people at least back to the ancient Romans were about as degenerate as we are, in my opinion, in terms of cognizing the need to actualize the Obligolnian strivings, or to make being-efforts in general. So it seems there has to be more to it than this.

Another possibility is that the first sentence is a teaching about suggestibility. About how easy it is for him to make us believe anything he chooses. After all, this isn't just *"Smith or Brown"* informing us about the sacred invocation, but Gurdjieff himself.

How automatic it is to want to believe an authority that I not only trust, but for whom I have the deepest respect. Why shouldn't I believe it? Gurdjieff said it, it sounds right, and he's my teacher. He would not mislead me. Except that like Coyote, he's a trickster.

The irony is that the stated aim for the whole First Series expressed in the page before the Table of Contents, is:

> To destroy mercilessly, without any compromises whatsoever, in the mentation and feelings of the reader, the beliefs and views about everything existing in the world.

However, he does this throughout *Beelzebub's Tales* not in the obvious way, as in *"You believed A, B, and C? What a jerk you are!"* but with *"entirely new principles of logical reasoning."* This latter phrase is a concept I don't pretend to understand in depth, but I caught a glimpse of it on the first page. He created the conditions by which we can see, if we dig deep enough, how we acquire beliefs in the first place.

How subtle is that, and how bold at the same time, to begin the first page of the entire book by slipping that curve ball past us, thrusting that new idea at the reader, and inducing us to believe it just by the force of a long, quintessentially Gurdjieffian sentence of prose. The point is, that I had always accepted his *"indubitable conviction"* passively, without questioning.

Isn't this in general how most of our beliefs are acquired? That is, by accepting uncritically what we've heard or read from an authority we trust. That would be the teaching in a nutshell. I will remind you, this is only a possibility for the understanding of this first paragraph, but there are also other aspects that should be considered.

First of all, how would an *"indubitable conviction"* like this be possibly be acquired?

Is this a conviction based upon a deep understanding of the human psyche? A conclusion he reached by active mentation? That every person, at some level of our consciousness, has the ability to make a connection with the creative force of the universe upon beginning, that is creating something new? Or is his conviction a result of extensive surveying and interviewing of individuals from many cultures - in other words, gathering of data. If the latter were true, it would have been necessary to sample people from all past epochs as well. This could only be attempted by someone whose level of reason was advanced enough to be able to consult the Akhashic record, or as Beelzebub calls it, the *"Korkaptilnian thought tapes."* (By which, for example, he accessed the thought process of Belcultassi, the first person to realize the necessity of Work on oneself.)

Because my own relationship to the Akhashic record is in its nascent stage - occasionally I tap into something, usually I don't, and I can't yet trust what I see - I cannot independently verify whether people in past epochs indeed had the tendency to verbalize these words upon new beginnings. In fact, this particular question, of how he acquired his conviction, has the quality of a dead end. Except it is a necessary part of the process to consider it.

Another aspect of any not-to-be-doubted conviction, from the point of view of how people influence each others' beliefs, is the following phenomenon: The more strongly and forcefully people believe and promote an idea, to the point of being dogmatic, even fanatic about it, the more likely their belief, later judged from a historical perspective, turns out to be based upon either confusion, lack of common sense, lack of data, some kind of prejudice (pre-judgment), or simply the consequences of the properties of the organ Kundabuffer. Two examples are, all prior beliefs about the cosmos (inevitably placing us at the center of the universe in one way or another), and all kinds of strange religious beliefs (that usually have as their central motivation the desire of a priesthood to exert control over their congregation).

In spite of this phenomenon, human beings, perhaps because we really are hard-wired to be suggestible, seem to have an irresistible desire to believe anyone with whom we feel a connection, when they express their opinion with enough force and repetition. That is why advertising is so effective, and political propaganda, and religious dogma, and *"educational"* training, and military indoctrination, and peer pressure, and on and on.

In recent times, I've seen people mindlessly pick up beliefs from radio talk-show hosts, from leaders of political parties, from the pastor of their church, from their doctor, from spiritual teachers, from scientific researchers, from the anchorman on the T.V. news, from facilitators of workshops they've attended, in short, anyone with whom they have the faintest trust, where there is some *"kinship of vibrations."*

In fact, the only way not to be suggestible is to be awake to a sufficient degree, and to base one's convictions upon one's own reason and experience, and not upon authority.

So, perhaps this is what Gurdjieff is trying to tell us in this first paragraph: beware of any unverifiable statements made by anyone - including me - who is convinced beyond a shadow of a doubt that they are true.

There are one or two more possibilities for understanding the first paragraph that I feel constrained to consider, before moving on to the equally fascinating third and second paragraphs of this first page of *Beelzebub's Tales*.

The next possibility is difficult for me to face, because this one is that maybe I misunderstood what he was implying. That is, on more careful reading I see that he wrote, not that there have always been many people who unfailingly invoke the three holy forces upon beginning something new, but that the tendency to intone these words arises *"among people"* of every degree of.. understanding. In other words, it might be a select few individuals *"among people."* Not every person. So if this interpretation is correct, the deception or exaggeration on his part that I inferred, was simply a result of my being unable to dig the real meaning out of a very difficult sentence.

For me, this means that the initial understanding that dawned on me, that he was deceiving us intentionally, might have been wrong. This possibility first appeared in my mind in the middle of the night, after waking from a dream. I realized that maybe I had misread that passage and I would have to abandon my newly acquired conclusion. It is so interesting how much more difficult it was for me to let go of an idea that I had discovered for myself, through my own deliberations, than it had been earlier to let go of the literal meaning that had been acquired passively. (The former often happens to scientists, by the way, who occasionally go to their graves refusing to give up a pet theory they've invented, even when the data against it eventually becomes overwhelming. Einstein's philosophical objection to quantum mechanics [*"God doesn't play dice with the universe"*] is the most famous recent example of this.)

This second dawning of mine, which threatened to overturn my new *"understanding,"* was not exactly like a light flooding in, but this time it was more like an early winter morning in Oregon when a thick fog has rolled in, and the first inkling of dawn is a very uncertain doubt about whether it's still pitch-black out there. Then the doubt become an ambiguity, and finally, much later there is a gray, foggy morning that never actually gets very light.

In other words, after all this contemplation, the whole question of the real meaning of that first paragraph became shrouded back into a foggy mystery, and for a moment, I doubted whether I had really learned anything after all.

However, upon further reflection, it became clear that I had learned a great deal (which I will speak more of later). Also I stumbled upon a way to read that is more active. Maybe one of the first steps of *"fathoming the gist"* of Gurdjieff's writing is to confront his assertions and convictions with data from one's own *"Work memory,"* and/or one's common sense, as I did on that late August night. If there is a dissonance in this confrontation; if something doesn't seem right, it is a question of trusting one's own experience, and probing further. The word *"fathom"* has to do with depth, and with understanding something profound and mysterious. A failure to ever come to this stage in one's reading of *The Tales* can lead to absurdities like literally believing that the sun *"neither lights nor heats."*

There are two further points that are important to note here. One is, that even if I were certain of the true interpretation of the first paragraph, it would not necessarily be a service to elucidate it completely at this time. If I did, I would be robbing the reader of his/her own experience of going through their own process of *"digging"* to find a deeper meaning. That was one point Mrs. Staveley (my teacher) was very firm about. Let people have their own experience. Don't just give them answers.

Therefore what I'm trying to communicate here is the process I went through, as much as any result I achieved, along with presenting possibilities instead of conclusions, and thus treading the fine line between mentioning a couple of discoveries I've made that have lain largely hidden on that first page for over 50 years, and not providing so much information that the reader might be discouraged from initiating their own investigation.

So in that sense it is good that I'm still in a fog about his meaning in the first paragraph, but the second point that I've understood is that it is lawful to be so. In other words, to resolve the question of whether some people *"always and everywhere"* unfailingly invoke the holy trinity on starting something new, there is a limitation on how much information can be gained simply by mentation alone, and by considering that one paragraph alone. The second two paragraphs of the first page represent the other two parts of a triad, and they provide data from the other brains or centers besides the head-brain.

For example, in paragraph three, Gurdjieff tells us how it *feels* to have pronounced the said words upon starting to write the book:

> "Having thus begun, I can now be quite at ease, and should even, according to the notions of religious morality existing among contemporary people, be beyond all doubt assured

that everything further in this new venture of mine will now proceed, as is said, 'like a pianola.'"

According to my Random House Unabridged Dictionary, *"pianola"* was a brand-name or trademark for a commercial player piano in the early twentieth century. So to paraphrase the second part of paragraph three: Now that he intoned the universal invocation, his writing will unwind quite automatically, like a mechanical, pre-programmed piano. And if this is the case, there would be no obstacles, no resisting force, no harnel-aoot, and no unforeseen circumstances to contend with; and again, he is *"beyond all doubt assured"* of this.

Even if I was too dull for many years(decades) to question his indubitable conviction in paragraph one, this tongue-in-cheek humor in paragraph three is so blatant that any *"even quite illiterate person"* should get the joke, but not necessarily with their left-brain.

But is his pianola analogy a message on the emotional level - a confirmation - that paragraph one also contained some *"monkey business;"* or on the other hand, is it that, as he does in other parts of the book, lighten things up with some absurd humor immediately after giving us a serious teaching? More possibilities.

One way to discern is to take an impression of the paragraph as a whole. When I re-read paragraph one, then paragraph three, I see that they have a very different tone. Again we come back to his declaration that this book was written according to *"entirely new principles of logical reasoning."* To discern truth, I may have to learn to use different parts of my mind - as uncomfortable as that may seem.

The first part of paragraph three, about being *"quite at ease"* after performing an obligation, is a whole study in itself that deserves some scrutiny, but I will try to limit this discussion to a couple of pertinent examples that come to mind:

Once I was listening to someone who knew John Bennett, telling me about her experience with a particular exercise where one decides in the evening - among other things - to perform a specific task the next day. She confided that she always was certain to complete it first thing in the morning, so she could be more at ease during the day and not have to worry about forgetting the task.

Is this how we succumb to *"contemporary religious morality?"* That is, if I have fulfilled my initial being-obligation, then I've been a good boy - nothing bad will happen - and I can calmly and peacefully fall back to sleep. When we begin in the Work we are so enveloped with these Judeo-Christian ways of thinking that for a long time its almost impossible to observe them. (By the way, isn't it amazing how he slipped that comment in there? Already taking a shot at one of our well-rooted sub-conscious beliefs.) For the mass of contemporary *"Christians"* in this regard, for most of the twentieth century, it was church on Sunday, then complacently assured that their spiritual duties were over for the rest of the week.

This may be what Gurdjieff is satirizing in the third paragraph, but there is probably much more to it than the above.

Many years ago, I also had an experience, the memory of which was evoked by this first part of paragraph three: It was in 1977, and my *"work in life"* at that time was in part, teaching Biochemistry to Chiropractic students. My group at Two Rivers Farm took for our weekly task one week, to make a sacrifice if we forgot to remember ourselves at a specified time each day. One morning of that week I decided that if I failed to remember myself while giving my lecture later that day at the College, I would intentionally not eat supper or anything else that evening. In those years I was a bit hypoglycemic, and missing a meal was a big deal, a real sacrifice.

During the lecture there was a vivid moment that I'll never forget, when I came back to myself while turning toward the blackboard with a piece of chalk in my hand. After a very brief second or two of being connected to something a little more essential, the first thought that came to my head was, *"Oh, Boy! I get to eat tonight,"* and in another moment or two, I was peacefully back to sleep.

Mrs. Staveley, amused by my effort, reassured me that my body knew that I was serious, so it helped me to remember. However this feeling of being *"quite at ease"* after an initial result (and yet underneath, not so much at ease) can go on for many years in students of the Work. As I recall there have been times, too numerous to tally, when I would perform a personal ritual in the morning, or say my grace before a meal, from a place in myself that was superficial enough that the predictable aftermath prevailed - total absorption and identification with the next thing, as in, *"Okay, I've done that, now lets get on with it."*

In any case, by going through the process of trying *"to fathom the gist"* of this first page, one practical outcome is that I have rekindled a wish, and received a taste of performing my daily rituals in a deeper way. For example, by being totally there in the moment of saying grace before a meal, and saying it with the whole of myself, I touch a higher level, a finer vibration, and when I'm finished, something from that level stays with me for awhile - permeates my presence as it were - and transforms my relationship with the meal. One does not feel complacent and *"quite at ease,"* after this quality of experience.

In relation to the above, the first page of *Beelzebub's Tales* has been surprisingly transformed from an enigmatic and quasi-humorous introduction to the first chapter, into a practical guide to deepen my inner Work.

I think Gurdjieff is telling us from the first sentence, that if one continues to reread this book passively and simply believe what is written, it will have limited value, and he will not have succeeded in his aim. But if the reader can delve and dig more deeply, as they become increasingly able, from their own acquired data and reasoning, there will be treasures buried where they are least expected.

The First Page of Beelzebub's Tales

Now let us consider one further possibility in order to expand our understanding of the first page: Perhaps Mr. Gurdjieff is sounding a *"DO"* in these first three paragraphs not only for the First Series of his writings, but for all three series at once. This idea came to me because the second paragraph seems to belong to the Third Series more than to *Beelzebub's Tales*. It is already a preview of how a more conscious human being would actualize the *"universal formulation:"*

> *"That is why I now, also, setting forth on this venture quite new to me, namely authorship, begin by pronouncing this utterance, and moreover pronounce it not only aloud, but even very distinctly and with a full, as the ancient Toulousites defined it, "wholly-manifested-intonation"*- of course with that fullness which can arise in my entirety only from data already formed and thoroughly rooted in me for such a manifestation; data which are in general formed in the nature of man, by the way, during his preparatory age, and later during his responsible life engender in him the ability for the manifestation of the nature and vivifyingness of such an intonation."

In this paragraph is the gem, the treasure that I have long overlooked right in the middle of the first page. So the first paragraph, seen in this light, could simply be a means to get our attention, a way to inform us that this *"trinity"* that is being invoked, is really universal, sacred and vitally important - not only a Christian expression, but simply that in this era we formulate it in Christian terms.

Actually, it is one of many formulations of Triamazikamno, the Law of Three, and it is significant that the whole first page is devoted to it.

The point is that the first paragraph now can be seen as a preparation, a way to galvanize our attention, so that we might notice that he is presenting us with an exercise in paragraph two, a ritual for beginning anything new that invokes the creative forces of the universe and that we can practice for ourselves.

It is quite humbling to face the fact that it took me this long to notice/discover this exercise, but the popular wisdom is that we find things when we are ready for them. Hopefully, in a community of peers, one makes a discovery like this when we are all ready for it.

The heart of the exercise is the phrase, *"wholly-manifested-intonation."*

From my experience, the above phrase is comparable to the effort of working in a *"three-centered"* way. The latter is something I strive toward, not something that can necessarily be done at will.

On rare occasions I can approach it in a movements class during very special moments when some kind of attunement becomes possible. I will try to describe one of those moments since this is my frame of reference for a *"wholly-manifested"* experience:

After much practice, and often after much resistance, there may come a moment when my body is completely at one with the rhythm and tempo of the movement, taking the positions in a relaxed but relatively precise way, and in synchrony with the people around me. My head-brain has overcome whatever distractions are present, and is quiet, following the body's movement and that of the class as a whole, always holding the overall pattern of the movement with a small part of the attention, and even aware of more subtle qualities of energy passing through me and the room. My feelings are connected to the music and the particular emotions evoked by the movement itself and sometimes intensified by the Work of the group as a whole. All of the above dances within the field of my attention in these unique moments when I find myself in this higher *"zone."*

For my Work to bear this kind of fruit, all the parts of myself need to be included. And whether this *"three-centered"* effort is attempted in order to participate fully in a movement, as I described above, or for example, to consciously stir a pot of soup, or even to actively listen to a reading, the principles are the same.

The exercise hidden in the second paragraph, that Gurdjieff is inviting us to practice if and when we recognize the opportunity, is to verbally invoke the three holy forces upon starting something new, with a *"wholly-manifested intonation."* To include every part of myself during this utterance; to include my whole being, if possible.

I can strive toward this possibility and not allow myself to be discouraged from trying because, for example, unlike Gurdjieff, I did not have the proper data rooted in my *"preparatory age,"* or for that matter, because of many other worthy excuses. (As an aside, this reference to data acquired in the preparatory age seems like a very brief preview of the second series, where the first part of that book (*Meetings With Remarkable Men*) is devoted to Gurdjieff's very unusual education.

So, after discovering this *"gem"* which I mentioned previously, now just before I begin something new, I first stand up in a relaxed yet erect posture and take a few moments to quiet myself.

I bring my attention to my feeling center in the area of my heart, and sense its connection to my throat and tongue. I remember briefly that I am about to begin, that is, to create something, and that I have a wish to make contact with the creative force of the universe. I feel the intensity of this wish and allow it to permeate all of me.

At a moment chosen by my intention, I speak the words, *"In the name of the Father,"* as distinctly and consciously as I can, and listen to where they resonate in me. At the same moment I allow a wave of relaxation to instantly descend through my body, to melt any tensions that may have reappeared. Then I say, in the same way, *"And of the Son."* I take a breath, relax again, re-establish my sense of presence, and focus my complete attention on pronouncing the final words, from a deep place in the center of my breast, *"And in the name of the Holy Ghost. Amen."*

I take a few moments, standing quietly, to let these words and the experience reverberate through me. Now I am ready to begin the new project.

The First Page of Beelzebub's Tales

This way of approaching the invocation, I feel, is only a beginning. Gurdjieff's way of intoning these words would have been derived from a higher level of consciousness and resulted in another level of *"fullness,"* but I am convinced that the only way to progress toward his level of ability is to practice. To practice what I understand.

There are two pieces of advice from Wan Su Jian, my Chi Gong teacher in China that can be an encouragement here: The first is that even if one only receives a part of a technique; practice it anyway. Proficiency will eventually come through practice - which also seems to magically attract the missing pieces. Secondly, in regard to data from the preparatory age - when I was in China I was totally awed by the abilities of twelve year olds, who began working with this teacher when they were eight. In America, children never acquire these skills of attention at all (except by accident or in rare circumstances) and as a result, very few adults here ever achieve any kind of mastery of themselves. But this teacher's encouragement was that though we missed these important preparations in our youth, we can still begin to learn what is needed even at the age of 50, if we are sincere enough and diligent enough. Hopefully, in this era of *"delayed aging,"* the advice would apply to people in their early 60s as well.

This would probably be an appropriate place to conclude this account of my recent rereading of the first page of *Beelzebub's Tales*, but so many questions remain.

For example, who were those *"ancient Toulousites"* that he tantalizingly mentions in the second paragraph? And for those who study the enneagram, why did he choose the moment when pen touched paper to intone the invocation? Why not when he first conceived the need, and then the idea to write the book? (DO? RE?) Or when he committed himself to the project, bought the paper and ink, and gathered all the materials? (MI?) Or when he was nearly drowning in the overflow of the ideas coming into his head? (Point 3?) Extrapolating from the meaning of the points of the enneagram according to Bennett and his pupils, the actual start of the writing would have been the point

4. Does this apparent inconsistency mean that my long-held beliefs on the subject of the enneagram also needs to be questioned? Back to beliefs.

The ancient Toulousites, by the way - if they were possibly the Cathars of the twelfth and thirteenth century - represent the first time in history that an independent Christian sect was mass-murdered by other Christians because of their beliefs (In the so-called Albigensian Crusades ordered by the Vatican in the year 1207).

In this theme about beliefs that is woven between the lines on the first page, the lesson here would be: Be careful how you express your beliefs. If they are perceived as a threat to the power-possessors, they can get you killed.

The stated reason that the ancient Toulousites were mentioned of course, was because of their *"wholly-manifested intonation,"* and it is coincidental in this regard that the Cathars were very much interested in the trinity. However, I have not yet had the time to research this question, so I will leave it to the reader to uncover this potentially very relevant information that could also have a practical benefit for our Work.

And finally, speaking of the trinity, what is this *"Holy Ghost"* all about?

In the formulation of the trinity, that is, the three holy forces presented on the first page, *"the Father"* would represent the active force, the creator. *"The Son"* would be the force associated with that which was created, which has a more passive character. And the *"Holy Ghost"* therefore must be the third force, in this case that which connects the creator and his creation. What could that be? That is, what could that be, from our own experience?

Beelzebub intimates indirectly in the chapter, The Arch-Preposterous, that we cannot perceive nor sense the action of the forces. They are forces, not material objects, nor *"formations,"* and as such are completely invisible. Especially the third force, because it is difficult even to conceive what it would be. It is ghost-like. It is like an apparition. It is there and it is not there. With ghosts, a few people claim to have seen them; most of us will never see one. Likewise, with the third force, a few individuals who understand the Law of Three may *"see"* it, that is comprehend its action; the rest of us do not, except for rare glimpses, or by assigning synonyms to it, or by passively believing someone else's interpretation. For me anyway, the third force is truly a Holy Ghost.

Hopefully, some readers of this commentary will come to understand it in a deeper way than I do.

In conclusion, there is one additional phenomenon to notice. That is, the amazing holographic nature of the book in general. Any individual page may contain material that opens as a window to the book as a whole, or at least to several other parts of the book. This may not be true of every single page, but of very many special pages, of which the first page is an example. It is as though in addition to the linear flow of the story, there is a non-linear movement, where the narrative sometimes projects ahead, sometimes jumps backward, repeats the same ideas in different ways in succeeding paragraphs, pages and chapters; and everything is interconnected through some other dimension of time as well as through the inner lines of the enneagram.

Therefore it is no wonder that the more one probes into the first page - or any of 600 others - the more the inquiry seems to lead deeper into the teaching, further into unexpected areas, and as I discovered, further into myself.

I now understand better how monks of one isolated Taoist sect in Old China could spend five years or more contemplating a single page, or even a single passage of their scripture.

One particle of truth, if pursued into its essence, can open up into the whole world.

© Copyright 2012 - Irv Givot - All Rights Reserved

The First Page of Beelzebub's Tales - Questions & Answers

Questioner: One more thing about my experience of the [Catholic] Mass, and I figure it must have been Gurdjieff's experience too; this Mass was in another language - in Latin for us, and when the sign of the cross was intoned in Latin we had to abstract it. We had to say, *"what does this mean?"* It put it out in front of us in a particular way.

The other thing was that when I read the second paragraph, and he talks about a *"wholly-manifested intonation,"* it resonated in me in the same way that some of those priests that I had experienced would intone those phrases. Finally, when I researched Toulousites I found them in Southern France as having been known for a special kind of singing, This reminded me, in both paragraphs he says, first aloud, then he says, this wholly-manifested intonation, so there's many things here, of course, but it resonated with me that the use of sound and particularly the reading aloud and the saying aloud of these [invocations] was a helpful thing to resonate within my organism and it evoked... sensing. Then finally, don't you see an octave in some of these paragraphs?

Irv Givot: Yes. And I also want to say that [it was not my fate] to be Catholic growing up so these ideas were all foreign to me. I had to rediscover these concepts (the invocation and the trinity) from his writing.

Questioner: Lets go back to the first page. Now this is only one of the seven aspects; I'm not saying its the only one, but the key to the whole thing is paragraph number three, the way I see it. From the first page of the book, Mr. Gurdjieff is telling us about the difference between a normal three-brained being and an abnormal three-brained being. For the abnormal, like us, everything continues like a pianola, because we are mechanical. But for the normal three-brained being, he is the player of the pianola. He is no longer the pianola. He plays the pianola. Because he understands the laws. And he can work with the laws.

And now lets go back to Orage. Because it was Orage who coined the word pianola. Mr. Gurdjieff asked him how is it going to continue [as such] like a pianola? It was Orage.

Irv Givot: I will read you what he says in the Manuscript Version (of *Beelzebub's Tales*) relating to that. It occurred to me that - just a couple of weeks ago I wondered how he phrased this part in the Manuscript when he first wrote it. And here's how the third paragraph reads the first time he wrote it:

"Having begun in this way, I ought to be quite assured and be able to count without any essence-anxiety upon everything further now gliding along as is said, on oil to an Italian Hurdy-Gurdy accompaniment."

All & Everything Conference 2012

Somehow it got changed from Hurdy-Gurdy to Pianola.

Questioner: Orage introduced Pianola.

Irv Givot: I think he felt that Western, [i.e.] English, French and American people couldn't relate to a hurdy-Gurdy.

Questioner: But now let's go to one further thing. A saying from Orage; he says, "be a pianist, not a piano." You see? Mr. Gurdjieff is a pianist; he's not a piano. We are the piano. So in plain English, play your own music. Don't let the piano play your music. And you know, this has a connection with the advice from the grandmother - in life, never do anything like others. Do your own way. Now my mistake in life, and I recognize it, is that sometimes I play my music and I forget about the people who are listening to the music. So I have to take it back and be very, very conscious of one of the most important things in the book: To enter Holy Purgatory, you have to put yourself in the position of others.

Questioner: Irv, I just wanted to say, Thank you so much for sharing with us the process of your reading and deliberation. I found a great deal of it echoed in my own experiences and actually as I was listening to the first half of your talk I thought to myself, Hey, that guy sounds a lot like that likeable Assyrian, Hamolinadir, of the Adherents of Legominism, who upon ascending the stage to talk about questions of the beyond relating to the soul, had a placard over his head: "the instability of human reason." And even though he was a highly developed individual and had gone to the School of the Materialization of Thought, he was just overwhelmed by the confusion of everything possible. And so, anyway, thank you so much, and I almost expected to see you run out the door; I'm glad you didn't. You seem to have brought the talk to a good conclusion.

Irv Givot: The irony is that sometime around 1980, Mrs. Staveley gave us an exercise of taking one of our favorite characters from *Beelzebub's Tales* and drawing a picture, an image, relating to that character. And guess who I chose, Hamolinadir.

Questioner: Perhaps I can make a comment. In the Islamic tradition where I was raised there is this invocation which many people do at the beginning of various activities. In Arabic it is something like this ….(?). Its very similar to the invocation [on the first page]. It has three parts to it and you're meant to do this to refresh your intention at the beginning of everything and connect, as it were, to a higher purpose when you begin something. So when I read this (first page) for the first time, I also had the impression that I understood what he was talking about. Not being a Catholic of course, it wasn't the same words, but like you I think on later readings I discovered the categorical nature - that he's saying this is true at all times for all people indubitably. It sounded so extreme, but somehow this didn't click until much later. So a very delayed realization, as you said. And there may be many other things there. So, thank you very much.

Irv Givot: Your Welcome. I'm going to read how he wrote the first paragraph in the Manuscript version; it sheds a little light on that.

The First Page of Beelzebub's Tales - Questions & Answers

Questioner: When did the Manuscript become available?

Irv Givot: Copies were made in 1931 when he finished writing the book, but does anyone know when he started writing?

Answer (from various people): 1924

Irv Givot: Anyway, the [manuscript] was at least 20 years before the published version. Here is the first paragraph:

"Everywhere on the earth, before beginning anything new, it is customary first of all to pronounce aloud, or at least mentally, the following words understandable by every contemporary, even illiterate person, namely: In the name of the Father, and of his son, and in the name of that Holy Ghost who if not understood by all ordinary mortals, is at any rate understood and beyond all doubt known by our priests and theologians."

So, not even getting into the second part of that paragraph, in the first part he said its *"customary"* to do this. He didn't say it was an indubitable conviction, that people said it everywhere and in all times, he said it was *"customary."* So what does that tell us about what transpired in his thinking during the next twenty years? [Perhaps] that he needed to make it a lot more definite so that readers would *"get"* the second paragraph. That's what I've come to, that he really wanted to make it so definite that even dull people like me might see what was there in the second paragraph. So (in the published version) he exaggerated - quite a bit.

Questioner: This first paragraph is changed twice. Two changes in the [1980's] revision by the New York foundation, and they are very important. First they put common presence in quotation marks. And the second change that they made is a more is a more practical change than profound, is that instead of saying, In the name of the Father and of the son, and in the name of the Holy Ghost, the revised version says, "In the name of the Father, the son, and the Holy Ghost." It doesn't have, "in the name of the Holy Ghost.

Questioner: I would make the point that In the circular letter, The Herald of Coming Good, there are two references to the invocation.

Irv Givot: Thank You.

Questioner: I have a question that came up when Will quoted the words over the gate to Purgatory:

"Only those may enter here who can put themselves in the position of the other results of my labors."
So the question for the group is, Beelzebub says that those words were formulated by His Endlessness himself. Is there any other place in the book where we hear the words of His Endlessness?

All & Everything Conference 2012

Irv Givot: At the very end.

Questioner: That's correct, and then there are the two [ways] foreordained by his Endlessness: conscious labor and intentional suffering. They come from Our Endlessness.

Questioner: It was already said that Endlessness is quoted directly in the ninth commandment and in the eighteenth commandment. The Ninth commandment is, I believe, the Golden Rule, *"Do unto others as you would have them do unto you;"* he phrases it a little differently, and I believe the eighteenth is: *"Love everything that breathes."* And because that's the ninth and the eighteenth - sounds to me like perhaps the ninth is a completion of the octave of the Kesdjan body, and the eighteenth is perhaps the completion of the octave of the higher being body.

Questioner: It's not *"Endlessness"* in the book, its His Endlessness. There is a big difference between those.

Questioner: It is most of the time, His Endlessness, but it is also Our Endlessness.

Questioner: I attended the conference in 2003, when I heard [someone] talking about *"Endlessness"*. I heard a sigh from some people, and I sigh, when I heard something about *"Endlessness,"* and I told them it is not *"Endlessness"* but His, or Our Endlessness and that is a big, big difference. *"Endlessness"*, the way I see it, comes from atheists. And *"His Endlessness"* comes from people who believe. I'm a Catholic.

Irv Givot: Be careful of those beliefs, Will.

Questioner: Just one additional comment. In the 1931 - the earlier manuscript version, *"His Endlessness"* does not appear. *"God"* appears, and that's a very, very significant change. But not completely. Not all references to the word *"God"* were removed because they are there in many places in the 1950 edition of *The Tales*. But in many, many places instead of *"God,"* it is *"His Endlessness,"* or *"Our Endlessness."*

Gurdjieff's Concept of the Function of Sexuality in the Evolution of Consciousness

David Brahinsky

Abstract

Gurdjieff, as far as I can tell from his writings and statements he is quoted as having made, believed that a healthy sex life is of fundamental importance for the process of spiritual evolution. He is quoted as having said, for example, that those whose sexual lives are governed by *"constantly working buffers, fears and strange tastes"* must eliminate them if they wish to get far in the Work. He says that the sex center plays a crucial role in creating a *"general equilibrium;"* is central in the formation of a *"permanent center of gravity;"* and that when it works properly, the sexual function represents the chief possibility of Liberation.

My paper will focus on how, according to Gurdjieff's understanding, this process works. Because Gurdjieff often speaks of the evolution of higher consciousness in terms of the formation of *"higher-being bodies,"* the paper will explore how the proper functioning of the sex center relates to the formation of at least the Higher Emotional Body and so will include a discussion of such ideas as Gurdjieff's concept of sex energy, how it relates to formation of this body via what he called *"the Second Conscious Shock"* and how this relates to his concepts of energy density, vivifyingness, buffers, identification and a number of other ideas that he discriminated. The paper will discuss what it means for the sex center to function properly and will argue that when it does so, it brings in impressions, or *"third-being food,"* that is required for crystallization of the Higher Emotional Body to occur.

My research indicates that Gurdjieff himself did not explain this process in other than symbolic terms and there is very little in the literature on it. For this reason, and because I am interested in trying to understand this process more concretely, I have attempted locate the relation of sexuality to the formation of higher being bodies within the realm of contemporary scientific investigation via the work of Wilhelm Reich, one of the few researchers who has attempted to study sex energy. At the end of the paper I will touch on this topic.

The paper is a condensation of some of the ideas that I explore in my book *"Reich and Gurdjieff: Sexuality and the Evolution of Consciousness"*

Gurdjieff's Concept of the Function of Sexuality in the Evolution of Consciousness

I

Gurdjieff, as far as I can tell from his writings and statements he is quoted as having made, believed that a healthy sex life is of fundamental importance for the process of the evolution of consciousness as he conceived of it. He is quoted as having said, for example, that those whose sexual lives are governed by *"constantly working buffers, fears and strange tastes"* must eliminate them if they wish to get far in The Work. He said that the Sex Center plays a crucial role in creating a *"general equilibrium,"* is central in the formation of a *"permanent center of gravity,"* and that when it works properly, the sexual function represents the chief possibility of liberation.[1] Gurdjieff often spoke of the evolution of consciousness in terms of the formation of what he called *"higher-being bodies,"* thus any discussion of how sexuality relates to such an evolution must confront this notion. He also spoke about *"sex energy,"* what he called *"The Second Conscious Shock,"* and used terms like *"energy density,"* *"vivifyingness,"* *"buffers,"* *"third-being food,"* *"impressions"* and *"crystallization,"* each of which need to be understood in relation to one another and The Work in general.

My studies of Gurdjieff's teaching indicate, however, that he did not explain the relation of sexuality to the process of the evolution of consciousness in other than allegorical and symbolic terms, and there is very little said about it in the literature. Jeanne de Salzmann, for example, in her book *The Reality of Being*, tells us, when referring to the relation of the Sex Center to the formation of a higher-being body, *"Gurdjieff never spoke of this delicate work, or even gave explicit indications about it."*[2]

For this reason, and because I am interested in trying to understand this process more concretely, I have attempted to locate the relation of sexuality to the evolution of consciousness within the realm of contemporary scientific investigation via the research of Wilhelm Reich, one of the few researchers who has attempted to study the energy involved in sex. Reich's work has not been accepted by established science as yet and has been addressed by only a few scientists. Nevertheless, I do not think this is a strong enough reason to reject it in the context of Gurdjieff studies, given Gurdjieff's own statements with regard to the scientific establishment, what he sometimes called *"science of new formation."*

The impression one gets from Gurdjieff is that this science in quotation marks is basically mechanical, does not take into account the whole organism, all of the centers (not to speak of the most general laws of world maintenance and world creation), and so leaves out a great deal of

---

[1] Ouspensky, P.D., *"In Search of the Miraculous,"* New York, Harcourt, Brace and World, 1949, pp 255-9. (ISM)
[2] De Salzmann, Jeanne, *"The Reality of Being,"* Boston, Shambhala, 2010, p. 182. (ROB)

what it claims to study.³ A study of Reich's research will show, I believe, that this is not the case for him, that his method (and understanding) is not mechanical in Gurdjieff's sense of the term, but is organic and holistic, takes into account the whole organism, all of the centers and the relation between the researcher and what he/she is studying. To verify this, of course, would require years of study of Reich's work itself.

II

Those of us who have been studying Gurdjieff for many years are familiar with his basic teaching that humanity, in our normal mode of consciousness, is not really awake, but rather in a state he sometimes calls *"waking-sleep."*⁴ This is, of course, an ancient idea, variations of which are found in many philosophical and religious works and traditions. Gurdjieff's presentation of the idea is expressed in relatively vivid terms via such ideas as the many I's, the difference between essence and personality and the buffers, his overall point being that in waking-sleep we are not unified selves but manifest in a variety of selves or I's, the totality of which constitutes our personalities or masks, and each of which is blocked from consciousness of the others by the buffers.

Given that this is true for what I call *"me"* at this moment, for example, I, in quotation marks am manifesting one of my I's, but because of my buffers my other I's are not aware of this condition and so this *"I"* takes this *"I"* as I, not in quotation marks, although it is, in reality, only one among many. In sum, the process of evolution of consciousness, as Gurdjieff taught it, is one where we become conscious of this rather schizophrenic (or, more precisely perhaps, to coin a term, *"mutiphrenic"*) state we think of as being awake and work to unify, to become one, conscious, awake I or self.

One way Gurdjieff spoke of such a unification is that the unified self evolves to a point where it can crystallize into one or more higher-being body that, when fully formed, can survive the death of the physical body.⁵ As we know, he spoke of three such bodies, the Higher Emotional Body, the Higher Mental Body and the Fourth Body, what he called the Soul proper. According to Gurdjieff, we are born with energy-matter out of which such bodies can be created, our essences, and via The Work can transmute this energy-matter until it crystallizes into a finer form of itself as it forms a higher-being body.

Given the allegorical and symbolic nature of Gurdjieff's presentation of his teaching in his own writings, however, it is not absolutely clear to me whether he meant that the notion of such bodies should be taken literally or symbolically (or in both ways), i.e., whether the concept "higher-being body" represents actual physical entities in and of themselves (in a finer form of energy-matter than our physical bodies), or states of mind within our physical bodies (which would also be a

---

³ Gurdjieff, G.I., "All and Everything: First Series, Beelzebub's Tales to His Grandson," New York, E.P. Dutton, 1964, pp. 275 ff, 755ff, 813-70. (BT)
⁴ See, e.g., ISM, pp. 142-5 and BT, pp. 78-9 and passim.
⁵ ISM, pp. 312-2, 40-44, 91-7, 180, 1293-7, 255-6.

form of energy-matter but conceived of differently than if they were seen as physical entities), or both. Be this as it may, I have attempted to present an account of how sexuality relates to this process in a way that expresses how it would work for either possibility.

III

As the last section implies, along with a psychological analysis of the human condition, Gurdjieff utilized an energetic analysis of reality and humanity. He told us in *Beelzebub's Tales to His Grandson*, for example, that the entire universe, and so every entity and function within it, is a manifestation of a prime-source substance, an energy-matter he calls *"etherokrilno."*[6] Differences between things and functions are said to be due to differences in the density of this substance. He also discriminated a number of centers or brains that make up the human organism, each of which is a function of this energy-matter and takes in impressions and expresses itself or manifests at or with various densities of this substance.

Gurdjieff saw the centers in a kind of hierarchy of functioning. The so-called *"lower"* centers regulate our everyday existence and the *"higher"* connect us with a more advanced level of functioning, a greater understanding, the Higher Emotional Center by feeling it, the Higher Intellect by knowing it. Still, Gurdjieff himself did not denigrate the lower centers. On the contrary, he emphasized that for the higher centers to function correctly, or for their functioning to be correctly utilized by us, our lower centers should be fully functioning or healthy. His teaching is, then, that when impressions from the higher centers are taken in by an organism that is balanced and fully functioning is his or her lower centers, the impressions can then be assimilated and utilized for the evolution of consciousness, which is to say that genuine understanding and crystallization of the higher-being bodies can proceed.

The centers or brains, like everything else for Gurdjieff, are concentrations of etherokrilno and function, in part, by making contact with forms of etherokrilno outside of themselves. Contact between organ and world results in *"impressions,"* another form of etherokrilno or energy-matter. Thus the model that Gurdjieff presented is one in which energy-matter at various densities, states of vivifyingness or frequencies, contacts other forms of energy-matter at various densities. This contact creates impressions or energy-matter at various densities, the function of which we call *"consciousness,"* a range of densities or frequencies of energy-matter, the accumulation of which we call knowledge or understanding.

The entire universe is thus seen in terms of energy-matter density, on the one hand, and in terms of consciousness on the other. All that is, on this model, is conscious to one degree or another, depending on energy-matter or etherokrilno density or vivifyingness. Food of any kind, including what Gurdjieff called *"first-being food,"* or physical food and *"second-being food"* or air, from this perspective, is a form of consciousness, which is most obvious with regard to what Gurdjieff called *"third-being food,"* or impressions per se.[7] But every kind of food functions as impressions

---

[6] BT, p. 137 and passim.
[7] See, e.g., Walker, Kenneth, *"The Making of Man,"* London, Routledge, Kegan and Paul, 1963, pp 78ff. (MM)

Gurdjieff's Concept of the Function of Sexuality in the Evolution of Consciousness

of one sort or another, taken in by one center or another. It's all energy-matter-impressions contacting energy-matter-impressions.

Buffers, for Gurdjieff, are functions that interfere with energy-matter functioning in our organisms.[8] In this process, the contact of center with center is blocked, a unified self is made impossible, and so we in quotation marks prevail: a body/mind/heart organism with, psychologically speaking, many I's, most of which are not aware of one another's existence. In terms of etherokrilno, this is a less vivified state than if we were unified.

Due to the effect of the buffers our organisms fail to vivify our etherokrilno to the point where it can make contact with the finer, more vivified energy-matter that the higher centers are said to utilize for food taking or impression gathering and which they emanate or manifest. Thus we are cut off from the functions that can lead us to higher consciousness, to a state where crystallization of a higher-being body, another form of energy-matter of course, can occur.

IV

As students of his teaching know, Gurdjieff presented it in terms of a symbol system where various energy-matter densities are given numerical values (as well as other forms of symbolic representation which, for the sake of simplicity, I shall ignore here). He pictured the process of taking in first-being food and digesting it, for example, as one where the food goes through a process of increasing vivifyingness or decreasing density as it is digested, from a numerically symbolized value of 768, through a value of 384 to 192 (which he calls, at times, "cellular energy"). Second-being food is represented as entering the organism (as we breathe) at the density of 192. The meeting and merger of air with cellular energy produces finer energies symbolized as 96 and then 48 where it meets and merges with third-being food, or impressions per se (sounds, sights, smells, etc. as organized by our complex nervous systems), and the meeting and merger of these energetic densities produces the finer energies symbolized at the levels of 24, 12 and 6. Each of these densities of energy-matter are said to be utilized by the various centers or brains to take in impressions and emanate manifestations.

Without going into great detail here, the point that I wish to emphasize has to do with the energy-matter density Gurdjieff implicated in the formation of the Higher Emotional Body and that used by the Higher Emotional Center and the Sex Center, viz, energy-matter symbolized as at density 12. In general, for Gurdjieff, for our consciousness to evolve, we need to be able to make contact with the manifestations or impressions of the Higher Emotional Center to the extent that is apparently needed to produce enough energy-matter 12 that can crystallize as a Higher Emotional Body.[9] To do so, we need to be able to make enough of this energy-matter density via the process

---

[8] See, e.g., ISM, 154-60 and passim. Buffers are mentioned symbolically in BT, p. 82.
[9] The symbols are discussed in a number of places, e.g., ISM. pp.71 ff. Also in Nicoll, M., "Psychological Commentaries on the Teaching of G.I. Gurdjieff and P.D. Ouspensky, London, Robinson and Watkins, 1970-2, pp. 379ff, and in MM, pp. 173 ff.

of taking in the three foods and digesting them. We need to make energy-matter 12 to make contact with the energy-matter 12 of the Higher Emotional Center. Their contact, their meeting and merger, can produce a sufficient amount of energy-matter 12 that can crystallize into the level of consciousness called the Higher Emotional Body. How do we do this?

For Gurdjieff, normal, every day waking sleeping consciousness is not sufficient. We need to trigger what he sometimes called the First and Second Conscious Shocks to wake us up to the proper level. Again, without going into all the details, basically what can happen is that we practice The Work, we observe and remember ourselves - this is the First Conscious Shock - and so produce more of a finer energy-matter than otherwise. An important function of this shock is that it can lead to dissolution of the relatively condensed or congealed form of etherokrilno that we call the buffers to some extent thus allowing more vivified energy-matter to pulse and flow within our organisms coming from the melted buffers and the fact that they no longer block the full functioning of less dense energy-matter already present within the organism. Via self observation and self remembering we gain a closer look at the *"society"* of I's we call *"ourselves,"* and can learn to distinguish which of our I's are essential and which are not and can be allowed to melt away. Triggering the First Conscious Shock is thus a significant step in the process of producing more energy-matter that can be vivified further for use by the Higher Emotional Center, the Sex Center and for formation of a Higher Emotional Body.[10]

Gurdjieff taught that a second conscious shock is needed to produce the requisite amount of energy-matter 12 for full and proper use of the Higher Emotional Center and for formation of the Higher Emotional Body, viz, what is called "The Second Conscious Shock." In *Beelzebub's Tales* he illustrated the process via the tale of the formation of the organ Kundabuffer and a description of what is needed to overcome or *"destroy"* its consequences, namely, by awakening conscience, which lies sleeping in our subconscious minds. The Second Conscious Shock is said to be the key function in awakening conscience, destroying the consequences of the organ Kundabuffer thus overcoming our tendency to see everything ass backwards (so to speak) and produce the requisite amount of the energy-matter 12 for crystallization of the Higher Emotional Body. This energy-matter, the energy-matter also used by the Sex Center according to Gurdjieff, is sometimes referred to as *"sex energy."*[11]

V.

Gurdjieff's teaching regarding what he (in places) called the Principle of Relativity is sometimes put in terms of sayings like *"every stick has two ends,"* or *"as above, so below."*[12] An implication is that the First and Second Conscious Shocks share a common function. Both help us gain impressions of the whole of ourselves, both produce energy-matter or impressions that function to

---

My version appears in my book, "Reich and Gurdjieff: Sexuality and the Evolution of Consciousness," U.S.A., Xlibris, pp. 37-50. (RG)

[10] See, e.g., ISM, pp. 117-22 and passim; BT, pp. 1209-11, 1066, 1109., and RG, pp. 16, 25, 29, 33, 248.

[11] BT, pp. 347ff, 87ff.

[12] BT, p 11.

Gurdjieff's Concept of the Function of Sexuality in the Evolution of Consciousness

do so. Both produce, in other words, a *"feeling of the whole,"* a form of self-remembering. The Second Conscious Shock enables us to connect with impressions of the Higher Emotional Center, impressions often described as those of *"ecstatic love"* (Rodney Collin)[13], or *"the feeling of religiousness,"* an awareness of the sacredness and divinity of everything existing, impressions said to occur with the awakening of conscience (Gurdjieff).[14]

Jeanne de Salzmann saw such impressions as those of Being itself, of the Presence, the only real reality.[15] Dhiravamsa, a contemporary Buddhist, characterized such impressions as an awareness of the very essence of the movement of the universe and claimed that such impressions are brought in at what he called the highest point of sexuality.[16]

Here we seem to have impressions of unity perhaps equivalent or very much like what is variously described in different traditions as Liberation, Satori, Nirvana, Samadhi, Awakening the Atman, Becoming the Christ, reaching one of the Higher Heavens, and so on. As a form of self-remembering, the Second Conscious Shock brings in impressions that connect us with the Greater Self. In that it helps to awaken conscience, it can lead to impressions of what Gurdjieff called *"remorse of conscience,"* a state that he implied puts us in touch with objective morality.[17] In terms of Gurdjieff's symbols, the Second Conscious Shock also produces more energy-matter 6, energy-matter said to be utilized by the Higher Intellect and is necessary to trigger a Third Conscious Shock, one that brings in impressions of the whole at an even higher level or finer quality. Here we gain impressions that we can call genuine knowledge of the oneness of everything existing, knowledge, in other words, we might wish to say, of the Absolute itself.

VI

Such impressions of oneness are often thought of in terms of impressions of spirituality that have nothing to do with our lower functions, including the sex function. Gurdjieff, however, apparently did not think this way, for, as mentioned, he emphasized that we cannot fully incorporate, utilize or understand impressions of the higher centers when our lower centers are unhealthy or not working properly. He also saw the very fine energy-matter used by the center that brings us the feeling of the whole as sex energy used by the Sex Center.

I have already mentioned that Gurdjieff appeared to think that when the sexual function is healthy it plays an important role in creating a general equilibrium, a balanced working of the centers, a

---

[13] Collin, Rodney, *"The Theory of Eternal Life,"* New York, Weiser, 1974, p. 98.
[14] BT, pp. 342-6.
[15] ROB, pp. 13. 16, 20, 31-52, and passim.
[16] Dhiranvamsa, *"A New Approach to Buddhism,"* Lower Lake, California: The Dawn Horse Press, 1974, p. 51.
[17] BT, pp. 342 and passim. Recent research with meditators has indicated that these experiences of unity can be attributed to brain states that can be stimulated via meditation or near death experiences, and possibly by other means as well. My favorite account is reported in *"The Mystical Mind,"* by Eugene d'Aquilli and Andrew B. Newberg published by Fortress Press in 1999, where they call the experience of unity an experience of *"Absolute Unitary Being,"* or A.U.B.

condition that can occur only when the centers work with the energy-matter density proper to them, and that it plays a central role in helping form a *"permanent center of gravity,"* a notion that refers to a permanent, unified I. This state, it seems to me, is what it means to be awake and to be in a process of crystallization of a higher-being body.

According to Gurdjieff, when the Sex Center works properly, all the other centers are able to work with their own energetic densities. He said that when healthy sexually, a person is already at a relatively high level of consciousness. He said that the Sex Center is stronger and quicker than the other centers and that the buffers can stop the Sex Center from working properly but cannot destroy its energy.[18]

What does this mean in concrete terms? I understand it this way: buffers can prevent a person from going through the full cycle from sexual excitation through complete gratification, and that when this happens the energy-matter that is not fully excited or released and transformed via a completed cycle remains within the body in a relatively dense condition. Anticipating our discussion of how Reich's work relates to this subject, we can say that the energy-matter that is left over is the very stuff out of which the buffers - in Reich's terms, the *"armor"* - is made.

In waking-sleep, for Gurdjieff, our Sex Center does not work properly - our buffers prevent this. Our sexual lives are characterized by what he calls a *"misuse"* of sex. The Sex Center is said to use energy-matter of other centers - *"borrows"* it - and vice versa, which expresses itself as a kind of sexual perversion. When we congregate at parties, in churches, at political conventions, e.g., the unspoken purpose is for what Gurdjieff called sexual *"titillation,"* a form of excitation that does not lead to gratification and that ultimately leads to frustration.

As I mentioned, Gurdjieff did not elucidate, in concrete biophysical or bio-energetic terms, the nature of sex energy. In *Beelzebub's Tales* there are symbolic references to it. What I think can be said is that it is a relatively fine form of energy-matter, in terms of what is available and/or created by human beings. It is highly vivified, highly excited, vibrating, for example, twice as quickly as the energy of the moving center as represented in the symbol system. This means that it has the potential to bring in very subtle impressions, impressions of the same density as those of the Higher Emotional Center and can result in crystallization of the Higher Emotional Body, triggered by the Second Conscious Shock. Thus the impressions of the Sex Center, when it works with sex energy per se, functions as the food, the shock that brings about the conditions necessary for crystallization of the Higher Emotional Body. This is how I understand Gurdjieff's teaching that proper use of the Sex Center represents the chief possibility of Liberation.

Gurdjieff is quoted as having said that sex energy is *"the matter with which sex works and which sex manufactures. It is 'seed' or 'fruit'."* The way I understand this is that, as the finest energy-matter produced from the transformation of first-being food, it represents its *"fruit,"* and as the

---

[18] See ISM, pp. 55, 115, 254-9 and BT, pp. 794-5, 974, 977.

energy utilized in the Second Conscious Shock for formation of the first higher-being body, it functions as this body's *"seed."*

Gurdjieff says that for crystallization of the Higher Emotional Body to take place, the cells of the physical body must become *"saturated"* with the energy-matter. Once the proper saturation level is reached, crystallization occurs. As we shall see, Reich's findings with regard to the relation of sex energy and our body's cells indicates that this way of speaking can be seen as more than just a compelling metaphor.

VII

To be able to understand how the Higher Emotional Body is formed, we need to understand how the Second Conscious Shock functions to saturate the cells of the physical body with sex energy, a process that was not explained by Gurdjieff in his writings or by his students and followers. But this puts us, as students of Gurdjieff's teaching or The Fourth Way, in a difficult position. We are told that a fundamental principle of this work is that nothing is to be taken on faith alone, that every idea must be verified, and that the practice of The Work should be undertaken with understanding of what the practice involves. Gurdjieff provided much of the necessary information regarding the First Conscious Shock, but not the second. Did he think the subject too *"hot?"*[19]

After studying Reich's work for many years and working with students utilizing Reich's and Gurdjieff's ideas, I can understand it if he did. As Reich used to say about the sex function (what he called *"genitality"* in general), everyone is scared of it. It is a function that has been severely repressed, tampered with and twisted by humanity over many centuries. Our anxiety regarding it is deeply ingrained in most contemporary cultures and individuals.

Gurdjieff does tell us that the Second Conscious Shock involves the transmutation of emotions and that the practice of non-expression of negative emotions is preparation for triggering the shock. Perhaps we can understand how this process works if we can gain a more concrete understanding of the energy-matter involved. I now turn to Reich to try and accomplish this aim.

In my book on the subject I go into some detail regarding the evolution of Reich's ideas and a description of experiments he conducted to test his hypotheses. For the purposes of this paper, however, I'm simply going to present some of Reich's findings in an attempt to concretize Gurdjieff's teaching regarding the relation of sexuality to the evolution of consciousness.

Reich began his career as a medical doctor in the early years of the 20th century. He joined Freud's team of psychoanalysts, rose to the top very quickly but soon went out on his own as he followed what he called the *"red thread"* of his research where neither Freud nor the other

---

[19] ISM, p. 191.

psychoanalysts would go. He came to a number of conclusions or hypotheses that are relevant to this discussion:

1. Orgastic potency is the capacity for complete excitation and release of that excitation in the orgasm. It is not simply erective potency, as many still think, or even just the ability to experience acme, or what most people call *"orgasm."*
2. The orgasm involves the discharge of the excited energy in an orgasm reflex in which the entire body musculature moves involuntarily in specific ways in both males and females.
3. There is a specific energy involved, which Reich eventually called *"orgone energy,"* energy he came to hypothesize prevails everywhere in the universe. He developed this theory as an extension and evolution of Freud's concept of libido (which Freud first called *"Sexualstoffe"*).
4. Due to many environmental and social factors over the past 6,000 years or so, repression and distortion of the sexual function has occurred and has made the capacity for orgastic potency almost impossible for most people.
5. People became armored against this function and the armor also functions to inhibit all kinds of emotional expression, especially the ability to love and accept love.
6. The armor is physical as well as emotional and intellectual. In energetic terms, it consists of condensed or chronically contracted orgone energy. When armor melts, however, more vivified energy is released into our bodies.[20]

---

[20] The evolution of Reich's theories and the reports of his experiments can be traced through the books and articles published from the late 1920's into the 21st century (by Farrar, Straus and Giroux mostly) as his publishers continue to bring out new material. The material is available from the Wilhelm Reich Museum Bookstore, Orgonon, P.O. Box 687, Rangeley ME., 04970. Here is a partial list with commentary (publication dates do not necessarily reflect first editions of these works):

"Selected Writings," 1960: Contains writings from various periods on nearly every aspect of his work.

"The Function of the Orgasm," 1961: Traces his theories from his psychoanalytic period through the discovery of orgastic potency and beyond. Contains an excellent description of his concept of orgastic potency.

"Character Analysis," 1976: Also traces his theories from his psychoanalytical period through the discovery of orgone energy with more discussion of his theory of character armor and the technique of character analysis that was adopted by many psychoanalysts and others who continue to practice as psychological or psychiatric practitioners.

"The Mass Psychology of Fascism," 1970: An excellent example of Reich's contribution to social and political science based on his experiences in Europe as fascism emerged out of World War I and took the world into World War II.

"The Invasion of Compulsory Sex-Morality," 1971: Reich's analysis of Malinowski's research in the Trobriand Islands. An important contribution to the discussion and study of the hypothesized transition from Matrist to Patrist society beginning sometime around 4500 B.C.E. Matrist culture apparently survived into the 20th century in the Trobriand Islands.

"The Cancer Biopathy," 1973: A description of many of Reich's experiments and theories pertaining to the development of cancer and other related illnesses.

"The Bion Experiments on the Origin of Life," 1979: A description of many of Reich's experiments that led him to the theory of orgone energy.

"Ether, God and Devil and Cosmic Superimposition," 1973: Here (in *"Ether, God and Devil"*) Reich applies his theories to the philosophy of science and religion, and then to cosmology and astronomy (*"Cosmic Superimposition"*).

A more complete listing of his books and articles is available from the Museum Bookstore.

Gurdjieff's Concept of the Function of Sexuality in the Evolution of Consciousness

IX

Both Gurdjieff and Reich spoke of functions that block freer movement and expression: Gurdjieff called this the buffers, Reich the armor. Gurdjieff is quoted as having said that we must *"destroy the crust of vices long accumulated"* and *"correct old sins,"* which means, I take it, that we must destroy the buffers if we wish to go on the higher forms of work. Reich's idea is that armor and neuroses in general have their source in a stasis of energy; that psychological blocks or defense mechanisms are rooted in biophysical, chronic muscular contractions. Merging Reich and Gurdjieff here offers the following perspective: buffers are manifestation of chronic muscular armoring. To destroy them, as Gurdjieff would have us do, is, in Reich's terms, to melt or dissolve the armoring.

Gurdjieff told us that our essence is ours by birthright but that false personality is not. Reich concluded that core impulses and emotions are ours by birthright whereas armor is laid on us by a human world that has been conditioned to fear and hate the core. Gurdjieff said that negative, destructive emotions have no center, are not a function of the essence. Reich learned that such emotions are a function of the armor, not the core (Freud had speculated that they are rooted in an instinct, Thanatos or the Death Instinct, a theory that Reich rejected). Gurdjieff taught that false personality operates with utter mechanicalness. Reich showed why, with respect to armor. It forms in infancy and childhood, for the most part, when we have no control or understanding of what is happening to us, thus becomes completely habitual or automatic.

Gurdjieff pointed out that if we attempt higher work before destroying the buffers, we evolve, if anything other than a life of fantasy, on what he called a wrong foundation. What crystallizes is the crust, the false personality, in Reich's terms, the aspects of our selves that are grounded in the armor. Thus, if we wish to evolve, in Gurdjieff's sense, it seems to me that we need to undergo a process of, in Reich's terms, dissolution of the armor.

Reich discovered that orgastic potency accompanies dissolution of the armor and concluded that orgastic potency is necessary for maintenance of an unarmored, healthy state. Gurdjieff taught that only people who are completely normal sexually have a chance in The Work; that people whose sexuality is governed by buffers cannot get anywhere via The Work; and that the Sex Center must work properly, i.e., with its own energy, for the organism to evolve beyond waking-sleep. Thus, merging Reich and Gurdjieff, we can say that establishment of orgastic potency appears to be essential for development of the capacity to work on oneself effectively.

Via Reich's writings, we have evidence gained through his years of working with patients and in the laboratory as to what the concept of sexual health actually means. Gurdjieff never told us what he meant by it, but his ideas regarding sexual normalcy, sexual fears, strange tastes and constantly working buffers can be seen, via Reich's research, in terms of orgastic potency (*"normalcy"*) underlying anxiety (*"sexual fears"*), sexual perversions due to in inability to experience complete genital gratification (*"strange tastes"*) because of the armoring (the buffers).

To say that in waking-sleep centers borrow unused sex energy, and vice versa, is to say that unexpressed sex energy becomes armor and is released unconsciously in activities as sexual titillation. Gurdjieff offers the following evidence of this process: when sex energy is misused by another center it can be recognized by a particular "taste," by a fervor or vehemence that belies the nature of the activity itself indicating that it is not only intellectual, physical or emotional energy-matter that is being utilized, but, inappropriately to the activity, unreleased sex energy.

X

The final concept of Reich's that I want to mention is his notion of *"cosmic superimposition."* The basic idea, as it relates to human sexuality, is that the orgone energy within emanates outside of our membranes or skin, forming an atmosphere or field and that when people are attracted to one another their orgone energy atmospheres or fields mutually excite one another or luminate. The attraction and excitation can reach a level of intensity where they feel an urge to come together and then possibly interpenetrate to the point where the two energy systems literally merge for a short time into one energy system. Each system can experience a loss of "self" or an experience of unification with the other; the two energy systems become one for a few moments. That the excited systems naturally come together and seek merger is, for Reich, a function of the energy when it vivifies in this manner. The excited energies seek contact and merger, and in the process, as the two merge, each system releases its excited energy into the other and the tension created by the excitation is released in the ecstasy we call orgasm. Reich called this *"cosmic"* superimposition because he saw this process as happening everywhere in the universe and thought of it as a key function in creation, including the creation of life.

This experience, of course, brings in impressions, in this case, impressions of loss of self, or unification with another, which involves, I imagine, a form of loss of identification. The theory here is that we won't experience such impressions if we remain identified or if we are buffered or armored against the full excitation, gratification and merger.

Reich hypothesized that our energy field is in direct contact with the energy within our skins, thus communicates its impressions throughout the body. The idea here is that the impressions associated with complete orgastic gratification and merger are transmitted throughout the body, to every cell, in other words. This may be one way to begin to concretely understand Gurdjieff's concept of cellular saturation.

Taken together, these considerations indicate that sex energy as Gurdjieff conceived of it, is, in Reich's terms, orgone energy excited to a certain degree of vivifyingness, namely to the degree that it luminates when two, oppositely charged or highly attracted, relatively unarmored people become sexually attracted to one another (Reich, by the way, hypothesized that this function of lumination between orgone energy fields is the basis for the phenomenon we call "light"). This implies that sex energy, in Gurdjieff's sense, exists only in potential prior to sexual excitation and is created when the energy present is excited to the requisite degree of vivifyingness and would explain Gurdjieff's teaching that buffers prevent the Sex Center from utilizing sex energy, for

Gurdjieff's Concept of the Function of Sexuality in the Evolution of Consciousness

when buffers are in place, the energy within the person cannot reach the level of excitation Gurdjieff refers to as sex energy and the Sex Center, as Gurdjieff taught, is forced to use a coarser energy. Via this idea, he is apparently telling us that we can have sex, even have what we think of as orgasms when our Sex Centers are utilizing this coarser energy-matter, but that the experience, the impressions, the activity itself is not one where a full or complete release-merger experience, which is possible only when the Sex Center utilizes sex energy per se, occurs.

XI

Identifying Gurdjieff's concept of sex energy as orgone energy luminating to the level of vivifyingness it reaches when two, oppositely charged or highly attracted unarmored three brained beings become sexually excited brings us to within one step of comprehending, from a purely theoretical point of view of course, how sexuality functions in formation of the Higher Emotional Body. When buffers or armor is dissolved, the freed up energy created and any other free energy within the body can luminate with another's energy. The energy-matter-impressions created can then pulse and flow throughout the body, which indicates that the cells can be at least put in contact with the energy and so be in a position to become saturated with it, to use Gurdjieff's term.

There needs to be another step, however, at least from Gurdjieff's point of view, for he taught that for crystallization of the level of consciousness called the Higher Emotional Body to occur, the cells must be saturated with *"transmuted"* sex energy, that is, energy-matter-impressions of a finer nature than that initially excited. This can occur, utilizing Reich's terminology, when the energy of the two organisms fuse in bio-energetic merger literally becoming one bio-energetic system. During the moments of fusion the fused energy-matter-impressions pulses and flows throughout both organisms, involving every cell, thus allowing the cells to participate in the impression of unity with another, loss of self, or surrender out of oneself (the literal meaning of ecstasy).

After periodic experiences of this kind, the cells are in a position where they may become saturated to the point where crystallization of the Higher Emotional Body can occur.

If Gurdjieff's teaching regarding formation of the Higher Emotional Body and the proper working of the Sex Center are correct and the understanding of this function gained via Reich's research is accurate, periodic complete bio-energetic merger in the genital embrace can provide the energy-matter-impressions-food necessary for crystallization of the Higher Emotional Body to begin. If Gurdjieff's concept of the formation of higher-being bodies is not meant literally but refers symbolically to a state of psychological awareness only, then what has been said here would apply solely to a level and/or a kind of awareness produced by the merger of energy systems. Of course, there are a lot of *"ifs"* here, and to go beyond theoretical understanding or speculation, to find out precisely what this might mean, I guess we'll have to make the experiment, take the journey, since there appear to be no humans as yet who have been able to provide the kind of evidence that would render these notions scientifically secure.

XII

In characterizing the difference between the four ways of spiritual or psychological evolution that he discriminated, Gurdjieff said that one who chooses the Fourth Way can evolve much more quickly than one who chooses the other ways because the worker in the Fourth Way learns a *"secret"* and via this secret can make a *"pill"* that when *"swallowed"* automatically leads to the transmutation of emotions or the Second Conscious Shock.[21] If he was not simply joking and we can take him seriously here, on my analysis, the function of bio-energetic merger in the genital embrace qualifies as such a secret. Of the four ways, that of the Fakir who overcomes physical pain, the Monk who overcomes emotional doubt, the Yogi who overcomes the monkey mind and controls thought, and the Householder, the Fourth Way, only the latter eschews suppression of sexuality.

That love is the secret, though not widely understood bio-energetically, has at least been noticed by some sincere seekers of truth over the centuries (not to mention the poets!) including the ancient Tantrics. Of course, many others have claimed (and continue to claim) that the kind of evolution we are speaking of here can only be stimulated via celibacy where the sex function is suppressed and its energy transmuted or transformed by its not being utilized in direct sexual activity. Gurdjieff's remarks on this topic indicate to me that he was not one of those.

© Copyright 2012 - David Brahinsky - All Rights Reserved

---

[21] See, e.g., ISM, p.50.

Gurdjieff's Concept of the Function of Sexuality - Questions & Answers

Q1: David, that was a very good presentation. I liked it. I totally agree with your opening statement that Mr. Gurdjieff said that the only way to Liberation is via transmutation of the sexual energy. For me, there is no other way. He says that the sex energy is the most sacred gift given by nature to men and women. So we must begin there somehow because it is the most sacred gift.

Now, he also said many times that there are only two ways for the transmutation of the sexual energy … total abstinence, meaning abstinence not only in sex but in thinking, feeling and organic instinct. Total abstinence. And I might give you an example of total abstinence is the greatest saint in India, Ramana Maharshi. Here is a man that not only doesn't have sex; he didn't allow anybody to touch him. Physically, nobody could touch him. And he obtained Liberation.

The other way is total sex. Immerse yourself in sex. I think he was talking more to men than women. Yeah. Believe me. I mean, that everything he says about sex in the exchange was for men, not for women. Mostly, I don't know about another woman, anyhow.

MC: Do you have a question?

Q1: I'm gonna ask him. This is the question. I disagree with you. I'm gonna ask him this question. When you say that there is no, that Mr. Gurdjieff never talks about how sex is. In fact, it's the most straightforward statement of sex. The third line in the poem on love by Ashiata Shiemash which says that love of body depends on type and polarity. We have to understand that in order to do the transmutation of the sexual energy.

Now my question to you is, what do you think about that?

David: I love the sayings of Ashiata Shiemash. I use them all the time, and I was just saying, obviously, that he didn't get into the concrete nature of the sex energy. Whereas Reich is doing that. That's what I meant. I mean, he says lots of things about sex but he doesn't get as concrete as I needed, personally, and when I came across Reich I felt that here was the concreteness that I needed for my own understanding. That's all.

And as far as complete abstention, as you mentioned, I don't mean to denigrate this great saint that you mentioned, but, again, being scientifically oriented, I say, well, how do we know that he never ever had a thought about it? You know the Zen story of the two monks who were walking on the road, you know, and it was raining and it was a muddy road. And one of them picked up this beautiful girl, carried her across the road and put her down. And they got to the monastery and the other one finally couldn't hold it in any longer and he said: "How could you pick up a beautiful girl? We monks are not supposed to touch young women." And the one who had picked her up said, "Well, I put her down on the other side of the road. Are you still carrying her?"

So what we carry in our heads is very private and …. So anyway, I don't know personally, I mean, Gurdjieff said it, that complete abstention might do it. Maybe. Is that harder? Is it harder to have complete abstention, without even thinking about it, than to actually have a normal sex life? Maybe that's a difference in the ways, right? Fourth Way versus, let's say, the third way or the second way or some combination of the ways.

Q1: No. But there are only two ways of Vedanta and Tantra immersion.

David: Ok.

MC: We have a question.

Q2: You mentioned a name earlier that I didn't know who you were talking about. Herbert …

David: Marcuse.

Q2: Yeah. Could you explain who that was?

David: Herbert Marcuse was a twentieth century philosopher and he became an activist. He was part of the Frankfurt School in Germany, came to America. He was sort of the elder statesman of the sixties activism. He was the teacher of Angela Davis. You heard of Angela Davis? She's still around. She just retired. They started a program over at the University of California at Santa Cruz which my son is graduating from called The History of Consciousness program. And that's about …. Anybody want to add anything about Marcuse that I didn't mention? And he's written quite a bit …. His most famous book is *"Eros and Civilization."* He wrote that book in the late 1950's. It was published almost at the same time as Norman O. Brown's book … what was that called? … the name has gone away from me for a second … (David's addition on transcription: "Life Against Death" is the name of the book). Those two books were very influential in my life. They got me on this path.

Q1 (again): And what do you think about *"One Dimensional Man"*?

David: That's a continuation of his theory in *"Eros and Civilization."*

Q3: Have you made any connection in your researches with the repression of our lower nature. What Beelzebub has to say about animal sacrifices.

David: Remind me of that. It's been a few years since I read *Beelzebub's Tales*. You are really up on it … everybody here. And I was up on it. What does he say about it?

Gurdjieff's Concept of the Function of Sexuality in the Evolution of Consciousness

Q3: Animal sacrifice is a huge topic.

David: Yeah. So what is the point you were trying to make?

Q3: I'm just wondering if you made that connection, that's all.

David: I probably would if you would remind men of that point (Laughter).
Can you summarize that really quickly. What did he say about that?

Q4: That's part of why Beelzebub came down to earth.

Q3: I guess that's the cause of … what was it? … the second, third descent? Second.

David: He came down to stop that process. Yeah. Right. Sacrificial offerings.

I don't know. Does anybody make that connection between suppression of sexuality in humans and that connection? I would have to think about it. Anybody here?

Q4: Feels right.

David: Fells right. OK. We'll work on it.

MC: Here's a question from ah …

Q5: It's very interesting, what you are saying. I use Reich's work a lot. But I have a question though. One thing that got me a little bit confused and that I, you talk about the formation of the higher centers, the higher emotional center?

David: No. The formation of the higher being body. The higher emotional center - we're born with that.

Q5: Yes. That's what got confusing when you were speaking because I … that's the reason it threw me off. The body is something one forms, the higher emotional center is completely formed already.

David: Right.

Q5: Ok, I just wanted to clarify that.

David: I kept throwing those terms back and forth.

Q5: You threw them back and forth at one point.

All & Everything Conference 2012

David: Maybe I confused the two at one point.

Q5: Exactly. And that's all. I just wanted to verify that.

David: Sorry. Right.

MC: We have one over here.

Q6: Just one thing that (a name) pointed out that I think is very interesting about the sacrificial offerings is that they could be understood as the first and second brain functions that have been sacrificed and as a result of that we would think that that would be pleasing to our gods. And to me that's an indication that we ... we... quote, *"wrongly"* sacrifice the normal functioning of the first and second brain.

David: Now you're making me think about it. Because historically, I wonder whether the beginning of the repression of sexuality which. I, at this point, adhere to the theory that about 6,000 years ago, and for thousands and thousands of years before, that the human race was Matrist, was sex positive. Women took lovers as they wished. We didn't know who the father was and it didn't matter. The tribe brought up the children. The uncle often served the function of the father. This continued to exist into the 2oth century in the Tribriand Islands. Malinowski discovered that in his study of the sexual life of savages (David's addition in transcription: this is the title of Malinowski's book) and Reich wrote a book about that.

Q5: That's how chimpanzees are?

David: I don't know much about that. So the question is: were they sacrificing animals in the days when there was no repression of sexuality? That's a long time ago and we don't have any written records. So I don't know. But if somehow we can find out ... the connection there. So if we can find that out we can see if there is really an historical connection like that, other than the emotional one that perhaps Gurdjieff was certainly talking about.

Does that make sense to you?

Q5: Uh, I'm not sure.

David: That's a new topic for us.

Q6: I just wanted to add that in current ... some current and traditional American Indian tribes ... might be described as culturally ... current practice.

David: Matrist.

Q6: Correct.

Gurdjieff's Concept of the Function of Sexuality in the Evolution of Consciousness

David: Yes.

Q6: And children are brought up collectively by the tribe. Very often. The uncle or mother's brother will be the male father figure.

David: Right. And, in general, the theory that Reich goes by is called *"Saharasia."* If you Google *"Saharasia"* this will come up. There's James DeMeo ... I just remembered the name ... I was trying to remember the name for somebody yesterday ... wrote this book *"Saharasia"* on this theory that Reich started and has been developed, that around 6,000 years ago deserts started forming in Central Asia and spread down to what is today the Middle East, and these deserts caused the Matrist tribes to begin to have to move to look for water. And eventually came in conflict with one another. And so started having to fight with one another.

The males, who were bigger and stronger, tended to be more important in those fights. And over the course of centuries it evolved into the males now needing to have the power in the tribes as Matrist turns to Patrist. And in order for the males to have the power and to continue their power they had to know who their sons were. So in order to know who their sons were they had to control the sex lives of the women. For the first time. And that's the beginning of the suppression of sexuality.

The first thing is you repress the sexuality of the women. That eventually leads to the inability of the men to have gratifying sex also, because it's not two equal people. It can't be gratifying according to Reich's theory. So the whole ... you know, the whole world is now suffering from this inability to have complete gratification. Which leads to violence.

Q7: Just one comment about addressing male sexuality. It's pretty hard to address the male without addressing the female. But I was wondering about ... it's puzzling to me to know how to understand Gurdjieff's own sexuality. After his wife died and he has relations with other women and fathers many children. What do you have to say about that?

David: You know, I don't think it's possible to understand a person's capacity for sexual gratification unless you know them really intimately, and maybe in a therapeutic situation where you can see whether their capacity for the organism reflex is there. It's impossible to know. So. And some people can have a gratifying life with one mate their whole lives, and other people can have it with serial monogamy, and other people can have it with more that one partner. Possibly. I'm saying possibly. There's no way to know.

Q7: I was wondering if he was trying to transmit some knowledge.

David: I have heard that one of the women who he did have sex with who did report on it in the literature said that she felt that, she said, that she really got Gurdjieff's teaching. (laughter) anybody else remember that? Remember who that was?

All & Everything Conference 2012

Q8: It was reported in one of Bennett's books. Bennett said that when he was around the Prieurie he heard women, more than one, I believe, indicate that there was a special teaching as part of that intimate relationship.

David: Which is not fair for us guys (laughter).

Q1 (again): What is fair if you want to imitate him.

MC: Stephen, you have a question?

Q8: Yeah. So you spoke of something can happen automatically.

David: Yeah. Gurdjieff put it that way.

Q8: And the sly man. And you've spoken about triggering the first conscious shock and even the second. And I think you also probably mean maintaining it, not jut triggering it.

David: Right. Triggering it over and over again. Maintaining it.

Q8: Because you've been in The Work so you know it's not just triggering it but I'm just assuming you mean maintaining it as well.

David: I do.

Q8: And what I've noticed is that through this repeated triggering and maintaining of this first conscious shock that the I begins to emerge and grow. The capacity to be there longer and longer and deeper and deeper and more and more. The different types of attention that result in the different brains deepens. Our ability to mentate actively and see and sense in the body and feel and see our feelings and allow them to really be increases … and increases almost automatically. This happens automatically when we allow for, receive and actively attempt this first conscious shock.

David: Like a pianola, right?

Q8: Yeah. I mean, it advances, it builds something. Just to do that first conscious shock. Something higher automatically blends with this new lower. The new lower is me being in the Work, so to speak. Triggering it and maintaining it so that becomes a lower for this new higher to enter and cause a new middle. The higher blending with the lower to actualize the middle.

So the question is: Is that sex? And then also, as I …

David: You sure you want to ask me another question? That's a tough one…

Gurdjieff's Concept of the Function of Sexuality in the Evolution of Consciousness

Q8: OK. Well, that's an easy one to remember but then, whether, uh, it's a sort of question that comes from listening to your wonderful talk and ideas is this: as we develop in this new way with this first conscious shock which is a glorious teaching, really. It's just amazing. How it's put to us. As we advance in this way we become more natural and many things become real, including gratification and what you're talking about, organismic connection and that kind of thing. Does it have to be just sex, sex that does it, or could it be a whole way. A holy way of being that does this?

David: Anything that helps to melt the buffers does it.

Q8: OK Then I have one more side to this whole thing. I don't fully understand what I'm saying and I don't fully understand the second conscious shock, but I see in myself, I become something when I work. I get this power. I can see, I can be, I can do, I can act intentionally. And this I becomes another I in a way that has to become completely let go in order to really receive something more. And I am taking that to be the beginning of the second conscious shock but I don't really know. That's it.

Q9: OK David, that was very interesting to me and I certainly don't want to let you get away without at least once at least bringing this back to the scientific side. We know that Reich was experimenting with clouds and accumulation, and maybe you have some answers that could help us with respect to some of the aspects of Gurdjieff Work in this regard.

So, can you say anything about the nature of the energies. Do you see this as some energy that s of an electromagnetic nature or completely separate from electromagnetism and chemistry and all those other things. An energy that is not known.

David: Let me explain. From Reich's point of view. For Reich, orgone energy is the fundamental energy of the universe and all the other energies are derivative of it, come from it. In the Gurdjieff Work you might even say descend from it because there …. Cosmic orgone energy, for Reich, if you want to take Reich and bring it to the Gurdjieff concept, is the One. It's the Oneness. So everything comes out of that. I think of it sometimes, I mean, without knowing, it's just a thought, as the Absolute itself. And that everything comes out of it. I think of it as we normally think of it as going down the Ray of Creation.

Q10: Did you say etherokrilno?

David: Yes. Perhaps that I would. You know. Perhaps. I would have to go back and study *Beelzebub's Tales* some more and see if I would want to say that definitely.

Q9 (again): OK. Well that's partially satisfying. To take it in another direction, we also know Reich was concerned with clouds, air, atmospheres and we know about exercises and Gurdjieff's reference to breathing. So do you think that. Well, tell us what the relationship is between this energy and the air.

All & Everything Conference 2012

David: Yeah. When we breathe we're breathing in orgone energy which Reich felt is ... oxygen molecules are attracted to orgone and vice versa or mutually, so when we're breathing in oxygen we're breathing in orgone. And the red blood cells that are carrying oxygen are carrying orgone. That's the basis of the Reich Blood Test. Testing people who had cancerous problems. You could take their blood and take a look at how long the red blood cells survive under the microscope. You time it. Then you put them in the orgone energy accumulator, which he built as an experimental device that he eventually started using therapeutically with terminal cancer patients, by the way. He never had anybody who wasn't considered terminal by the medical establishment.

They go into the accumulator and their energy system would interact with the accumulated energy if the accumulator because of the way it's built with organic material on the outside, metal material on the inside in layers, so little by little the accumulator accumulates the energy, and now it's in the box a little more so than in the air. You go in there and your energy interacts with the energy of the accumulator and that raises your energy level. You don't suck in the energy. You luminate with it.

Just like with two people. And that raises your energy level. And then you go out and you have your blood taken, and the red blood cells last longer. That's the Reich Blood Test. I've seen that. That's one of the few experiments I've actually seen.

Q9: And there's a limit for the tolerance of that?

David: Of being in the accumulator?

Q9: OK.

David: There's such a thing as being overcharged. And you can start feeling bad, yes. So there was a ...

Q9: So the animals die?

David: Well, there are agreements. You don't die. You just feel a little sick and you get out.

Q9: We saw a room at Rangely that had had multiple layers of ...

David: The Orgone Room, yeah.

Q9: And they had. And he had built it too powerful.

David: Accidentally, some of them died? I didn't remember that.

MC: Before we continue, I'd like to mention that we have a long list of questioners. We have about 15 minutes left. So here's trying to be brief with your questions.

Gurdjieff's Concept of the Function of Sexuality in the Evolution of Consciousness

Q11: Yes. My question would be: let's say, in your opinion, let's just say that we are able to get rid of the blockages that are there muscularly, and have this orgastic energy, this orgone energy flow within us. Why would there be any need for work on oneself? Would one reach any sort of permanent state of …. I don't mean to say enlightenment … of being, if that were true, because that's the piece that seems to me that is completely missing in Reich's …

David: Reich was not involved in that at all.

Q11: Right.

David: That's not part of his work. Reichians who know about my work and who are not at all sympathetic to Gurdjieff or anything like it are not interested. However.

Q11: I'm just talking about your opinion.

David: Here's my opinion about it. I would really like my neighbor to be orgonotically healthy. They'd be much better neighbors. They'd be healthy. They wouldn't be repressive. They'd be sweet. They'd probably not be violent. But if they are not working on themselves it might not go beyond that. That's why I decided to do both. Because I feel the need to work to evolve what you were talking about, that I. And so that's why I think you need both. But that's only if you are interested in both.

Q12: So David. Back up for a second. This question has to do with what I am interested in, more about your special interest within philosophy … how Gurdjieff was …

David: Well, I was studying philosophy in college, and the only thing that a person who studies philosophy in college can do with it is either become a lawyer (David's transcription addition: if you go to law school afterwards) … this is before computers (further addition: lots of philosophy majors go into computer work) … or become a philosophy teacher.

So I went in that direction and in the middle of that process I came across both Reich and Gurdjieff. I told this story at lunch yesterday. Where I had studied Buddhism and I was practicing Zen and I had given up words. I said I'm not going to read or write anymore. I wanted to just develop my being.

And I was sitting on a couch at a friend's house in California and I forgot my vow. There was a book sitting next to me. And I had forgotten my vow and I picked it up. And it was *In Search of the Miraculous*. And you could say that there was an angel there who put it there because it sure felt like it. And that changed my whole life. And I said this is what I've been looking for. This is the source. This is what all the philosophers are trying to get to. And some of them have gotten somewhere close to it. I think Plato … the talk on Plato yesterday and Pythagoras was very interesting to me and I think those guys were really working in that region.

All & Everything Conference 2012

So I decided I can teach philosophy and use The Work as the underlying thing, because I think many of the philosophers I teach, all of the ones I teach in my introductory classes, have something of The Work in them, and I can bring that out in my students.

You know Heidegger. Heidegger! Trying to understand Being. Ok, that's The Work. Sure he went through despair and Nothing to get there. You don't have to do that. So I show that to my students. So those are the kind of things.

Kierkegaard, you know. The *"leap of faith"* into freedom. Sure he was a twisted, unhappy, miserable soul … particularly sexually. He had one sexual experience in his whole life and …

Q1 (again): It was bad?

David: It wasn't only bad. He said *"The shame of it, the shame of it,"* with a prostitute. But you know so they each have a little piece (delayed laughter). You understand what happened … they each have a little piece of it and some more than others, so that's how I do it.

And when I teach religion, it's the same thing. You know. *Beelzebub's Tales* … Moses … Saint Moses, Saint Jesus, Saint Muhammad, Saint Buddha. I teach all of these religions. But I show what happened to them … as soon as the saints died, so to speak.

MC: There's a question here from …

Q12: First I have a comment. Your presentation, the chronology, the way that you presented the concepts sequentially were very assimilable.

David: Thank you, thank you.

Q12: Thank you for the structure. My question has to do with one comment you made early on and I'm trying to get an association … It was just a statement about objective morality.

David: Right.

Q12: I don't recall how that is connected.

David: For Gurdjieff, the contact with conscience which is part of the second conscious shock is what puts us in contact with … when we do wrong and so we feel a remorse of conscience. If we did wrong. Objectively wrong. So there's a sense in Gurdjieff that there is such a thing as objective right and wrong. It's not just a matter of opinion. And it's not because God told us what's right and wrong through one or another scripture which may or may not have it. But there's something … in other words, right and wrong is objective as facts.

Gurdjieff's Concept of the Function of Sexuality in the Evolution of Consciousness

Now we know that facts can also be …. You know, it's not simple, but it's objective. That was Plato's attempt. He attempted to do that in *"The Republic,"* to teach the objectivity of morality.

Q12; And to clarify: that was leading into what?

David: Well, that's part of the experience of the second conscious shock … of contact with the higher... that's what the higher emotional center teaches us, which enables us to form the higher emotional body. You get that straight?

Q1 (again): I just want to address a question of my friend here: the importance of sex in men. A disciple asked Mr. Gurdjieff: *"why is sex so important among us men?"* and Mr. Gurdjieff said: *"That is a very subjective question because not all men are interested in sex. Only a few men, or some individual men."*

And to finish I'm going to tell you this little story about Isaac Newton. This is the greatest scientist who ever lived. They asked Newton one thing before he died. What is the greatest accomplishment of your life? He said, *"my greatest accomplishment, I'm gonna die a virgin."*

David: Let me say something abut Reich. You reminded me of what Reich said about men and women. I didn't have a chance to say it before, but now that we brought it up again …

For Reich, men and women can have the same experiences in sex. Perhaps the reason why women's experience has been different for the last 6,000, 4,000, whatever years is because of the repression of women. That once women are unrepressed their experience is not different from men's. Their capacity for orgastic experience and for gratification is the same. So, for Reich, two healthy, unarmored organisms can have the same experience. I mean, how do you measure experience? But, theoretically, generally speaking.

So I think a lot of the differences between men and women perhaps have to do with the fact that we've been living in an armored world for thousands of years. How do we know what it would be like to be in a world of unarmored people? We don't. That's why Reich dedicated his work to the children of the future. Because every child that's born is a potential unarmored being if we can change our way of bringing children up.

MC: Next question.

Q13: On this business of Cosmic Orgone Energy, and getting back to The One, the source of all and everything, there's a lot of validation for that, and I wondered about the impetus, and how you got to that realization. It's in Rumi, and there's one poem in particular that resonated with me, The Dying Laughing, where this man is declaring to this woman, I love you so much, I've done everything for you, I've given you everything, what's wrong with you? Why … what's wrong? What's wrong? What's troubling you? She says, well you haven't died, that is, surrendered completely.

All & Everything Conference 2012

And it's also in the Bible, in the King James version, in Song of Songs, when Solomon comes to claim his maiden and he says well how do you want me, and she says, betwixt my breasts, in perfect balance, in perfect balance.

So I wondered, my question to you is, how you came to understand this, when did it click in for you?

David: I can tell you this. I'm not sure I can tell you when it clicked. But I can tell you that it continues to evolve. I've been having little epiphanies just recently on this subject about the relation of The One and The Many.

When reading something from what's his name? the playwright who studied the Gurdjieff Work … Peter Brook … who was talking about the inner play in Shakespeare's play about sex couples … Midsummer Night's Dream. He wrote about the inner play saying that in that inner play the sex problems that they have all get solved in the end. Which Brook was saying was Shakespeare's way of saying sex is important for the propagation of the species because the species is what is evolving. That we need to look to the children to keep evolving that way. So the Many, the differences, the individuals that was talked about at lunch yesterday, which I really hit upon, is crucial, is just as important as the Oneness. Because the Oneness and the Individuals are all The One.

That's what I have been … that's been happening to me lately more … feeling that connection more. But I don't remember when it started.

Q14: Well, my interest is in the sex energy because he tells us in *Beelzebub's Tales* that sex energy is the same as creative energy or work energy. So I can really see that in a practical way in the food chart, because you know you eat food and it goes around, gets digested and ends up as exioehary. Exioehary is the sex energy, but it's also the energy we need for work. So that, to me, is the essence of it … is that more is produced than I can use for work.

David: That's Reich's theory.

Q14: Yeah.

David: That the sex function is the release of the excess energy of the cells.

Q14: Right. So more is produced that I have the capacity to use for work, but, if I surrender it too much in other ways …

David: You can have too much sex and use it up.

Q14: No, but see, the point is, that it gets squandered before it even gets to exioehary. That's the practical part.

Gurdjieff's Concept of the Function of Sexuality in the Evolution of Consciousness

David: Right.

Q14: The point before that, piandjoehary, point 7, which he calls the cerebellum, and that's the form thinking, visualization, imagination, and so forth, and so the main problem that I see in people today is one squanders that piandjoehary with negative imagination, with worry, with day dreams, with fantasies. All these picturings that are wasting that precious energy that could become exioehary that I could use for my work. That I can squander with my day dreams. And fantasies and imaginations. And, um, the me that's. that's like a big obstacle for using the sex energy for my work. So anyway, do you have any comments on that?

David: I … just … check (hand motion showing total agreement). (Laughter)

Q15: I have a question in the context of this talk. Do you have anything to say about homosexuality?

David: Here's the way I've come to understand it. That it doesn't matter whether it's male and female. It only matters whether there's a polarity excitation between the two. So that if a person is homosexual, and they have a strong polarity attraction to another person of the same gender, the same kind of thing can happen. As far as I understand it.

I don't think Reich understood it that way. I think he was still caught … He died in 1957, so, I don't know how he would feel today.

Q15: In jail, let's not forget.

David: Right. At the age of 60. Imagine, at the age of 60. A young man as far as I'm concerned.

Does Gurdjieff talk about that? I mean, some people think that's what he meant about people with strange tastes. I've seen that ….

Q1 (again): He said to Fritz Peters, homosexuality as a career is a dead end.

David: Yeah. So, you know. See, I don't look upon these guys as gods, as perfect. I think … The kind of respect that is shown Gurdjieff here is very, very heart-warming to me, but I'm sure that you don't think of him as a god, that he made mistakes.

Q16: He wants us to question what he said.

David: Right. Exactly.

Q16: He did have the women of The Rope which he …. He wasn't discriminating in that case.

David: And that's another thing too which is important in the Gurdjieff Work, and that is that he is talking to a particular individual or a group at a particular time for a particular reason for a particular need. It doesn't mean he's making a universal statement. So that's something that we have to take into account.

The Inner Trauma of Kundabuffer

Russell Schreiber

Abstract

This paper will address three interlinked psychological strands that G. I. Gurdjieff presents in All and Everything. In the first strand of this weaving, I examine deeper psychological repercussions of the introduction into humanity of an organ represented by Kundabuffer. We need a more complete understanding of the inner psychological trauma produced by Kundabuffer. Gurdjieff presents the foundational negative behavioral changes he observes in humanity due to Kundabuffer. However, there are important psychodynamic repercussions to be explicated that can help us understand the impressions we receive in our self-study. The second strand is the unexamined relationship of the psychological trauma produced by Kundabuffer to the subsequent design of religions or *"ways"* to correct for unexpected negative changes following Kundabuffer's removal. The third strand involves the inadequacy of these *"ways"* to foresee, understand, or compensate for the psychological, homeostatic dynamics created by Kundabuffer and the inherent difficulties of trying to correct humanity's negative, violent emotional behavior through *"ways."* We need to better understand the interactive mechanism of these three strands. A new approach to working with our negative emotions is needed and I will outline this in my presentation.

The Inner Trauma of Kundabuffer

Mr. Gurdjieff encouraged, advised and, at times, admonished us to know ourselves in order to approach the possibility of inner evolution, the development of an inner life. In order to do this, we must understand the psychological structures formed within us as a result of the trauma of Kundabuffer. In this presentation, I will examine three interwoven aspects of human psychology stemming from what Gurdjieff considered the abnormal development of the human psyche caused by the introduction of the organ Kundabuffer in our early ancestors. The first aspect to be examined involves psychological and behavioral changes due to Kundabuffer. The second aspect is the relationship of these behavioral and psychological changes to the religions or 'ways' formulated to correct for the deleterious effects of this organ. Finally, the third aspect pertains to the unexpected complications that occur due to premature attempts at changing human behavior without fully understanding underlying psychological structures resulting from Kundabuffer.

Gurdjieff as Beelzebub presented the roots of unexpected negative behavioral changes he observed in humanity in *All and Everything*. Beelzebub observed that this bizarre behavior was unexpected following the implantation and subsequent removal of Kundabuffer. Here, an exploration of the psychodynamic repercussions of Kundabuffer will help us understand the extreme difficulty of psychological change and evolution facing us even though various 'ways' or religious traditions have been developed to help us evolve.

Gurdjieff states that what characterizes our lives is not a state of consciousness where we are actually awake and for which we were designed, but rather a waking-sleeping state uncharacteristic of normal three-brained beings. The world we live in today is the result of centuries of people remaining unconscious and the playing out of behaviors generated by the remnants of Kundabuffer. In simplest terms, Gurdjieff's work was to help others experience the sleeping-waking state of consciousness in which they live. If people could be aware of their state of sleep and make the necessary efforts to wake up, then they could provide the required vibrations that human life was designed to produce. *All and Everything* describes the developmental history of our disregulated psyche that results in the 'fall' of humanity from its path of normal evolution.

Why Kundabuffer was Needed

According to Gurdjieff, our current situation is not due to the fault of Adam and Eve. It is ultimately not entirely the fault of humanity at large, but was due to an unforeseen cosmic event: *the genesis of the moon.* A massive cosmic body collided with the Earth which broke off large fragments that in turn coalesced into our moon. In *All and Everything*, Gurdjieff states that our dilemma arises from the implantation into us of an organ, Kundabuffer, at the time of the moon's genesis. This organ prevented humankind from seeing reality correctly. In *In Search of the Miraculous*, Ouspensky recounts what Gurdjieff said about humanity's predicament. Due to the organ's implantation, humanity is unable to realize its actual purpose which is to produce certain vibrations, or '*food' for the moon,* along with the rest of organic life on earth. This 'food' is more sophisticated than simple physical food and is comprised of the sum of all vibrations that organic life produces, and especially those produced by human beings as distinct from other instinctual animals. The total vibrational output of life on earth is necessary for the further planetary development of the moon.

As Gurdjieff explains, three-brained beings, as he called humans, were already evolving on the earth. If the natural order of things had prevailed, they ought to have acquired what Gurdjieff calls 'objective reason,' or an accurate perception of reality. In time, they would develop 'higher bodies,' or souls. In describing the genesis of the moon, he introduces beings he calls angels. They are a kind of cosmic bureaucracy concerned with overall maintenance of larger systems, but not with the fate of individual creatures. The angels and archangels calculate that the fragments broken off the Earth might leave their position and produce instabilities or 'irreparable calamities' in the solar system. To offset a possible catastrophe, they decided that organic life and three-brained beings would be required to produce specific radiations for the emergent moon. However, the 'cosmic authorities' were still anxious. They feared the three-brained beings on earth might become aware of their objective situation - that their main purpose was only to produce a special substance or radiation for the moon. They feared that humanity would react with such horror that they would choose to destroy themselves en masse.

The Inner Trauma of Kundabuffer

To guard against the possibility of humanity's mass suicide, the cosmic administrators implanted an organ called Kundabuffer at the base of each person's spinal column, reducing human beings to nothing more than 'thinking animals.' I want to repeat - they were reduced to thinking animals. More specifically, the organ reduced them to only be able to see 'reality reflected in their attention upside down.' And so, what is trivial seems important and what is important goes unheeded. Humanity's situation is all the more poignant because, while the higher individuals removed Kundabuffer later on, its effects continue on to this day. *All and Everything* is full of examples of the *"maleficent consequences of the properties of the organ Kundabuffer."* What are these consequences? Overwhelming egoism, heedlessness, waste, war and delusion. Ironically, the very organ that was supposed to prevent us from destroying ourselves has resulted in a situation where we are in a perpetual state of war, continually destroying each other's existence.

One important element we may take from this historical allegory is that life, human life, is intertwined with the development of cosmic systems, particularly our solar system. Our evolution is not some epiphenomenon or accidental by-product of blind mechanical forces. Gurdjieff always insisted that, willy-nilly, humanity is part of and must serve the purposes of Great Nature. Because we are composed of matter and energy like everything else in the cosmos, we must fulfill our duty and purpose by giving back to the whole. However, he proposes that if we serve Great Nature consciously with intention (being-partkdolg-duty), we may retain something for ourselves, for our own individuality and development. We can participate in one of two ways: unconsciously, where we retain nothing real for ourselves; or intentionally, where we become useful as part of the larger cosmos, and where we can achieve self-consciousness.

Behavioral Changes due to Trauma caused by Kundabuffer

Self-perfection and the evolution of humanity is a noble aim, but it is extremely difficult to accomplish and this is not due simply to a lack of effort on our part. If we accept what Gurdjieff has told us, that an organ was placed within our ancestors to limit their consciousness, it is important to ask what are the psychological repercussions of having an organ that limited our inherent capacities. What happens to human beings when they are restricted from exercising their full potentialities for long periods? Kundabuffer was designed to limit certain experiences in the human organism and yet resulted in abnormal behavior patterns such as war, hatred, egoism, vanity, greed, etc., It is imperative to ask how this occurred and what were the psychological changes produced in us that resulted in these negative behaviors.

When I first became interested in the repercussions of Kundabuffer, the concept that arose for me was *trauma*. Symptoms found in many of the anxiety disorders, and even posttraumatic stress disorder (PTSD), are similar to many psychological aspects and behaviors indicative of Kundabuffer.[1] I began to realize that Kundabuffer's implantation may have profoundly

---

[1]. *Diagnostic and Statistical Manual of Mental Disorders*, (Washington, DC: American Psychiatric Association, 1994), 393-444.
Anxiety Disorders, 393-444.

traumatized the human species. If that were true, then it seemed important to look at some of the known, predictable results of psychological trauma to better understand the consequences of Kundabuffer.

Psychology is increasing its awareness of the deleterious effects of trauma from war, societal violence, and other unexpected, painful or abusive aspects of life. If we believe Gurdjieff's description of the history of Kundabuffer, it might represent a fundamentals trauma to the psyche that would affect all subsequent generations, including our own. It is especially important to recognize that trauma, whether abuse, an auto accident or war is usually known to the individuals that experience it. Trauma by its very nature produces a defensive psychological posture in people who experience it. However, Kundabuffer's experiences would have been unknown to those experiencing it due to its activity lying beneath ordinary consciousness. In my practice, I meet with clients who have been traumatized, thus causing their life force and behaviors to be restricted. They are afraid to drive on a freeway, go out with a man, walk down a dark street, all as a result of something that has happened to them in the past. In short, trauma often results in behavior being restricted. But what happens if we reverse this situation, that is, what happens if the restriction produces the trauma? What are common responses to being restricted?

As an example, take a child who is restricted from activities because her parents are over-protective. She may react with aggression, rage, despair, or simply follow the dictates of her parents. Aggression is often an expected result and we see this is many adolescents and young adults whose lives are restricted. Aggression has become such a characteristic of human behavior that you may say it is now a typical habitual response. Keep in mind that according to Gurdjieff, Kundabuffer reduced three-brained beings to the status of 'thinking animals.' Higher mammals tend to become aggressive or depressed when restricted - you can observe this behavior in any zoo. In the wild aggression for protection and to assert dominance and order. Of course, I am generalizing here, but is it not plausible that the human response to psychological restriction, either known or unknown, might be a predilection to aggressive behavior? In jails throughout the world, inmates attack each other and their guards. In jail, people realize they have been restricted; since the implantation of Kundabuffer were unknown to its earthly inhabitants, **people would**

Posttraumatic Stress Disorder is characterized by a number of symptoms: recurrent and intrusive recollections of the event, in rare instances, dissociative states that last from a few seconds to several hours, or even days during which components of the event are relived and the person behaves as though experiencing the event at the moment. Intense psychological distress or physiological reactivity often occurs when the person is exposed to triggering events that resemble or symbolize an aspect of the traumatic event. Stimuli associated with the trauma are persistently avoided. The person commonly makes deliberate efforts to avoid thoughts, feelings, or conversations about the traumatic event and to avoid activities, situations or people who arouse recollections of it. Avoidance may include amnesia for an important aspect of the event. Diminished responsiveness to the external world, referred to as *"psychic numbing"* or *"emotional anesthesia,"* usually begins after the event.

The individual has persistent symptoms of anxiety or increased arousal that were not present before the trauma. These symptoms may include difficulty falling asleep or staying asleep that may be due to recurrent nightmares during which the traumatic event is relived. Hypervigilance and an exaggerated startle response may be evident. Some individuals report irritability or outbursts of anger or difficulty concentrating or completing tasks.

experience Kundabuffer's restrictions only unconsciously, but yet they would still experience them and such restrictions would likely make profound changes in their behavior.

It follows that Kundabuffer was an organ to restrict consciousness - cognition, recognition, sensation, emotions, all the functions of a human being. That there are negative reactions to severe restriction still lurking beneath our 'normal waking state' is an important psychological possibility to keep in mind when pursuing psychological evolution. It might mean that within our *unconscious* we may have a strong impetus toward negative behaviors we have neither knowledge, understanding, nor control over.

Gurdjieff leads us to believe that we did not have a separate *unconscious* part prior to the introduction of Kundabuffer. We can speculate that Kundabuffer in this scenario caused the development of the unconscious part, the splitting off of one part of consciousness from the whole. Gurdjieff states clearly that real consciousness resides in our subconscious part, which makes sense, if our true consciousness was split off.[2] This may mean that before this split in our consciousness, we were aware of all the motivations for our behaviors. Kundabuffer formed a barrier within people that left them with only certain basic life functions, while their higher functions remained suppressed and unavailable to them. We must now ask what are results of a barrier that restricts consciousness?

Paranoia is one response to restriction. Paranoia is more than just suspicion that something bad will happen. It is a state of hypersensitivity and vigilance usually due to a psychic, emotional or physical injury/trauma. Paranoia can often result in aggressive behaviors. It then follows that restricting people's consciousness from its full potential might increase the tendencies in human beings toward both aggressive and paranoid responses.

Another behavior connected with aggression and paranoia is anxiety. Robert Sapolsky, writing in *Why Zebras Don't Get Ulcers,* points out that human behavior in the face of danger is different from that of other mammals.[3] If a zebra senses a lion in the bush, it is immediately on full alert until the danger passes. That is, the lion either chases down the zebra and kills it, or the lion moves off and the zebra goes back to grazing. The zebra does not remain a state of high alert, remain in a state of anxiety continuously. People on the other hand, show a marked tendency to remain in an anxious state for days, months, years and even an entire lifetime following a threatening or traumatic experience. In addition, a potential threat of an accident or personal injury, disease, or the stock market's decline can also evoke a state of anxiety. Anxiety can also be triggered when we learn about a friend's sudden illness or injury - the point being that it is not occurring to us, but someone else, and yet we feel anxious. Because of our power of imagination, anxiety can become a chronic reaction. We worry - even fear - that our behavior may be restricted, for example, if we lose money on the stock market. Whether we realize it or not, a great deal of our anxiety about money is really a concern that our options will be restricted, or our security threatened.

---

[2]. G. Gurdjieff, *All and Everything*, (New York: Harcourt, Brace and Company, 1950), 24.
[3]. Robert Sapolsky, *Why Zebras don't get Ulcers,* (New York: W.H. Freeman and Company, 1994), 5-8.

The longer we are restricted from natural behavior, the greater our tendency to become anxious, aggressive, paranoid, or sometimes depressed. You can see this for yourself if you are restricted from physical activity even for a short time period due to illness. The tendency is to become either anxious or find a way to numb out, fantasize or sleep. Numbing out, fantasizing and sleeping are states that appear in children who are forced to sit still for long periods in school. In this way, schools may unconsciously foster an atmosphere that leads to behaviors characteristic of or accompanying aggression; for example, either anxiety or an inability to remain attentive.

The restriction resulting from the properties of Kundabuffer appear to produce a generalized state of anxiety - a state that closely mirrors the symptoms of PTSD when an individual is continually anxious and afraid following a trauma and is unable to integrate material that is either partially obscured in memory or has been repressed due to feelings of overwhelm. 'Generalized' in this case means a background state of anxiety now embedded in the individual and even in culture. It is as if culture itself is traumatized and fosters behaviors we see in PTSD.

PTSD is often characterized by repeated flashbacks of an incident that requires defensive behaviors in response to a stressful situation. When we are traumatized, we fall back on survival mechanisms that include the more instinctive, animal side of our nature - the 'thinking animal' of the Kundabuffer period. We tend to react like a cornered animal, an animal filled with anxiety and fear. If a woman is raped or a man is robbed and beaten, they may suffer for years from the trauma induced by such experiences. Why can't the human being be more like the Sapolsky's zebra, running for its life from the lion, but later grazing peacefully on the plain?

The stressed human 'thinking animal' does not behave like Sapolsky's zebra. The addition of the third brain - the thinking brain - provides a different response to life-threatening situations. The zebra's responses are limited to freezing in place or running away. A person's responses to a threat, either perceived or imagined, might include aggression, defensive behavior and/or planning for future attacks. In addition, traumatic experiences might elicit responses of paranoia, aggression and anxiety that might continue long after the danger has subsided. Carrying the possibility of danger forward in memory, people take precautions to prevent further danger. They form armies, build forts, and even attack others preemptively. They sense aggression from others, have the response of anxiety or fear to the aggression sensed, and then respond like an 'animal' without any ability to bring in the third brain to equalize their response due to the split between their conscious and unconscious.

When a person is stressed for long periods, it is very normal for him to feel overwhelmed and act out that overwhelmed feeling in a negative manner. Overwhelmed here refers to the common human experience of feeling like one cannot handle any more stimulation, especially emotional or cognitive problems. The most common reactions to overwhelm are depression or violence. It is important each of us to learn about our responses to stress - to notice the movement toward violence or depression. Reactions to stress such as the restriction in consciousness often include a breakdown in logical thinking characterized by confusion, anxiety, fear, irrationality and often emotional overwhelm and/or violence.

The Inner Trauma of Kundabuffer

Another likely effect of Kundabuffer similar to the break between the conscious and unconscious, and perhaps directly related to it, is the partitioning of the psyche into many distinct 'I's.' Gurdjieff explains that this partitioning kept the different parts of the psyche from overwhelming the person with their incongruities. At first glance, the partitioning may be a mechanism to decrease anxiety, since, being unconscious of one's inconsistencies, a person would not have to face them. However, my guess is that having many 'I's' leads to increased anxiety. If a person cannot explain - even to himself - why he seems to have so many contradictory behaviors, feelings and thoughts, would it not be only natural to be confused and anxious?

I see the extreme results of such partitioning in therapy clients. Dissociative identity disorder (DID), formerly referred to as multiple personality disorder, is a disorder where an individual may develop two or more personalities that are so separate that they remain completely unaware of each other. Often the disorder involves the sufferer experiencing at least two clear identities called 'alters,' each of which has a consistent way of viewing and relating to the world and can emotionally exhibit different ages, that is, one a child and another an adult. Some individuals with DID have personality states that have distinctly different ways of reacting in terms of emotions, pulse, blood pressure, and blood flow to the brain. The separation can be so complete that one personality suffers from some physical illness such as diabetes while the other has no symptoms of the illness.

There is also a broad range of other 'dissociative disorders' that are indicative of the partitioning of the psyche. Further examples of partitioning are found in schizophrenia and other psychotic or delusional states. Psychotherapy clinics and inpatient hospital settings are filled with individuals who suffer from the extreme effects of the partitioning of the psyche into many 'I's' and also the larger division of the psyche into conscious and unconscious parts.

I hope that you can see that Kundabuffer may have had many psychological repercussions that need further reflection and study. We have looked at just a few, paranoia, anxiety, aggression, depression, and the partitioning of the psyche into distinct parts. These now inherent habitual behaviors generated by Kundabuffer act as a resisting force to the normal development of people. The effects of Kundabuffer need to be taken into account when individuals are following a 'way,' such as Gurdjieff's system of self-study and self-evolution. Each of the great religions has attempted to correct for the effects of Kundabuffer, and yet each has run into psychological roadblocks that I propose flow naturally from a homoeostatic system created by Kundabuffer. Let us look at a few of the reasons why the very systems developed to 'cure' Kundabuffer have not produced the desired results.

Religions to cure Kundabuffer

The great religions, Judaism, Christianity, Islam, Buddhism, Hinduism, Taoism and Lamaism have been, until the modern era, the primary vehicles for self-perfection. According to Gurdjieff, each was a means based on a specific human capacity such as reason, hope, faith or love, to correct for the unexpected negative changes observed in human behavior following Kundabuffer's removal. Each religion or 'way' employs different methods and practices; each in their original form stressed the need for conscious labor and intentional suffering. The problem is each of them has failed to produce the desired results. It may be that certain psychological factors were not anticipated, those factors that we are discussing here. So far, humanity, or even discreet portions of it, have found it quite difficult to develop consciousness and objective reason, and fulfill the purpose for which three-brained beings were designed. Nor has religion been able to correct humanity's abnormal manifestations - especially war, a mass insanity bequeathed intact to each succeeding generation.

Humanity now stands at a place where the degradation and deformed justifications of Christianity, Judaism and Islam appear to be leading the world once again toward a major war. Why have these great religions not achieved a more benign result? Why has religion itself become a factor that increases rather than lessens our predilection for war?

It would be very easy to say that the failure of religion is simply because human beings are too weak-willed to follow religion's precepts. But perhaps, isn't that like saying famine victims are too weak-willed to abstain from fattening foods. Gurdjieff in *All and Everything* makes constant reference to the unbecoming nature of humanity. He clearly splits the responsibility for the abnormal development of humankind between Kundabuffer's results and the unbecoming behavior of human beings over many centuries. One could make a good argument that he lays the bulk of the responsibility on humanity, and if that is so, then it behoves us to ask, *"Is there something happening within us which preordains our efforts to fail, to turn into their opposite?"*

Religion often becomes a set of rules instructing people to behave in certain ways so that they can reach their highest potential. But, it is one thing to tell people what they should do, for example, tell them they should perfect themselves through various forms of abstention or by doing good works. However, it is quite another to understand the impediments they face, both outer and inner. I propose that a lack of understanding of human psychology has contributed to the abysmal outcome of the teachings of great religions.

If people have truly suffered severe psychological restriction for generations because of Kundabuffer, it is no wonder they distort and misuse the very tools religion gives them for their development. I am not in any way excusing or justifying why human beings in general have been unable to use religion for their benefit, but I am interested in the problem of what is missing. How is it that religion fails on such a large scale? Is there a mismatch of religions doctrines and people's interior landscape?

One aspect of the failure of religion is its inability to understand the inner trauma of the psychic world of individuals. Religion has not studied the major obstacles in the human psyche and has perhaps unintentionally created more trauma for its adherents. If part of Kundabuffer's result has been to create a human being where aggression, paranoia and anxiety are core building blocks, then these qualities must be understood and included in the corrective measures designed to circumvent Kundabuffer's tendencies. When religion asks people to 'stop certain behaviors and do others,' often more of the same trauma is generated. Without understanding the mechanism of inner anxiety and fear that we live in, religion is bound to fail. When we create a 'heaven and hell' and ask people to stop certain behaviors without understanding either the behavior or how to 'stop' them, we further traumatize people by creating more fear and shame, and stifle natural impulses. More traumatization in the form of misunderstood rules produces just the opposite. Thus, we see an increase in many countries in fundamentalism, terrorism, and evangelism with its adherents wreaking havoc in their societies.

We need to consider all the underlying forces when are trying to heal trauma. It is important to note that one common human tendency already in place is to try unsuccessfully to repress certain negative emotions such as anger. Children are told not to be angry. Adults feel that is wrong. Laws try to curtail it, but we do not know enough about anger. This is a topic that this presentation does not provide the time to explore, but which is important to those in work. It concerns attempts to prematurely stop the expression of negative emotion without fully understanding this natural affect. The ways to observe anger, work with it constructively, and the repercussions of repressing it, represent an important area of study.

Worse than the failure of religion to help people perfect their being, is the fact that many times, religions often have just the opposite effect. Often, religion degrades people's inborn qualities, as a means of social control. For example, Catholicism prohibits its clergy from having sex with a partner and procreating. These strange prohibitions began in the Middle Ages, and we see their results in such unconscionable aberrations as the continued sexual abuse of children and young adults rather than the possibility of such individuals procreating. Religions can also promote and even deify aggressive behavior, as clearly demonstrated by wars, crusades, jihads and ideological wars of sects within a particular religion. Let us look now at some of the ironic messages that religions have given us and see how they perpetuate and collude with the very psychological qualities that they were meant to correct for.

The Myth of the Soul & Humanity's Sleep

Almost without exception, religions perpetuate the false message that people have a *soul* or that some part of them will continue beyond death. Some religions even tell us that we need to put forth little effort to develop, that is, our soul is already complete. This message of a future life after death has degraded people's intuitive sense that they actually need to work to achieve inner development. The life-after-death message of religion - that our lives will somehow continue following the death of our body - is a disaster for the few who have within themselves the possibility of self-development. The rationales for these erroneous messages are manifold. However, they primarily serve to calm the anxiety of a religion's adherents, putting them into a state Gurdjieff called, 'self-calming.' Of course, this helps the religion or 'way' grow new adherents. Religions instill this self-calming from a very tender age. They tell children and young adults that by following certain precepts - for example, praying to Allah five times daily - they will be taken off to some paradise following the demise of their physical body. Adherents of a religion hope anxiety is thus banished, but of course we know it cannot be banished this way.

It is interesting to juxtapose the Darwinian notion of accidental evolution alongside the life-after-death message of religion. The Darwinian tells us evolution is an accidental phenomenon guaranteed to take place. The priest guarantees us that our soul will be saved if we just believe. These two simplistic notions, one from Darwinism and the other from established religions, illustrate how from their youth people are programmed with the message, 'You don't need to make any effort!' This is one place where religion and science are in lockstep.

The myth that something will survive the death of the physical body is found in every religion. Hinduism, for example, elaborated the idea of life-after-death so much that fail to make any effort and justify their inability to control many aspects of life. What difference does it make if one will come back again anyway? The same belief in an afterlife fuels Islam, keeping its followers in constant hope of a better life following death, rather than seeing and understanding the objective causes of their oppression, fear, and aggression right now.

Buddhism suffers in a similar way in its admonition to 'free oneself from suffering.' Many of its less-sophisticated followers believe they may avoid suffering by thinking their way out of it. To escape from suffering appears to be a noble aim and a means to achieve salvation, but even devoted Buddhists frequently misunderstand the message. Some Buddhists believe that by meditating for hours, they will somehow achieve a state of non-identification that will help them survive death. Or, they believe that if they can think their way out of suffering, they will somehow avoid it in actuality. Eckart Tolle's *The Power of Now* is a great example of the so-called 'effortless way' - simply think about things differently. Then all will be well, and you will be able to give up your suffering. This can be for some a beautiful means of self-calming.

I would hope that everyone in the Gurdjieff work realizes that the aim is not to free ourselves from suffering, but to differentiate and learn to use the 'mechanical' suffering we are subject to in a conscious and intentional manner, first by observing it. We need to understand our reactions to suffering, to the violence aroused in us, and to the fear and anxiety all cultures suffer from.

Shame-based Religion

There is another inherent reason that religion has failed so many people so miserably - and perhaps it is the most glaring defect of all: it often devolves into a set of doctrines based on shame. Religion is not alone here. Governments with laws and even families with rules do that same thing. Religions attempt to keep their followers in line by relying on the human affect of shame. Shame is a very poor, if not impossible, basis for a religion of consciousness or a religion based on faith, hope or love. Shame, when used to coerce behavior to conform to the precepts of a religion, is bound to produce poor results.

Organic shame is a naturally occurring affect, hard-wired into the human species. It is meant to work hand-in-hand with objective conscience. However, according to Gurdjieff, objective conscience has been driven into our subconscious, and organic shame has also gone underground with it. In society, 'pseudo-shame' has replaced organic shame. That is, I feel a form of shame for forgetting a certain social convention or speaking the truth because it embarrasses someone else, or getting caught in a lie. However, I don't feel shame for treating another person badly, or killing them. We must examine the affect shame more closely since it is so important.

Objective and Subjective Shame

Psychologists say that shame is a 'natural affect,' one of the nine biological affects. The other eight affects are anger, disgust, dismell, fear, joy, sadness, interest/excitement, and startle.[4] Shame is an emotion in which the self is perceived as defective, unacceptable, or fundamentally flawed. It often follows a moment of exposure where something hidden is revealed. Here, when speaking about shame, I will be referring to pseudo-shame, the type of shame modern people generally experience. Otherwise, I will use the term 'instinctive' or what Gurdjieff refers to as *"organic shame"* when referring to the pure affect of shame that is hardwired in us.[5]

Shame is perhaps one of the most important areas of self-study we can engage in, and yet it is one of the most difficult to study. Shame is now mixed with so many of our manifestations - intellectual, emotional and even somatic - that it has become an integral part of our being. As such, we are usually unaware of its influence upon us. Without realizing it, shame has developed a deathlike grip on us. Our culture has wielded it as a behavioral weapon since we were children to force us to fit in. Use of shame coercively in this way wounds and brutalizes a child's essential nature.

In *All and Everything* Gurdjieff directs our attention to the affect shame and the de-evolution it has undergone. When discussing some of the deleterious effects of Roman civilization, Gurdjieff says:

And the Romans were the cause why as a result of successive changes, the factors are never crystallized in the presences of the contemporary three-brained beings there, which in other three-brained beings engender the impulse called 'instinctive shame;' that is to say, the being impulse that maintains what are called 'morals' and 'objective morality.'[6]

According to Gurdjieff, instinctive shame has gradually disappeared and been replaced by a pseudo-shame that governs our manifestations. He says the following about pseudo-shame:

Here it is very interesting to notice that although, as I have already told you, thanks to the inheritance from the ancient Romans, 'organic-self-shame' - proper to the three-brained beings - has gradually and entirely disappeared from the presences of your favorites, nevertheless there has arisen in them in its place something rather like it. In the presence of your contemporary favorites there is as much as you like of this pseudo being-impulse which they also call 'shame,' but the data for engendering it, just as of all others, are quite singular. This being-impulse arises in their

---

[4]. Donald L. Nathanson, *Shame and Pride*, (New York: W. W. Norton & Company, 1992), 73-147.
[5]. Gurdjieff, *All and Everything*, 424.
[6]. Gurdjieff, *All and Everything*, 417-418.

presences only when they do something which under their abnormally established conditions of ordinary being-existence is not acceptable to be done before others.[7]

Our caregivers are our teachers of cultural or pseudo-shame. The rest of the people who influenced our lives, families, teachers, friends and others, reinforced it in us. We learn pseudo-shame by imitating gestures, facial expressions, postures, tones of voice, and most importantly, emotional reactions. In short, we master all the manifestations of those around us. In psychological parlance, a child *introjects*, that is, creates within herself, the various negative affects of its caregivers. She unknowingly becomes similar to them in the way in which they manifest emotionally. Even if a child hates the way her mother or father acts and swears she will never act that way, she nonetheless picks up certain parental traits she remains unaware of and which manifest during her life.

Having introjected the emotional attributes of the caregiver, teacher, or friend, the child then proceeds to police herself by inner talking, that is, by self-criticism. She can even cause herself physiological pain when she does something she feels ashamed of. Thus, pain accompanies shame, and sets in motion certain endocrinological changes. This triggering of the endocrine system by the emotions occurs instantaneously. The study of emotions and endocrinology has given us a basic knowledge of the relationship of the adrenal glands to fear and anxiety; however, there has been little study of the endocrinological effects of shame. Organic shame and pseudo-shame feel the same to the body, neither feels good, but one is real and the other is not.

By the time we are in our late teens, pseudo-shame has developed into a mechanism that inhibits our behavior and causes internal pain. One need only witness teenagers' addiction issues. They use drugs not solely because they wish for ecstatic experience or to fit into a group. Drug addiction is a way to handle pseudo-shame - if you are not handsome, beautiful or smart as some of their friends, or you disappoint your parents. Teenagers use drugs to repress their contradictory feelings due to multiple 'I's and their pain from pseudo-shame. Finally, lack of support from a society that uses shame to belittle them, fuels the need either to release their rage or quell it through drug use as a means to quiet the emotional disharmony or the pseudo-shame they feel.

Pseudo-shame is also used to repress and limit children's emotional expression. Children who are taught to repress their real emotions by being shamed when they express them, are often emotionally crippled as adults. Parents tell children not to be angry, not to show sadness, not to be afraid. They say, *"You have no reason to be angry," "You shouldn't be afraid,"* etc. In these cases, pseudo-shame combines with the repression of emotion.

Clients I see in therapy are tortured by the pseudo-shame they carry around. It can be activated by thinking about their past, their life, their body image, their age, the negative feelings they experience toward spouses, children and others; or just about anything else. Their shame links up with past failures and decisions, or the fear and anxiety they anticipate as failure lurking just

---

[7]. Ibid., 424.

ahead. It is especially painful and difficult to sort out when pseudo-shame, mixed with repressed emotion, is activated in close relationships like marriage.

Examples of pseudo-shame abound. For example, most people experience it if they are on the toilet and someone inadvertently opens the bathroom door. Or, if I say or do something incredibly stupid in front of my peers. Just imagine going into a restaurant on a date, eating an excellent meal, and when the bill arrives, realizing you have left your wallet at home. You can easily find countless examples in your experience.

Religions have further distorted the human psyche by adding more rules and regulations that people are unable to follow and when they cannot follow these rules the affect shame is activated. Through repeated activation of shame, people are for short periods able to keep their behavior within certain guidelines, mostly by repressing, denying or subduing their pseudo-shame. This is all of course mechanical and often the result can be catastrophic. If shame is repeatedly activated either by an individual or by a parent or leader, the human response can be rage and violence. Yet, our religions, our laws, our attempts to control ourselves and others devolves when we use shame and blame.

Instinctive or organic shame is different from pseudo-shame. Instinctive shame is a natural function, arising from activation of conscience. It should act as an alert system for our behavior, to help us change behavior that feels counter to our essential nature. It could prompt us to ponder the repercussions of our actions. However, culture has hijacked the essential roles of conscience and instinctive shame. A child is taught to be ashamed only when her behavior violates social taboos. The artificial taboos that activate pseudo-shame gradually mix with the real affect, instinctive shame, and its physiological cues. Inevitably, pseudo-shame replaces organic shame.

Shame has become a means to control oneself and others. We constantly employ it in our close relationships with our children, family members and significant others. We need to sniff out our experience of shame and study it. Often, it masquerades as blaming someone else or making others feel smaller by cutting them down or humiliating them. You can realize for yourself the ubiquitous nature of pseudo-shame by trying some of the exercises listed at the end of this presentation.

The Third Aspect - Changing without Understanding

The third aspect we need to examine occurs when we try to compensate and correct for the psychological, homeostatic dynamics created by Kundabuffer - humanity's negative, violent emotional behavior. What are we to expect when we try to change the now inherent psychological structures using practices without understanding psychologically the structures and tendencies produced by Kundabuffer? Let us look at a number of rather unexamined aspects of kundabuffer: homeostasis, modification of the mechanism of our attention, and the self-hatred.

To understand Kundabuffer's effects necessitates that we examine the concept of homeostasis. Homeostasis is the tendency of a system, especially the physiological system of higher animals, to maintain internal stability, owing to the coordinated response of its parts to any situation or stimulus that would tend to disturb its normal condition or function.[8] This concept is perhaps the most overlooked concept in psychology and certainly in the design of the 'ways' of being self-perfection - religions and practices. The homeostatic nature of psychological patterning in people produces what we refer to as habits. In short, human beings learn behaviors and then behaviors become habitual and take on a life of their own. How does homeostasis affect a process of self-perfection and why is it so important?

The primary characteristic of homeostasis is one of resistance, specifically resistance to change. A system itself, whether a mathematical one, a simple or complex machine, or a computer program is a system due to its attribute of including certain elements or relationships and excluding others. Once existing, a system due to this inclusion/exclusion characteristic will resist change. The system maintains itself through exclusion of infinite possibilities and inclusion of a relatively few possibilities. Once operational, a system resists change. When a change is made, homeostasis attempts to reestablish the original structure of the system.

Psychologically, we see this mechanism in action when we look at addictions such as smoking and drinking or drug use, but it holds for almost all psychological processes. Smoking is considered one of the more difficult addictions to modify and people continually fail to quit. A core reason is the stability of the homeostatic system of smoking. There are physiological, cultural, and personal aspects of smoking and any attempt to change this pattern will be resisted. In many ways smoking is an enneagram in action.

Smoking is a relatively simple pattern compared to the intricate system of patterns operational in us. The human organism is extremely homeostatic, that is, all of its parts represent a complex system that resists change. All its parts working together are a structure that is self-maintaining, and if one wants to change some part of this system then this resistance to change must be considered. If it is not, then the change wished for may be impossible to achieve.

Although Gurdjieff pointed out to us that we have no permanent real 'I' and that we are changing one moment to the next, this tendency toward impermanence or undependability is also homeostatic. That is, our tendency to be thrown off balance by any small change in our inner or outer environment makes it extremely difficult to create any lasting change. Gurdjieff speaks about this problem and the gradual adaptation nature was required to make. Nature had to reduce our potential, to create a more primitive homeostatic system in our psyche.

---

[8] ., retrieved 1/12/12.

The Itoklanoz and Foolasnitamnian Principles

Gurdjieff begins to tell us of nature's plight and how in particular our psyche was adjusted to produce the required vibrations. He describes a gradual major change. He says:

To begin with, you should know that throughout the Universe there exist two 'kinds,' or two 'principles,' of duration of being-existence. The first principle of being-existence, called 'foolasnitamnian,' is proper to all three-brained beings arising on any planet of our Great Universe. And the fundamental meaning and aim of their existence is to serve as the vehicle for the transmutation of cosmic substances necessary for the 'common-cosmic trogoautoegocratic process.' The second principle of being-existence is the one to which all one-brained and two-brained beings are subject, wherever they may arise. And the meaning and aim of the existence of these beings also consists in the transmutation through them of cosmic substances, which are required, in their case, not for purposes of common-cosmic character, but for that solar system alone, or even for that planet alone within which or upon which these one-brained and two-brained beings arise.[9]

I remember being intrigued when I first came across the concepts of Itoklanoz and the Foolasnitamnian principle in *All and Everything*.[10] I noticed Gurdjieff referred to them as 'systems.' It seemed to me he was justified in inventing such outlandish neologisms. He was describing something no one else had understood in quite the same way. According to Gurdjieff, three-centered beings (humans) were to be governed by the Foolasnitamnian principle, and *"They were obliged to exist until there was coated in them and completely perfected by reason, the body-Kesdjan."* [11] However, due to the unbecoming manner in which human beings behaved, Nature had to modify the human organism to follow the principle of Itoklanoz. Thus, our faculty of attention was modified, so that it was activated and received the impressions of just one center at a time. In other words, according to Itoklanoz, any old association in any center could distract my attention at any time. On the other hand, when the Foolasnitamnian principle functioned, it required impressions from all three centers equally, to activate my attention. When our attention switched to functioning according to Itoklanoz only, we lost control of the direction of our attention. I have noticed such a lack of control over my own attention repeatedly, and anyone can verify it quite simply.

Experiments in Experiencing the Principle of Itoklanoz

Walk down the street and try to notice, without attempting to modify, the movement of your attention. One moment you are thinking of something; the next, your vision alights on a car, person or sound, and then your attention is drawn there. Next, your attention moves to the

---

[9]. Gurdjieff, *All and Everything*, 437-448.
[10]. Ibid.
[11]. Ibid., 131.

temperature outside, then a worry passes through you. Do not take my word for this wandering, but verify it for yourself.

Next, try to walk down that same street and keep your attention on some subject you wish to think about. What happens? I'll bet your observation is almost identical to what you found in the first experiment.

Next, try walking again, but simply count a number sequence such as 2, 4, 6, 8, 10….up to 150, and back. What happens then? Or try counting, 1, 4, 2, 5, 3, 6, 4, 7….up to 150, and back.

We need to conduct experiments like these because then there is certainty that we have little or no control over our attention. We are at the mercy of the associations that are triggered by the environment or by the inner flow of our thoughts and emotions or sensations.

Thus, we see that Itoklanoz is a system whereby any chance stimuli, outer or inner, elicits associations from one center or brain that continue until others from another center replace them. The energy of your life and being is used up and is wasted in the flurry of activity in each center, stimulated by nothing more than chance impressions. Nature spends your energy this way without your knowing it.

Is there a way out of this situation? Gurdjieff says there is. He says we need to resist, or learn how to *"not give ourselves up to the associations of just one brain."* [12] I must admit, I never liked his formulation, but Gurdjieff is telling me something very important. So important that I pondered this conceptualization for some time. I believe it to be one of the cleverest means for the simultaneous development of both *will* and self-knowledge. I am using the word 'will' here as the ability to my direct attention, although it can have greater implications.

My experience has shown me that people have a great difficulty not doing something; i.e., to *"not give ourselves up to the associations of just one brain,"* might seem difficult. I express to myself the effort in language that is more positive. Instead of trying to not give yourself up to the associations of just one of your brains, I try the following: *I try to maintain simultaneous awareness of the associations coming from each of my three brains*. This kind of awareness may not be possible all at once, but we can try to get a taste of the experience. The exercise below can help.

Experiment in Resisting Itoklanoz

Sit alone quietly.

---

[12]. Ibid.

The Inner Trauma of Kundabuffer

While sensing just your right hand, simultaneously notice your emotional state. Note, I have *not* said 'try' to notice. There is a reason. Yoda in *Star Wars* was correct when he said, "Don't try, just do!"[13]

Practice this exercise on a regular basis for a week for just ten minutes each time. Your aim is to simultaneously have an inner part of you aware of your body, by sensing, and your emotional state, by noticing. Through this simple practice, you can develop the ability to be aware of two centers simultaneously. You will have an awareness of yourself that is closer to the way Nature intended you to be. I have found it useful to expand this experiment gradually, and practice in quiet circumstances. Practice this experiment gently, do not force your attention or awareness. Instead, direct your attention deliberately, yet gently.

Gurdjieff said that because of the 'unbecomingness' of our ordinary existence, Nature had to change us so we would automatically give off the correct type of vibrations necessary for the general, cosmic good, vibrations that are produced only by mechanical, unconscious suffering. However, Nature actually requires the quality of vibrations produced by conscious labor and intentional suffering. Not being able to receive the required quality of such vibrations, she increases the population in a vain attempt to receive what is required. However, as we are, we are not capable of fulfilling the required role for Nature because first, we live by taking the ephemeral for the real (seeing only what is visible as having permanence and importance in our lives); second, we have no ability to intentionally direct our attention; third, we live according to a principle of existence designed for one and two-brained animals - Itoklanoz; and finally, rarely do we develop higher bodies that the Foolasnitamnian principle provides for three-brained-beings as unique means of self-development. The chaotic movement of our associations is typical of our unconscious life. Just noticing the flow of these associations changes something in my consciousness. What has changed? It is that awareness exists. Awareness is separate from the chaotic vagaries of my attention and can be increased through the simple act of noticing.

Self-observation, noticing, self-remembering. They all regulate the chaos of my flickering, unorganized attention. Awareness in itself contains an organizing quality. Itoklanoz is random, chaotic. We can live our entire life in Itoklanoz, unless we develop a regulating function. Living under the influence of Itoklanoz is similar to a dream state where waves and currents of anxiety, pleasure and sensation repeat themselves for no apparent reason. By contrast, in following the Foolasnitamnian principle, I am able to direct my attention, to focus. The energies of the three centers can be coordinated, and each can supply simultaneous impressions to sustain my attention. The possibility exists that I can live in three centers at once, rather than one after the other.

The Need for *Gradual* Transformation

I wish to emphasize that the process of self-study and self-development is a *gradual* one. We cannot accomplish change rapidly in an inner way, but only by taking incremental steps. Real

---

[13]. George Lucas, *Star Wars*.

thinking, or 'mentation' as Gurdjieff refers to it, requires gradual and *balanced* development of our human capacities. He says:

In short, only by a gradual change of the tempo of one part of the whole is it possible to change the tempo of the whole itself without injuring it. And now I find it necessary to repeat that active mentation in a being, and the useful results of this mentation, are in reality actualized exclusively by the functioning to an equal degree of all three of the localizations of spiritualized results in his presence, called the 'thinking center,' the 'feeling center,' and the 'moving center.'[14]

Each person's psychological makeup is configured around his or her experiences and dominant patterns. I need to change gradually so that my organism will not fall radically out of balance. However, even small changes that occur because of my increased self-awareness can lead to profound transformation. Therefore, my message is, go slowly and be interested in your own inner structure, notice it, understand it, and then make small changes and notice the results.

Self-Hate

Over the years that I have studied myself, I have become familiar with a distinct part of myself, a distinct 'I,' that hates me; moreover, I have found out this part is not unique to me. At first, my interest in studying self-hatred was motivated by my wish to understand myself. Gradually, I realized if I could understand my own self-hatred, I might better understand it in my clients. As I moved forward in my study, I even began to wonder how self-hate manifests in the world among people in conflict and among countries at war. Generally, it is understood that war is a manifestation of hatred; but does *self*-hatred also play a part in war, in what Gurdjieff calls the *periodic process of reciprocal-destruction of the common presences of others*?[15]

I have studied self-hatred in two distinct arenas. I first familiarized myself with current psychological thought about causes of self-hatred and how it manifests in individuals and in myself. Then, I examined humanity's current and historical conflicts through the lens of self-hatred.

Hatred can be conceptualized as anger with such a charge that it seeks to annihilate its object. I think that most of us who are involved in work have observed an 'I' within that guards the repository of my disapproval and negativity toward myself and others. When this negativity is directed inward, it manifests as self-hatred. Mainstream psychology refers to this part of the self as the 'inner critic.' For me, the term 'inner critic' is not really strong enough. Self-hatred generates emotions so strong at times they result in suicide. Let us look at self-hatred in action.

Recently, a client I'll call 'Alan,' returned from a visit with his somewhat elderly parents in Europe. He described how negative they both were in the ways they treated one another and

---

[14]. Gurdjieff, *All and Everything*, 1172.
[15]. Ibid., 1055-1118.

treated him. When I asked how it had affected him, he replied he also had become very negative. He found himself feeling angry toward his mother, but was unable to express his anger, and instead began to hate himself. He had become critical of everything he did and felt depressed and hopeless, believing he was powerless to change anything. It is interesting to note when Alan was unable to express his angry feelings to his mother, he turned them inward, just as he had as a child. He also said that upon returning home to his wife, he was angry with her too, and provoked a number of quarrels.

When Alan was a child, he had convinced himself that his parents' continual anger and negativity toward life and him meant there was something wrong with him. Otherwise, he reasoned, why would they be so constantly critical of him? Part of him was extremely angry at the aggressive way his father treated him and the fact that his mother never stood up for him, but always bowed to her husband. Due to his fear of physical harm from his father and without any outlet for his anger, he began to stuff it down inside himself. Eventually, his anger turned against him and he hated himself. His un-released and impermissible anger had nowhere to go, and it began to come out in distorted ways. He did poorly in school and got into fights as an unconscious way of getting back at his parents. Through drug use, he gained some temporary release from his increasing self-hatred; drugs also allowed him to stuff down and numb his feelings of rage toward his parents.

Many men carry such self-hatred out into the world. They join the military or become police officers, fields where they can legally release their aggressions. Others release it through violence against others, hit their wives, become criminals. But Alan was lucky, he became interested in the painful feelings he couldn't understand and eventually came to therapy. Our societies try to control anger through laws, but anger has not been understood. It suffers the same fate as shame, it is now distorted.

Shame and anger without an appropriate outlet turn and without my understanding it, can turn upon me and interweave to form self-hate. The inner critical 'I' within us (the part of us which judges what we are allowed to do, think or feel) becomes the instrument that determines when we feel ashamed or angry with ourselves. The inner critic has a repository of memories that trigger feelings of shame, self-hatred and anger. If I fail a test, I feel ashamed, disgusted and angry and blame myself. The inner critic keeps the scorecard.

We were not taught about the natural affects of shame and anger or the other natural affects. We do not realize they have been corrupted. We remain ignorant of self-hate and how to deal with it. These areas of human behavior have been left to academia and psychologists, who for the most part write about the natural affects in relation to their research and their clients. Rarely if ever, do they study and understand these emotions in themselves. Is it not time now to understand how these natural affects work within us through our self-observation?

All & Everything Conference 2012

Summary

In summary, I have found that it is extremely important to understand that we now have natural impediments that are part of our psychological structure. Violence and aggression, paranoia, pseudo shame and self-hate, and all their manifestations caused by these human experiences can be seen as a logical outgrowth of restricting our potential psychological attributes. The attempt to correct for the abnormal behavior due to Kundabuffer has proven more difficult than anticipated. The cures have been distorted and produced other abnormal behavior. I propose that the way out of this dilemma lies in becoming familiar with the psychological structures inside us, studying them to their very roots. The tendency in the Gurdjieff work has been one of dismissal of psychological ideas. Often, Gurdjieffians feel that mainstream psychology has little to offer them if they are in the work. I believe that a completely new attitude is needed if we are to garner a greater understanding of own interior processes and find a means to reconcile our inherited tendencies due to Kundabuffer.

A greater understanding of the mechanism of violence within us and the reasons for it will increase our self-compassion and compassion for others. Gurdjieff entitled his major work, *All and Everything*, but it would be foolish to believe that he considered himself to be the last psychological researcher. One can find examples within *All and Everything* that point to just the opposite. Beelzebub is always adjusting his research, meeting new obstacles and finding and presenting new information based on his practical research and observation of himself and others. *All and Everything* is a book foremost about psychology. I believe it is Gurdjieff's call to us to continue the work he began. The treasure he brought back is not simply to be worshiped or repeated in a formatory way, but to be utilized as a tool to go deeper into our psychology. Our psychology ultimately is the source and means of understanding our predicament and the means to transform it. We are the ones who need to do this, each of us individually, and working with others collaboratively. Gurdjieff brought us a treasure with practices to be used along with a mandate to dig deeper and develop new understanding and new means to spread and increase the possibility of inner evolution.

Exercises for the Observation of Shame

Personal Study:

In discussions and arguments, notice how individuals may try to make others feel and appear stupid or ashamed about their behavior or what they are saying.

At work, when your supervisor speaks to you about something you did incorrectly - or when you speak to a subordinate - notice the attempt your boss or you unconsciously make to make the other person feel ashamed for his error or stupidity. You can find the evidence in the person's tone of voice, the emotional message behind the words, or feel the tension that comes about during this conversation. *Do not try to change your behavior at this time. That is not the point. Just gather impressions.*

When you have made a mistake at work or in another situation, notice how you defend your position, decision or action to yourself or others. See if you can notice and feel the shame you are experiencing. We do not like to make mistakes.

When you discipline your children or redirect their behavior, notice how you may subtly shame them as means to get them to follow your directions.

Cultural Study of Shame:

If you follow politics, notice how every remark made by political figures in speaking about their opponent is an attempt to shame them.

In church or any place of worship, notice how shame may be evoked during the sermon.

© Copyright 2012 - Russell Schreiber - All Rights Reserved

The Inner Trauma of Kundabuffer - Questions & Answers

Questioner: Change. I want to ask about change. My sense about the teaching is that when we immediately want to change something that we see in ourselves we're supposed to use that moment to see more. The whole thing about *"don't change the breath, don't change the thinking,"* I think change, that could be a distraction from this thing of *"seeing."* What do you think about that?

RS: I agree with you completely. In other words, that's our tendency, we see something and we, I hate to say it, but very often we don't like it ok? But we have some sort of sense about what it's about and we naturally go ahead immediately and do something with it and the difficulty is, more often than not, it becomes associative, in the mind only. What is so difficult is to stay with it?

Here is an example. I have gotten angry at you. Can I be angry with you and stay in relation to you and actually experience in the moment, as a negative emotion, the fact that I'm angry at you and actually feel what that's about and how dysregulated it may be? If I can do that, then I end up having a possibility of awareness. And we are going to remember during our lifetime, from my experience, I am only going to remember those moments of awareness. The other moments are going to flow out, be gone. So, if you continue to notice what is happening even if negative, you will be living here [indicates solar plexus]. You will actually have experience, you won't need movies to distract or dissociate from your inner trauma, you will be living, interested in the present moment. But what happens generally" We want to think about it, we end up not liking what we see, we want to do something with it, it makes us feel powerful to do something. I saw this about myself, and then we are back asleep! And I'm not making this entire automatic process good or bad, we have to see this process too, it is habitual. That process of wanting to immediately change something we see has to happen, but you're absolutely right, that's my experience. Did I answer your question?

Questioner: You nailed it.

Questioner: Could you speak a little bit more about more about the danger of stopping thoughts?

RS: Absolutely. I remember I worked for a very short period of time with Robert de Ropp. DeRopp and Ouspensky tried this too, they said we have to learn to stop our thoughts. Ok. I ask you, try to not think about a pink elephant, try it, try not to think about a pink elephant, really work on this. You cannot do it. This organism, and the associative head brain, has been active for a very long time. I don't pretend to know how long, but even dogs have this associative mechanism going on. These mental associations will continue right till the moment of one's death. When you try and stop thought, well first of all, we try to do it all the time, it's part of dissociation. What do we do when we dissociate, what the dissociative person does is they go (points to diagram with many *"I's"*. and they are off here, (pointing to outer edge of diagram).

The Inner Trauma of Kundabuffer

They are trying to move out those *"I's"* that are present to some extent, that are thinking perhaps about something painful. An extreme example, somebody kills another person in war and they surprisingly end up with PTSD, right? What they are doing is to try to block out the thoughts and images of what they have actually done, and it is so difficult and at such a deep level that they can no longer function. They are trying so hard not to think, to stop their thoughts, that they are internally dysregulated. Later they get flashbacks of what happens, breakthroughs.

Stopping thoughts would be equivalent to taking your car engine and jamming a wrench into it when it is running at high speed. If you're doing a sitting or you do meditation, or even if you work at movements, the reason you get a slowing down of the associative mind is because your attention is occupied with something that is meaningful. You might pay attention to your breath, you pay attention to an arm movement, whatever it may be. The attention has something that it is focussed on and thoughts occurring in the associative, formatory apparatus, just gradually winds down. You are taking energy away from it. So these (yoga, meditation, movements) are integrated methods, ways of integrating who and what you are versus, "I'm going to stop my thoughts - with my thoughts!" I believe it is very harmful and I have seen harmful results. I really liked Robert de Ropp, but some of the stuff he would do with people. It was unbalanced, you know, and I have met people who are very balanced in the work and those who are less balanced, and I can only judge by who I am, and I'm not always balanced so I have a pretty wide spectrum to judge by? So I really recommend against attempting to stop thoughts. I think it created problems for Ouspensky.

Questioner: A very short comment and then one very specific question.
The story of the crystallisation of the cause of the consequences of the properties of Kundabuffer is necessary; but it is not sufficient.

RS: Say more, it's not sufficient?

Questioner: The sufficient condition is the study of the cosmic laws. So the necessary and sufficient condition is a psychocosmology.

RS: Absolutely.

Questioner: Now my question to you? Why, instead of freeing ourselves from this list (points to the list of the psychological consequences of Kundabuffer), I think the whole list, and I work with one aspect all my life. Why, instead of freeing ourselves, why do we not use them (the list) for the process of inner transformation or alchemy?

RS: That's exactly what I'm suggesting. You are talking about freeing yourself from this list of consequences of Kundabuffer. You don't need to free yourself. I don't want you to free yourselves. If I am able to be who I am in the moment, including if I'm angry, sad, whatever it may be, short of hurting somebody, let's say, and I am not completely attached to my state, attached means identified, same meaning, whether you're a Buddhist or a Gurdjieffian, if I am not completely attached to it there is some part of me that's going "Oh, I've just gotten angry at

Marlena," alright? But I'm present with my anger - then another force enters. In other words, the reconciling force can come on in and teach me or show me, or open the situation up so that "I'm attentive to my state. This is the indirect way to transformation.

Then I could respond differently to her right now. I could say to her, "You know I'm realising something you said got me really upset." It opens up my emotional part so I can be in relation to her rather than simply, I'm angry and then I attempt to cut off the anger and don't say anything. And that's a problem not only in individuals, but in countries. The Palestinians and the Jews, they are getting very close and then something is said and it is taken in a certain way, somebody feels shamed by what has been said, they are projecting onto each other their fears, and what they do is they back up and they are feeling attacked and in this interactive field, similar to the one right here between you and me, they get turned away so that instead of people coming closer, they get further away.

So, in order for you to get transformation you have to be able to tolerate what anger feels like. Or, you have to be able to tolerate the fact that you have a lot of pseudo-shame going on, all right? If you can tolerate it then there is something that is tolerating it, something is separate from what's going on. If you can't tolerate it, then you say to yourself, "I have to have a drink," or "I'm going to go for a cigarette," or "I'm going to go shopping," or I just dissociate. I just start to go somewhere else, 'I'll think about something else, I can't experience about how much I feel shamed by a particular situation. For example, I lost my job or this person treated me in a bad way and I'm angry. So they, all these affects here, [pointing to the 9 affects], these affects are interlocked, you could put them if you wanted to on the enneagram. I don't bother to do that, because they're all interacting together. And that's one of the reasons we get hung up in this area here, the negative affects.

It is important to note Gurdjieff didn't speak directly about negative emotions, he said, according to Ouspensky, and only in Ouspensky do you see it, he said "Hold back the **immediate** expression of unpleasant emotions." The second time Ouspensky mentions this he takes out the words "immediate" and "unpleasant" emotions, and refers to negative emotions. Very subtle, unpleasant doesn't exist the second time he brings it up.

But Gurdjieff was saying "immediate," well why would he do that?' So instead of just being reacting when I'm angry at Marlena, I go inside, and say "Okay, I'm angry at her, right? I'm staying right with it." Well, I might go on then to learn, I am angry, because she said something that embarrassed me or she didn't consider me enough or I didn't get appreciated enough or something like that. Oh? Now I know what it was. Immediately I am informed. Then I might actually say something to her, such as "I realize I am angry." So, I am guessing here, but Gurdjieff appears to be suggesting that to hold back a little might teach me what is happening and give me some space to respond rather than just react, to see my mechanicality.

Questioner: Yes, but in *Views From the Real World,* he says something different.

RS: Say more.

Questioner: OK, he says, "All these negative emotions are all organs, are the basis for future organs. Fear is Clairvoyance and Anger is real Strength.

RS: Absolutely.

Questioner: So that's the way I work with it.

RS: Correct, you are absolutely right. Fear is a human capacity. If we can look to see what the other side of fear it, it would be force or strength. If looking at shame, what would the positive side be? I am trying to think of the right word expression for it. For shame, it might be true pride, in the sense that you are living by your true conscience, and then you're unified. If I'm unified inside, and no matter what anybody says, if they don't like me, I can be like Judas, I can take that place, a place of pain. And you're right, this we are talking about the psychological here, but the only thing I would suggest to you is, is there is also a cosmic element to it.

Notice I've put down and asterisk next to certain affects to signify they are extremely dysregulated. I suggest we need to study these in particular, fear, anger and shame, the most dysregulated affects. The way to work with these is to remain present with them, to notice them. Not by stopping the experience, but by being present, which is what Steffan was really getting at, to stay with it. The affect shame, we could spend the entire seminar on. I could have just spent the entire time talking about shame. Ninety five percent of the people we see in psychological clinic where I work have shame dysregulated, and it can lead people to kill themselves and it leads them to kill others, it leads them to take drugs.

Gurdjieff points out the importance of this affect and how organic shame disappeared in us and a strange pseudo-shame replaced it. We don't have organic shame any more. We have got a strange thing, it's an artificial shame and we suffer from it. People in our group in California, who were Catholics and who have gone through this pseudo-shame, they suffered and they can talk about it. They cut themselves off. They stopped their religion because of it because they can't take it any more.

Questioner: I speak of this because it's from experience. Several years ago, maybe about seven or eight, I claimed something in myself, and it had to do with the fact I have a right to be perfectly relaxed in every situation. You've been talking about having that little space in what you are saying. Now whenever anything happens something inside of me, a part says, "You don't have to go there, you can, but you don't have to." And I think that unless you claim that space, your subconscious won't give you that choice.

RS: I agree. So you claimed it and you had a familiarity with it.

Questioner: Now I experience it all the time.

RS: You do experience it all the time. Exactly, I think that's exactly right because you are willing to go there. This is true, that experience is there, and you say, *"I'm going to own this."*

I personally have had to look at myself in terms of my competitiveness, prejudice, all these different things, and stay there with these traits, and the more I've done that, the more it is transformed. I have learned to say, *"Isn't this is interesting. Where did this come from?"* And I start understanding that and feeling it, and then when I have such emotions come toward me from other people or see it in other people, I understand it.

This is what work does, and I put these difficult emotions here, these affects here, because it this work of owning and being with our identification, our difficult feelings that gives one self-compassion. You can stay with the emotion or thought so you can see the truth. Self- compassion then comes, you really have this trait you see, you see it in others. It will allow you to actually hold others in a bigger, broader, way.

I put this in here, [pointing at chart at different aspects of trauma]: *"Becoming aware of my inner trauma,"* which could be any of these dysregulated affects; you don't have to use the word trauma.

Sensing is also an incredibly helpful tool here. The movements also. Sensing is experiential, not just cognitive. The cognitive part plays a point in terms that we are directing our attention, but sensing it's physical. In other words it's embodied. I bring up sensitive energy in my body and then have my head brain pay attention to this sensitive energy. The ability to pay attention to this sensitive energy and experience it as a body experience, and something in me knows I exist in the moment. Then, I'm not wearing out one center at a time, just using one center alone, because two centers and even three can be involved simultaneously.

[Pointing back to shame on the chart] I put shame down here because it has been helpful for all the people I have worked with, that is noticing and studying how shame can become self-hate and automatic hatred of others. This has to be studied to the core. Gurdjieff, I think, was repeatedly directing us to this topic of shame. We even see it in how nations behave, how they make these immediate negative decisions, shame plays a part. Gurdjieff even shows this in relation to himself in the Ekim Bey chapter. Ekim Bey was from a culture that he **automatically** did not like and yet he was able to make a deep friendship with him.

[Looking at the chart again]: These are all results of Kundabuffer on us. Aggression, projection, paranoia, anxiety, these negative emotions. Anxiety, this is a negative emotion, and it is spinning in the entire society today. Everybody suffers from it.

I thought I might do an experiment, have each person turn to just look at another, make eye contact for one whole minute, but then I said to myself, *"I am not sure if we can handle it."* All these different emotions come up in us, all results of Kundabuffer, they are habitual in us. We can try it at some point, but immediately these emotions will come up. And if you pay attention to these inner feelings you'd feel constriction in your body - fear.

The Inner Trauma of Kundabuffer

[Pointing at chart again]: The study of blame and shame is a huge topic for us. I believe it is again the result of trauma.

[Pointing at chart again]: I listed hypnotism as a result of Kundabuffer also, and the hypnotic state is very similar to the dissociation you get in PTSD. Hypnotism is a type of dissociation. People sort of space out. This is what I do all the time. However, I can notice it when I'm doing it now. I notice it at times and at moments, and so I can taste the difference between this hypnotic state and real presence, anyway, that's the hope. But it is about fuller integration of my centers, not just knowing I am hypnotised in my head, but experiencing this state in my emotions (pointing to the solar plexus), owning it, as you were saying. Noticing it, and then being able to be in your body.

Questioner: I think of Kundabuffer. I like to remind myself, and others, how this is what I love about Gurdjieff, about regardless of how negative a picture he paints, there is always hope. We need to remind ourselves that the organ has been removed and now there are just the consequences and that is all.

RS: Absolutely. I agree totally. In other words, by painting the picture black and it's not completely black - it is just the material we have to work with. Without this material (pointing at chart) at this point, we wouldn't be able to move and grow, we would be stuck and that's the reason I want to be able to pay attention to all this psychological material, the results of Kundabuffer, because Gurdjieff, he didn't live long enough. You know, we suffer from the same problem, we don't live long enough too. I believe Gurdjieff would have gone into all of this. But instead he said that these are the consequences and the more familiar we are with these the more we will see them, the more we can see, *"Oh! Consequences of Kundabuffer."* Not good, not bad, just is. Just is. It is very helpful to see and experience these consequences.

Questioner: Russell, Gurdjieff mentions transformation many times. What is your sense of what is it that gets transformed?

RS: I think that a wonderful question. My sense of what is transformed from my personal experience, is my whole being is transformed when I've been able to be with the truth of who I am. I don't want to simply say that the reconciling force enters and so forth and so on, but there's an expansion of my consciousness, an expansion of my understanding. That's what I find transformative and there's also harmonization, a dissolving of buffers.

You know, I've had to work with my pride and realize it just is there in me. That's the transformative part. There's a part of me that opens up and there's the strength to both tolerate my pride and to have compassion for myself, I am caught. Because compassion for me was the big shift. I began to realise that unless I am bringing compassion, self-compassion into my work, that I am going to end being negative about what I see, maybe positive about other things. This is not useful. I have to be able to hold both sides of who I am here, and compassion is one of the few things that can do this. And I don't think it's a silly or shallow compassion.

Compassion comes as an experience, *"Oh, yes, this is right, this is exactly the way I am."* Ok, this is the way I am, I can't get away from it, I'm like this every single moment, you know, and I'm not getting away from it.

What are people going to make of me? Are they going to like me, are they going to appreciate me, think that what I said was smart? It's a dis-ease, the whole thing when you're with people, meeting them, so it is continuous, it just doesn't go away. Anyway, I hope that answers you.

Questioner: Gurdjieff differentiated one thing earlier, one thing that I think all of us would benefit from if you could comment on it. It has to do with seeing the degree of dysrhythmia that appears. All of us who have been involved in group-work have had to make decisions about people. About people entering seriously into work. There are many stories by people close to Gurdjieff that tell how often he sent people to see a psychologist to get help. He said, *"when you get well then you may come back."* Could you comment on that because that's something we are all involved in. We all bump into people who are marginal… how do we make decisions and what do we do in that situation?

RS: I have to make the same decisions. I think to a certain extent you have to trust your experience. You must trust your experience because it is the best you have to work with. Gurdjieff was obviously caught in this dilemma. I have had to say to certain people that they cannot come to a meeting, and it's painful and difficult because a person needs a certain level of balance, or perhaps only a certain level of imbalance, let's say. Beyond that certain level of imbalance it's problematic. I mean at the clinic we once in awhile have a therapist who is has what we refer to as having borderline tendencies. One minute you are the most wonderful person in the world for this therapist, and then, the next minute, they are hating you. It has to do with their whole psychological configuration. The whole clinic gets crazy. In other words after a while everybody's going *"what's happening?"* So when you're working within a group, especially a Gurdjieff Group you have to pay attention to this type of problem. You don't have to make the group exclusive, but you have to watch for it when your intuition, your internal part says *"You know, I don't think so. Something's off here."* You need to say to the person, *"You need to go and have that issue looked at,"* or, *"Come back in a while, let's see how serious you are."* I think you have to do that. That's my experience. Because they are too dysregulated. They are dysregulated so much they are not trustworthy. I think that's what you're saying, isn't it?

Questioner: Yes, the dysregulation as you pointed out, it is just so severe that they need help in another direction.

RS: Right, and you can't do that in a group, no you can't. In other words the group is not meant for that. A certain amount of such problems for people do get regulated in a group, people may become more flexible. I mean I'm sure that's what I always admired about Two Rivers Farm. I wish I could have lived there, but my obligation to my son, where he lived and our kids, made it impossible. We couldn't move but we always went to visit. At the Farm, they had friction, this having to adjust to all these different people. That challenge and being collaborative at the same time, could create real flexibility in people, a flexibility one might not have developed in other ways. I might not have developed this flexibility as much as I could have, so I was always jealous of that.

Questioner: This is a comment for all the teachings in *Beelzebub's Tales*. Kundabuffer is of the Earth. The Choot-God-Litanical period is of the Cosmos. Before Kundabuffer appeared on the Earth there was the sins of the soul. So the work is very long. We get rid of Kundabuffer, we are free, then we have to clear ourselves from the sins of the soul. And for that we have holy Kundabuffer.

Seminar 2: Chapter 8 - Meetings with Remarkable Men

Ekim Bay

Facilitator: Russell Schreiber

Introduction

Facilitator: As a way of getting started on this chapter, I thought that we would do something just a little different. It requires people to stand up, but we will do it a little bit differently than you would ordinarily do it. Please put your packages or what you have on your lap down. You do not have to do this, you can just sit if you want to. I want to do this out of respect for this vehicle we live in all the time. And possibly we can learn something from it. So, you need to put down your books underneath your chairs because you are going to need to concentrate on what you are doing when you are getting up. I would like you to get up very slowly and as you get up slowly to just be with the experience of what your muscular system is doing in order to go from your habitual sitting posture that you are in to your next habitual posture of standing. Just see if you can go a little bit more slowly than usual.

So we are just going to be getting up slowly paying attention to the experience of what the muscles do as we get up. Go as slow as you can. Now I would like people to close their eyes, or you can have your eyes slightly open. Start simply by bringing your attention to your breath. You are just breathing in and out through your nose following a particle of air down into your lungs and back out. As you are following your breath in and out, just notice your balance, notice what the body is doing in order to keep you upright so you are not falling. And notice if you can that the entire musculature of the body, of all the major muscles, are involved so you can stand. Notice how the breath moves the body fractionally, just the act of breathing.

Somewhere in this balancing process, there are three forces. This balancing mechanism is automatic, its instinctive, everyone is born with it. Now when you sit down, sit down slowly and notice what your balance needs to do. Experience the musculature of the balancing system working in order so that you do fall. You can open your eyes if you need to. But just watch what the balance has to do in order to compensate. The reason I thought that might be interesting is because the Ekim Bey chapter has quite a number of things about the human body in it.

I am going to open this discussion by suggesting a possibility. People may say anything they wish to about the chapter and let us see if we can find any major themes within the chapter. I am going to ask David to list them on the white board so as other things come up we can see if there are some theme weavings going on, some threads going on in this chapter which we as individuals might miss, but as a group we may begin to take note of.

Seminar 2: Chapter 8 - Meetings With Remarkable Men

Discussion

Questioner: I am embarrassed to say that I have not read this chapter in two or three weeks. I have forgotten how it goes. As soon as people start talking about it, it will come back to me, but I thought that if we could take a minute or two to summarize it, it would bring it back to those like me who are negligent.

Facilitator: In the first part, without going into a lot of detail, Gurdjieff, in need of money, finds a way to make money by diving for coins thrown into the water by cruise ship passengers. And a man of means in one of the ships drops his chaplet into the water. Ultimately, Gurdjieff dives down, finds it, and returns it to him He is then invited to lunch with him. Soon after leaving his house, he gets sick and he assumes it is from the salt water. Gurdjieff is brought back to the wealthy man's home and stays for a few days. And the wealthy man's son is Ekim Bey. What struck me is the pure coincidence of it. I was thinking what is that about, it occurs at this place, at this time, with this particular person and the man's son turns out to become an essence friend of his. What is the chance of that happening? someone else could have found the chaplet and then maybe the connection would never have happened. Does this have to do with magnetic center? Gurdjieff, no matter where he went, seemed to attract just what he needed in the middle of nowhere - serendipity, so that struck me immediately in reading the first part of the chapter. Does someone else want to summarize the balance of the chapter so that we will all have it? Have most people read it or not read it? All right I will finish it out.

A friendship is made between these two men and at this time Gurdjieff is planning an expedition with quite a number of his comrades. They are looking for ancient towns. Ekim Bey at some point, although he is planning to go off to military school, changes his mind and decides to become a physician, to go off to Medical school. Midway through this process, Ekim Bey writes Gurdjieff and says that he would like to come and visit him and comes to pay a visit. He meets with all the people who are friends of Gurdjieff and as Gurdjieff says, Ekim Bey falls into their psychopathy, their Dervish psychopathy.

Ekim Bey gets very excited and gets permission to take a year off and go an expedition with them. About 20-25 of them set out on this trip, and during the trip they have many difficulties. They hear about a very old dervish and go to meet with him and sit down with him. At first, Gurdjieff does not think very much of the dervish, he is sitting in tattered clothing and Gurdjieff does not think he has anything to offer. As he sits with him, he begins to realize that the dervish might in fact know something. At one point they are eating together and Gurdjieff is asked by the dervish why he chews his food so thoroughly? And Gurdjieff begins to explain this and the dervish interrupts him and says that he bets that Gurdjieff does yoga also, and Gurdjieff admits he does. Then the dervish begins to explain to him about his eating practice and Gurdjieff is taken aback because this man appears to have incredible knowledge. This begins to change his belief patterns about everything he had previously thought. There is another exchange in which the dervish tells him about breathing. This is the overall direction of the chapter.

All & Everything Conference 2012

There is some other information given, but then Gurdjieff goes on to explain Ekim Bey's ability with hypnotism because Ekim Bey becomes and expert in hypnotism. Gurdjieff goes on to tell how they both make money so that they can return home. He also explains different aspects of the human body and how these are used by the hypnotist, and how the mind affects the body. That is the general framework of the chapter.

Questioner: Inspired by Irv's approach, is it possible for us to just read the first paragraph of the chapter, just the first paragraph?

Questioner Reading: *"I wish to devote this chapter to my reminiscences of another man whom I consider remarkable, and whose manner of life in his later years, either by the will of fate or thanks to the laws operating in a 'self-developed individuality,' was arranged down to the smallest detail like my own. At the present time this man is in good health from the ordinary point of view, but according to my view, and speaking between ourselves, only his physical body is in good health."*

Questioner: Each chapter in meetings represents an aspect of Mr. Gurdjieff. We cannot separate this book from the first one. What it says in *Beelzebub* is corroborated in *Meetings*. So this Ekim Bey is about hypnosis in a way. Now I am going to give you a complete example here. If you go to page 903 in *Beelzebub*, you will find the experiment of Hadji Asvatz Troov on the vibration of dogs. He says that dogs which we have eon earth, two brained beings, have higher vibrations than three brained beings. He shows the vibration of a dog to have more quality than the vibration of a human being.

Now let's go to *Meetings* and find the corroboration of that. Mr. Gurdjieff writes in Bokhara, where Hadji is also located, that he finds a room in a house. Now in that house, there is a woman who is running the house and the way he describes her is very disrespectful; he calls her a *"fat Jew woman."* So, what happened with this woman? She has four barrels of food in the hall, but she does not offer anything to Mr. Gurdjieff who was hungry. Now, next morning, he gets up and he sees that his dog Philos has gone to the market and has stolen a Jerusalem artichoke. Every day the dog brings Gurdjieff food and the fat Jewish woman never gives him anything. So the vibration of the dog is higher than the vibration of the woman.

Questioner: It does seem like Gurdjieff depicts himself a lot in *The Tales*, and I think that it is extremely interesting in this first paragraph that we read that Ekim Bey's details of his life are exactly like Gurdjieff's down to the smallest detail. And he also says speaking between ourselves, that his health is poor in spirit, but good in his physical body. And it seems like this might be almost the opposite of Gurdjieff. It is like some kind of antithesis of him in Ekim Bey and he becomes a hypnotist just like Gurdjieff. But he tends to use it for his own celebrity in a way, and eventually he has the same problem as Gurdjieff and has people flocking around him. So he goes off to retire in some place remote. But it struck me in that opening paragraph that Ekim Bey is almost a nemesis of Gurdjieff. The opposite side of him. I don't mean to make Ekim Bey an

Seminar 2: Chapter 8 - Meetings With Remarkable Men

enemy because obviously he is a remarkable man who is a friend, but there is something different there.

Facilitator: So do you see that as a possible theme? There is something here about someone who has taken life in a way where he is disheartened? I am curious if that is a possible theme.

Questioner: Yes, I think so. This is somehow the opposite path in a way. It is the same path in that they are going the same way, but they have treated it differently.

Facilitator: Is there a way you could phrase that theme in a sentence or so?

Questioner: From what you were saying Brian, the image that comes to me is that of a mirror. It is like a mirror image.

Questioner: He questioned if Soloviev ever existed. Moore says that he never existed. Its just Gurdjieff, an aspect of Gurdjieff in the book. And I agree with him.

Questioner: Another theme that Russell mentioned is the folly of free judgments. Gurdjieff really tells us about himself. He was really thinking that this dervish doesn't know diddily and he then realizes that he is extraordinarily knowledgeable. It reminds me a bit when I came into this group and I looked around and prejudged everybody and then I got to know them.

Facilitator: The theme of the folly of prejudgment.

Questioner: I think a theme of this chapter has to be warnings. It opens up with a warning. At the end of the chapter there is the warning of falling into the trap of celebrity. Then of course, there are the warnings which Gurdjieff himself receives related to mastication which are interesting symbols as well because not only to you eat the food whole and swallow the bones to exercise your stomach, but you take ideas and concepts entirely in chunks, not easily digested and that readies you for further activity later on and digestion in the future.

Facilitator: A theme?

Questioner: Warnings and Symbols.

Questioner: Can I ask a question? What is this chaplet, is there anything we can say about this chaplet? This thing that falls into the river. It is like a rosary.

Facilitator: One thing I would say is that it is something of great value and goes down very deep. Most people don't make the effort that Gurdjieff makes to go and get it. And it is deep, it is in the water, which somehow is esoterically connected with truth. It is also connected with Gurdjieff becoming sick. He almost dies in that process of getting this valuable thing and that is what starts the entire process of him meeting Ekim Bey. So, for me there is something there about resourcefulness and willing to go deep. That is what I saw. We will need to go all the way for what is valuable.

Questioner: I may be wrong about this, but my understanding of what a chaplet is, is that it is usually a piece of string that hangs about the neck and attached to that is usually a piece of fabric and inside of the fabric is often a bone or something that is sacred which is sewn into this piece of fabric. And there may be different definitions.

Questioner: So where is the fabric in there?

Questioner: This is not what I was describing, but in the Catholic Church, usually a chaplet is a piece of cloth and sewn into it is a relic or the bone of a Saint or something like that. And I think that among the Indians they were chaplets that people were given or carried.

Questioner: A Muslim, the Pasha, had a chaplet.

Questioner: So, if he assumed the owner of the chaplet was of the Muslim faith, this chaplet may have been designed along the lines of having a multiple of 11 or 33 beads in it.

Questioner: Associative mind working. Chaplet, bone, buried, dive. I don't know where that is as a theme, but it is in the book.

Questioner: I just wanted to say, this chaplet, whichever origin it has, it has the same significance of praying and reminding.

Questioner: Also, there is the connection with the loss of Atlantis in the waters, which you know, no grandmother reminded us about this. Also, Annulios is conscience. There is that connection too.

Questioner: I am reminded that the purpose of *Beelzebub's Tales* was to uproot mercilessly everything we have ever believed. And to my way of thinking, this is directed toward our historical personality which is the product of heredity and environmental conditions, nature and nurture as we grow up. Gurdjieff wants to uproot what we have come to believe about everything. The purpose of the second book, *Meetings with Remarkable Men*, is to provide constructive material for the building of a new world. And within this context, bearing in mind that what he is attempting to do is to help us resurrect our essential self, the non-phenomenal part of ourselves which has been submerged within our historical personality. Each of these characters, who may be literal, but I take them more allegorical as a teaching device, is intended to show us different aspects of our essential self, new constructive material that will help us to re-invigorate and resurrect our essential self so that it may become the active affirming force in our personal law of three, rather than how it is now where our historical personality is the dominating force. So, Ekim Bey becomes, if we will remember what Beelzebub said about hypnosis, our historical personality in what we regard to be our consciousness. We call it waking-sleep, but that our real

consciousness, that is, the consciousness of our essential self has been submerged and called our subconscious. And only when there is a change in the tempo of the functioning of our blood circulation, can this center of gravity be shifted from the consciousness of our historical personality to the consciousness of our essential self.
So, in Ekim Bey, as he says here in the second paragraph, there gradually arose a close friendship and later they went through all kinds of incidents when their inner worlds had been drawn together like two arisings from the same source. So here he is talking about the reconciliation of the essential self and the historical personality.

So, just one more point I would like to make. To my way of thinking the Bey, the governor who lost his chaplet, becomes symbolic of Beelzebub. Marlena, I was interested in what you were saying about a chaplet. I always took it to be what she (another participant in the group) handed you, a rosary of sorts. The Bey was doing his prayer beads and they dropped into the ocean. So in a sense, in *Beelzebub's Tales*, Gurdjieff has created a chaplet, a rosary which has fallen into the world, the water. We are required to bring it all up, return it to Beelzebub, at which time we need the governor's son, since Ekim Bey is the governor's son, who becomes subsequently an expert in hypnosis. And so we see that aspect of ourselves as we learn to befriend the essential self within ourselves and learn about how to change the blood circulation in ourselves in order to facilitate the activation of our essential self to be the predominate center of gravity which our historical personality follows.

Facilitator: How would you put what you said into a few sentences as a theme?

Questioner: By hypnotizing our historical personality, we can activate our essential self or we can search for the essential self through the practice of hypnosis.

Questioner: So I remember right now that I was in a group in Paris, a group of Henri Tracol's, and I said something in French and he replied to me in Spanish. He spoke Spanish and do you know what he told me, *"You are becoming like Ekim Bey."* So far, I do not know what he meant. The only thing that I can think of is that he was tell me, *"You are getting crazy."*

Questioner: This is not so much a theme as a question which I feel runs throughout *The Tales*; it runs throughout the music, it runs throughout the movements. And it is the question of tempo. Because he speaks about the importance of the tempo of the functioning of the lungs, the stomach. They are there first in *The Tales* when Hassein has these questions about his functionings and Gurdjieff says that he is not old enough and has not reached the required tempo so *"I don't put these questions to you yet."* I was speaking about this with Trevor today. At the end when Hassein has this experience, he inherits his place from Beelzebub one could say, and then Beelzebub speaks so precisely about tempos. One part has now accelerated and you need to allow the others to harmonize. We see it over and over in the movements, especially the Obligatories, the three tempos. I feel like he is pointing very much to this question and I do not think very much is understood yet about tempo and about what you just said. It is the tempo of the circulation. What does that mean? How do we understand tempo? It is not speed obviously, but there is the tempo of

each center, the tempo of the functionings, the harmonizing of the tempo. So this is for me a question. What is he trying to tell us about tempo, what is tempo? What is he trying to tell us when we worked on the first obligatory last night, the three tempos? I feel like he is pointing to something. If anyone understands something about this I would be most grateful to hear.
Bonnie Phillips: Something I would like us to keep in mind during our discussion is this sentence in *The Tales* about the second series which you brought up: *"To acquaint the reader with the material required for a new creation and to prove the soundness and good quality of it."* I would like to keep that in mind. I would like understand I think this proving has to do with verification, but how do we prove that, especially collectively?

Questioner: I wanted to answer your question regarding tempos, and in this instance I am somewhat indebted to de Salzmann's *The Reality of Being* where she discusses an aspect of this, but it is also verified in my own experience and Dave echoed this very thought in his talk this morning. We have different centers vibrating at different frequencies. And for us as historical personalities, we are dominated by our thinking, and our feeling, and our moving centers of our physical body. But I think that our essential self, that is, the life force that animates the physical body is experienced initially as a vibratory sensation, like a vibratory chord running through our bodies which when amplified perceives itself as light in infinite extension. The problem is that because nobody educates us to look in that direction or develop that, it never does develop, it atrophies. But, the intent of being aware of tempos is to learn how to accelerate our essential self so that it becomes the dominant perception to which the other centers ultimately become sublimated. And Jeanne de Salzmann talks about that in her *Reality of Being* toward the end of the book where she is reaching the end of her conclusions about how we achieve harmonious being of all these different centers operating on different frequencies.

Facilitator: I would like to come back to what Bonnie was just mentioning, and Trevor also just raised it, and I am going to raise it again. In *All and Everything*, you have this entire section which we haven't touched upon in this particular get together. It has to do with the Atlanteans and how they went out and studied things. They knew something was going to happen. Mr. Gurdjieff in this section here gives us a hint here about self-initiation which Mr. Gurdjieff did, but also, this whole group of men went out and searched to find out about these things. And I think this has to do with finding new material, it is not passive, but is actually active. It is not simply sitting at the feet of the guru, although they do that, but rather even to get to there, they had to go through incredibly difficult hardships. In other words, conscious labor and intentional suffering. That theme in running around in the fabric of this chapter. Gurdjieff may make it sound like it is no big deal; we just took our forty camels and 23 people. But, Gurdjieff also says he is worn out. He says very specifically, I am worn out, I am exhausted. Ekim Bey is also exhausted and worn out. I am bringing this up because it relates to the story about how those from Atlantis went out and did their work to find out what was happening. I see this as a theme.

Questioner: I just had a comment about tempo. Every time I see that word it is like a shock to me. I do not know what he is talking about and I know it is important. But, the image that just came to me now was of an automobile engine and how if you are in second gear the engine has to be going

Seminar 2: Chapter 8 - Meetings With Remarkable Men

at a certain tempo and if you give too much gas, its going to wind up, and if you do not give it enough gas it will stall. So, it needs to have just the right amount. And the tempo that the engine has to run has to be right or you screw it up. And I think that our stomachs are like that. If we eat, get the food in there too slowly, it is like being in second gear and not giving it enough gas. It is disharmonizing. And the same with breathing. If we take in too much oxygen, it is like giving it too much gas and that has to do with the same kind of tempo that we experience when we drive a car having it in different gears and going at the right speed through the different gears. We have an experience of that. We sort of instinctively understand it. Whereas with our organism, we are out of touch with those instincts. We try to manipulate nature and that is one of the dangers. Don't manipulate nature. You can screw it up because we are out of touch with our instincts.

Questioner: So in a way we do not know what tempo is, but recognize lack of tempo in way.

Questioner: Here are a couple of brief comments on a couple of topics that I think actually might be related. Just a thought on chaplet; etymologically, the word sounds like a little chapel to me, to my ear. It makes me think of one's own personal bit of the sacred, the holy. And here is a thought regarding tempo. In terms of music, very often a tempo is indicated by a word that has some emotional value, like grave or vivace or one like that. So I am thinking that tempo in that sense indicates timing that is tied to a higher state or perhaps higher emotion. It is tied; it is a timing that is tied to another force in a sense. So maybe this is totally out there and I don't know how they are related, but maybe our tempo is tied to our little chapel. Just a thought.

Questioner: I just wanted to tie in tempo with A, B, and C influences; this book providing material for our actualization of the work needing these beings, perhaps C influences. And, the only way you can get at the influences is indirectly from the person, the tempo of the C influence, communicated through meeting these remarkable men. There is a tempo of the higher consciousness which is different from the tempo of our personalities.

Questioner: I want to tie this in with the activity of the centers. The tempo has to do with the activity of each center, of the three centers. You know I am an engineer and I love to measure everything. I would say tempo is the quantity of associations in the center. Now, what is the secret to regulate tempo? It is called Iraniranumange, not to give yourself up to the association of only one center.

Questioner: I have some questions. The dervish. After hearing him speak, Gurdjieff immediately changed his opinion.

Facilitator: Are you trying to point out that Gurdjieff accepts too quickly what he is told?

Questioner: It is also mentioned here; this element of thinking and muscle tension, and this might be related to tempo as well. I am just pinpointing that.

Questioner: Hypnotism. I don't know much about it, but I think that our inner exercises that we have studied from Gurdjieff are actually self-hypnotism. So, Gurdjieff said earlier, that through hypnosis one can get to essence and make a change in oneself. I think if I am putting this together probably, it could be connected with that.

Questioner: I guess we have come to the dervish. I see a theme the actual instructions of Gurdjieff in how to take in the first and second being food. And I was wondering, I myself did not find anything about the third being food. Maybe someone wants to answer that. I could not find anything about how to take in the third being food; I can see the first and second.

Facilitator: There is something there if we look at our beliefs, about the way he sees the dervish to begin with. He is taking in the food of impressions in a certain way, and then he has to look again so that he gets a new impression of him. So there is something there. That is all I can see.

Questioner: It is striking to me that the dervish's indications, which are given in detail, really seem like common sense. And Gurdjieff immediately senses the truth of what he is receiving. There is no hedging his bets or doubting, or is he conflicted about these new impressions he is receiving. It seems clear that this is common sense, that this guy has got more than what I thought.

Questioner: I don't know if it is a theme, but he spends about a quarter of the chapter talking about breathing, and the last admonition is, after going into all the hows and whys, is to stop all artificial breathing. And for me personally, whenever someone gives me an exercise where it has any kind of breathing in it, I am very suspicious and I have only found one indication of the right way to breathe and will share it. It is in the last three pages of the *Search*. And it I has to do with movements and the breathing that is induced by the movements, where it is not artificial.

Facilitator: Bob, I am going to add one thing there which I feel is important and that I have noticed from years of working with different sittings, exercises, and movements; there is actually a *"work"* involved in order not to play around with breathing. Especially if you are observing your breathing or noticing it; to allow the breathing to continue unconsciously. I have also felt the same about the heartbeat. In other words, to allow that to be, and even in the *Oragean Version,* it is one of the things that is mentioned by Orage where there are certain exercises given. So, there is an effort needed to notice, and yet not do anything to change it.

Questioner: I have been raised dogmatically and I am also a building inspector. From modern science and physics we find that anything that is observed is changed. So, even in movements, I find that even if I am not observing my breathing, but I notice it occasionally, but there is so much else going on that I am not paying attention to it. And somehow if the tempo of that is being regulated through the efforts at the movements, then it is not being observed by one of my "I's." It is induced.

Questioner: I don't want to be contrary of course, but. You know at the end of the book, *Life is Real, Only Then When I Am,"* Gurdjieff does give a very specific breathing exercise for the

Seminar 2: Chapter 8 - Meetings With Remarkable Men

division of attention. Actually in the middle of the book. This is in order to develop attention in order to pacify our thought while at the same time attempting to perceive the transmission of finer particles of second being food being pulled down into our lungs as a source of nourishment. So clearly, this is a balance between the advice of the dervish who says, hey don't do anything unless you know what you are doing with Gurdjieff's indication, presuming that you have mastered *Beelzebub's Tales* and understand the principles and presuming that you have mastered *Meeting with Remarkable Men* and understand the new constructive material. And then at this point, you see, it all boils down to attention and one never sleeping reminding factor is breathing which can be used as a way to divide attention and consciously ingest finer particles of air which we normally inhale and exhale without appropriate attention.

Questioner: This is a follow-up on what you guys have been talking about. I felt exactly like you did for many years until the year 1999 and 2000, when I accidentally or by chance, however you want to say it, found myself in a workshop with a bunch of doctors or healers. And I found myself doing this rebirthing breathing technique where everybody lies on the floor on their backs and breathes as deeply as they possibly can for almost a whole hour. There is a technique to it. Afterwards you are in a state that is very different from your ordinary state, for a half hour to an hour; it even goes on longer than that sometimes. It wasn't exactly like taking a psychedelic drug, but it was definitely a different state and a higher state too. My only concern was that I was maybe poisoning my brain with too much oxygen. From my scientific background, I thought to do something about that. But anyway, after doing this a couple of times over a period of two years, it occurred to me how wonderful that was. It was not a negative thing. It was a very positive experience. One night I woke up, or maybe it was in the morning, and I was in bed, and I found myself breathing that way and I realized that I always breathe this way when I am sleeping. We breathe more deeply when we are sleeping. It hit me like one of those dawnings I was talking about yesterday, a dawning of understanding. Oh, I get it, I repress my breathing. I mechanically repress my breathing and I have done so since I was a little child because that was what I was taught by adults. You don't go around going …(makes heavy breathing sounds). It is not socially acceptable to do that. So we have repressed our breathing. Everyone right now is breathing artificially because we have repressed the way human beings would normally breath. And the way we would normally breathe is the way we breathe when we are asleep, I believe. There is evidence for that. I could be wrong.

Questioner: I read the chapter four weeks ago, right after my depression, and what struck me the most was the last paragraph of the chapter so I am going to read it because it is tell us something about America and Europe. This is about Europe and America.

Their ideas about its size are very vague; they are always ready to compare it with European countries and do not suspect that Asia is such a vast continent that several Europes could be put into it, and that it contains whole races of people about whom not only Europeans but even Asiatics themselves have never heard. Furthermore, among these 'savage groups' certain sciences, as, for example, medicine, astrology, natural science and so on, without any wiseacring or hypothetical explanations, have long since attained a degree of perfection which European civilization may perhaps reach only after several hundred years.

Now what is he telling us here is one of seven aspects, I am not saying that I am right. He is telling us exactly what Orage said. Asia is the essence, Europe is the personality and America is the body. America is the *"I"* descending into the planetary body. So, we think we know and we don't know. Questioner: I just wanted to mention that one way that our breathing tempo is changed is when we laugh and certainly there is a lot of laughter in Gurdjieff's writings and perhaps we take things in differently at that time. And another thing is that it took him quite a lot of practice in order to hold his breath a long time to dive down to get these coins and to get the chaplet. And there are a lot of people in the world who do deep sea diving for sponge and various things, and I am not sure what ill effects they suffer from; not that I am advocating breathing exercises by any means. But, I also know that in some Buddhist traditions, the holding of breath is part of a way to gain some sort of different awareness. And what is the meaning of salt in that story, because he becomes ill from the diving and he has to keep his eyes open despite the salt in his eyes. There is so much there.

Questioner: As far as breathing goes, I have experienced screwing my breath up with breathing practices, and as far as breathing goes, and to be honest, it corrects itself pretty quickly. The organism is pretty resilient. So, I have done the rebirthing breathing. If you practice that every day, you will experience it throughout the day, but within a week of not doing it, your breathing just corrects itself.

Facilitator: The thing that I would like to add about the breathing is about a gentleman named Stanislav Grof who is a psychologist. He has taught holotropic breathing for many years. He has groups where people do holotropic breathing. It is a very strong breathing. I wish to point out the human system is a fully integrated system. So if you change something in the biodynamics (that is a Reichian term), if you change something in the musculature, then you change the tempo of the thinking, you change the tempo of the feeling. So breathing can be a direct way to punch through psychological buffers and people do that in holoptropic breathing and sometimes they become psychotic, sometimes they just drop a defense system, sometimes they have an out of body experience, sometimes they have a very positive experience or sometimes very negative because it depends on the person's ability to tolerate the energies that are released. Because the body is an integrated system, if you do something to one part, it affects the whole body. Also, the heart beat and breathing and pulse are interrelated and respond to the impressions coming in. If you were driving on a two lane road and a car came directly at you, everything would immediately shift in your body, the emergency would cause the breathing to change. If you change breathing, you change thinking and feeling. We see this all the time when you do somatic psychotherapy or Reichian work where you can change feelings and thoughts that have been there for years by just having someone breathe more deeply for four or five minutes.

Questioner: So back to hypnotism and something perhaps related to that with the magic tricks that Ekim Bey performs. The hypnotism that Gurdjieff speaks about I presume is the hypnotism that he found so worthy through Mesmer, and then was polluted because people did not like Mesmer's

Seminar 2: Chapter 8 - Meetings With Remarkable Men

approach to pulse and flow, magnetism of the blood, and that sort of thing. But within this chapter, he also speaks at considerable length about how to perform magic tricks by feeling the finer muscle movements in the body or in the wrist. And it becomes very difficult at times to know which parts when Gurdjieff writes about things, which part are we to take literally, what do we take as allegory, and what do we take as a transitional device, a literary device as we try and go from one subject to another. But it is was interesting to me each time that I have read this chapter, the time, the care, the energy and the focus that he places on this inability to modify or deceive other people who can then tell what our intention is through these fine muscle movements. I have no idea at this point what he was trying to get at if he wasn't just being literal and giving us some instruction for the sake of the story.

Questioner: You brought up Reich so I want to mention Reich started as a psychoanalyst and then became more proactive, moved around to face the patient and over time realized that they were not breathing. All of his patients were inhibited in their breathing and eventually he started to ask them to breathe and that is the so-called Reichian breathing technique which would in his theory eventually stimulate the orgone energy in the body. Then this energy would run into the armor and the armor would clamp down. Then you could see the armor and then you could work with it physically and verbally. So that was the origin of the Reichian breathing technique.

Questioner: I hope that I am not remembering this from the film and that it is in the book. One of my favorite lines from one of those two is when the dervish first starts speaking to Gurdjieff, he prefaces it by saying, *"May god kill him who does not know, yet presumes to show others the way."* Maybe that is really the point.

Questioner: I think that if we were looking to get back to themes for the chapter, we would really have to include the physical body of man, its needs according to law and possibilities of manifestation. He promises as he does one of his famous paragraphs where he says I will not record here in my second series of writings what these are, and obviously that means there is a lot of material right nearby, and we have been talking about it you know. Even in the hypnotism part where he is talking about the manifestations of your physical body that you can't control.

Questioner: I said that *Meetings* was a corroboration of *Beelzebub* and here is another example that just came to my mind. Remember the chapter on Russia. We spoke about turkeys. Here in this book *Meetings*, we have and example of a turkey that became a peacock. That is the prince.

Questioner: I will just read David Kangas' quote. *"Shaking his head, the old man slowly and with conviction uttered the following saying which is known throughout Persia: Let God kill him who himself does not know and yet presumes to show others the way to the doors of His Kingdom."*

Questioner: I just want to mention along with the theme that I first mentioned, I really do think that this (Ekim Bey) may not be an historical personality. It may in fact be the other side of Gurdjieff because he talks in his writings about when he misused hypnotism to a certain extent, when he had a traveling road show basically. We know that these are historical things about him personally. And I think that he also at times had gotten off on the wrong track when he was interested in sex and food, and things like that. I think that this is a manifestation actually of Gurdjieff himself and it is a little bit disguised, and it is not who we want it to be.

Questioner: To support your theory, the word Ekim, it sounds very much like hakim, which means physician. So a physician-hypnotist.

Questioner: Well then this follows on the question. Why does he say that he is only in good health with his physical body? So why did he even say that? What is wrong with Ekim Bey?

Questioner: Well it is showing the mirror, the two sides of a man. He put it in quotation marks and when I read it, *"a self-developed individuality,"* and what can become of them. You can become a self-developed individuality and not pass on the teaching to other people and go out and abuse people and make money. And he and Gurdjieff are even laughing and splitting their sides with laughter at the people's naïveté and stupidity. And there is something wrong with that. It is not the Gurdjieff that he ended up, although he was like that at times. That is who he could have been and it is showing that Gurdjieff did not go this way. Gurdjieff was in fact in bad physical health and in excellent physical health. He was the flip side of this thing.

Questioner: To follow up on the position that this chapter may be a reflection of Gurdjieff himself. I think, I do not know if anyone else has looked at this, but I think the whole book on one level can be taken as a self-portrait of various aspects of his inner life. I think it is more than that, but I think it is a really interesting way to read it. The last time we read it, we kept returning to that theme. It holds up pretty well.

Questioner: So if that's true, then we are meeting Gurdjieff and we are getting his tempo.

Questioner: My take on it is that Ekim Bey is Gurdjieff. I actually have that written in pencil at the end of the chapter the last time I read it. And that all the other characters are not Gurdjieff, but they are people who existed in one form or another that he greatly admired and in that admiration tried to emulate those characteristics, and he was able to do so. And then when he wrote the book, they were part of him.

Questioner: I think one of the remarkable things about Gurdjieff to me is that he has tried very hard in his writings to preemptively prevent that we turn him into a hero, into a super human. And when I read his writings, and when I see a passage like the *"body is in great health,"* but the spirit is suffering, I assume that Gurdjieff went through those phases himself and that he is talking about himself. And then in the third series, there are many passages where he talks about depression. So he has made this effort that I do not see in other teachers and messengers much. He has made this effort for future generations so as not to put him on a pedestal. Forget about the person Gurdjieff, forget about the body that came through this world. Think about the teaching, see what is in there. The other thing that came to my mind when we were talking about the advice of not altering the breathing and the other passages where breathing exercises are given, I think that any good teacher will teach in paradoxes because that is how the world is. You cannot say well this is the only true

Seminar 2: Chapter 8 - Meetings With Remarkable Men

thing. As soon as you say something, the opposite of that is also true somewhere else. So you have to teach in paradoxes. It is the only way. We have an inclination to remove the contradictions in his writings, and I think we should see that and not change it, but we should see that and try to leave that alone and just keep going.

Questioner: Just one thing in relation to what he just said. Paul Taylor said, *"Make sure they write the worst things about me."* Make sure, and you know who did it, his own son, *Daddy Gurdjieff*, is the worst book ever written about Gurdjieff. You read that book, it is on the internet, you do not have to buy it. You say, this man was the devil. So he was not god. People do not want to know that he was not a god.

End of Session

Seminar 3: Chapter 35 - Beelzebub's Tales

A Change In The Appointed Course Of The Falling Of the Transspace Ship Karnak

Facilitator: Bob Godon

Introduction

This session was begun with reading the 2nd paragraph of Chapter 1, *"The Arousing of Thought"*, followed by the group reciting the *"utterance"* at the end of paragraph 1; *"In the name of the Father and of the Son and in the name of the Holy Ghost. Amen."*

Chapter 35 was read in its entirety.

Discussion

Questioner 1: Something that has always puzzled me with this very minor thing, I think, and which has always caused me to laugh out loud when I read it is when he wants the ship to move to the left. I think that people knew in that time that there's no left and right in space. What is he referring to? Probably not a political position.

Facilitator: Does anyone have a clue? From the presentation about Plato, wasn't the door to heaven on the right?

Questioner 2: I'm not sure this is a clue, but there are sometimes switches from right to left. The Amu Darya flows to the Caspian Sea, but after some tremor, a minor planetary tremor, it switches flowing. If you look at the map it is flowing to the left, then it is flowing to the right and there may be other switches of that nature.

Questioner 3: In one of the seven aspects from which this chapter is written, Mr. Gurdjieff is telling us: I left Russia, I'm going to France and from France I'm going to America. Now why? Well, first, the chapter is in between Russia and France, followed by *"Just a Wee Bit More About the Germans"*. Now that has a different meaning. I spent three months, almost without sleeping, trying to decode the paragraph about Deskaldino, Zilnotrago, Salzmanino, Trogoautoegocrat and Karnak. I wrote a paper about that but I never publish it, because it is very hard and may be my subjective opinion. I don't want to talk about it but will email to you if you want. One day after I finish paper and I send it to friends I feel like little devil and send it to Mr. Sinclair, the president of the New York foundation, and wrote to him saying here is the categorical proof that Jeanne de Salzmann betrayed the living teaching of Mr. Gurdjieff. And he replied to me a week later that not only did Madame de Salzmann not betray Gurdjieff, she was appointed as his successor by Mr. Gurdjieff. I replied to him, you got it wrong Mr. Sinclair, it is not Madame de Salzmann and Gurdjieff, it is Gurdjieff and Madame de Salzmann, you got it backwards. And you know what he replied a week later - never again write to me, and I never did.

Questioner 4: Well maybe it's a warning there of our trip through the universe. We are all to pass through environments which are not very easy for us and which can be catastrophic if we are not careful.

Questioner 5: This has been a burning question for a long time, especially in relation to the next chapter, which I believe is intrinsically tied to this chapter, but one thing that struck me today is that he says that here lies the solar system Salzmanino in which there are many of the cosmic concentrations which for the purposes of the general Trogoautoegocratic process are predetermined for the transformation and radiation of the substances Zilnotrago. He tells what Zilnotrago is earlier, but what is the transformation of it? What is predetermined?

Questioner 6: We had an incomplete definition of Zilnotrago. Can someone read from earlier in *The Tales* when they come upon the Madcap? In there he gives a very precise definition of Zilnotrago. He gives what it does. Someone reads from chapter 3, pg 56: "Your Right Reverence….", and the footnote on that page. That's the point, it is not a permanent thing, the inference is pretty definite, it dissociates things, it disorganizes things for a while, it doesn't destroy them, that was the implication that came up yesterday, and that's not true. Here we're talking about a process that lawfully it's there, it's there by cosmic law, and it will do this and Gurdjieff obviously knew this, knew the great stresses that were going to be placed on his teaching. and where are those stresses going to come from? Is that what we are pursuing in this chapter?

Questioner 7: Something occurred to me for the first time when I heard the reading a few minutes ago. It has to do with Beelzebub taking this opportunity to visit his teacher because of the being impulse of gratitude that arose in him. And perhaps if we are like Beelzebub, Gurdjieff is like the great Saroonoorishan and Gurdjieff is giving us the opportunity to express our gratitude to him at this point in the journey, not because he wants the gratitude necessarily, but by expressing the feeling of gratitude we are better prepared to receive what he is giving to us, as that is part of conscience.

Questioner 8: It may or not be significant that cyanic acid is composed of the same elements from the hydrogen table that represent the matter that are the carriers of the forces. It might be significant that he throws cyanic acid in there.

Questioner 9: I'd like to read this passage again: pg 659, 2nd paragraph. So, if I ask myself what are the parts of me that radiate Zilnotrago, what resonates for me is for example, when I wiseacre, when I inject something into the conversation that distracts or takes things off the point, or disintegrates the conversation or the direction of the energy at the moment. There's some part of me that does that, once in a while, shall we say. And I can take that idea and work with it. Is there also a part of me that processes these disrupting influences when they come into my neighborhood? Is there something I can do to avoid being destroyed by that sort of energy that is destructive? Isn't that reminiscent of work efforts? Isn't that reminiscent of efforts we sometimes make in life to digest things coming in from outside that might be disruptive and distractive to us? When Gurdjieff says cosmic concentrations I often think of parts of myself.

Questioner 3 again: Anyone here understand Greek? (silence) Okay, the word trago in Greek I cannot pronounce this, is the merde of the God, the merde of the God is trago, so for me Zilnotrago means impulsiveness, and that is Zilnotrago. What is Deskaldino? In my paper I concluded that Deskaldino is America. Now how did I get to that? Very simple. I will read the last paragraph on pg 917 in the Bokharian Dervish. Reads *"Whereupon...."* Now turn the page; page 918 is *"Beelzebub in America"*. So, Deskaldino is America.

Questioner 10: Can I ask a question? Why does he have to go through Salzmanino to get to America?

Questioner 3 again: Beelzebub is travelling, travelling to America, but one paragraph before is Deskaldino, this is where he is going to find a teacher.

Questioner 11: Getting back to the question Questioner 9 was raising, which is an interesting one, and I'm not sure on this, but if I heard you right, maybe you were suggesting an opportunity to transform Zilnotrago, and yet in the text isn't it indicating wherever the ship encounters Zilnotrago there is no attempt to move through it, but rather a great effort is made to avoid it. But I think what's interesting here is that you can avoid it. Isn't that in the text that the captain always figures out a way to avoid it, and maybe that's a teaching for us, first to see it and then to avoid it.

Questioner 12: I think it's important that he says unhindered falling of the ship through the system would scarcely be possible. So he's going to find a way to go through it anyway. After he's telling the driver, the intellect, We've to go this way, and telling the driver he has got to figure out a way to do that, he's going to figure out a way to avoid the Zilnotrago. I think Gurdjieff is saying yes, there's going to be some disorganization, but we're going to punch through this thing.

Questioner 6 again: Also the solution the first time in *The Tales*, the solution is to fill up the time of waiting with something useful.

Questioner 13: I'd like to read one more reference to Zilnotrago, this is from chapter 3. The question is wait or detour? This reminds us that we should spare our ship useless damage. I would like to remind us that Choon-Kil-Tez and Choon-Tro-Pel discovered that there was a difference between emanations, which are the product of the Sun Absolute, or any one of us, in being able to separate these forces that heterogeneously comprise us. That is, when we go through Djartklom, we emanate. Whereas, for the most part, because we don't, because we are not able to perform that Djartklom. We all radiate in order to create a specific atmosphere which keeps everything at a proper distance from ourselves. So, for me, this Zilnotrago refers to this atmosphere of historical personality which creates all kinds of trauma and all kinds of dissonance for us. And so, as Beelzebub is falling now towards Purgatory, Beelzebub is in a sense bringing us to the laws of world creation and maintenance. Only he may enter here who may enter into another one of the works of my hand. And then we have to, once we can enter into the place of another, then we are prepared to go back through this Zilnotrago and Salzmanino to Deskaldino, which is to say we are able to enter into the emanations of Beelzebub himself, or our teacher, whoever that might be.

Questioner 14: Through the chapters at the beginning of the book that deal with the spaceships and the way they are organized, I begin to see an analogy between the ships and the teaching. So now I'm thinking that Zilnotrago might stand for wiseacring. That makes a lot of sense because wiseacring is definitely destructive to a teaching.

Facilitator: Sometimes it's interesting to look at the roots of the words he creates and the different meanings depending on the languages you go to. For example: there is a possible connection between Trogoautoegocrat and Zilnotrago. Trogo, trago has a meaning *"to eat"*. Zil, Zilno possibly meaning no. Hence, No Eat, Zilnotrago.

Questioner 5 again: I will make a request to the planning committee for next year to work again on this chapter and to include the following chapter number 36 also.

Questioner 15: Wouldn't it be a good idea to include chapter 3 as well?

Questioner 5 again: It's a perfect, quote, mi fa interval, although I'm not interested in putting everything on an enneagram. It is because of this first delay that we have *The Tales*. As was said earlier, they filled the time with something useful for us all. Without Zilnotrago *The Tales* would have never happened.

Questioner 16: I would like to mention that if you want to start reading any chapter in the book you should read the last two pages of the preceding chapter, as the DO for the chapter to be read is often contained in the last two pages of the chapter before.

End of Session

Seminar 4: Where Do We Go From Here?

Facilitator: Bonnie Phillips

WDWGFH Session Notes:

Item 1:
It was also often suggested that the reading in *All and Everything* be conducted like the Wednesday evening session. This session was more 'a going around the room' with comments and discussion. All attendees seemed to want more reading and discussing *The Tales*.

Item 2:
The humor at the conference was great. I did not hear a bad joke and was glad to revisit old ones. Steffan Soule really set the tone for us to have fun together - play was alive and well. The attendees voiced this during the closing session and in other conversations.

Item 3:
As the Movements continue to be brought up from participants as a needed part of A&E, Stefan Maier had quite a good suggestion. It was that we assign 2 hours each day for *personal study time*. Examples of the possibilities to use this time would be:

   1) movements and movements assistance among demonstrators and participants that are present,
   2) reading/study groups to focus on a chapter/issue/question
   3) with people interested in further discussion with a particular presenter
   4) music study group
   5) laws study group

Item 4:
And finally, the first being food at the hotel was okay but could have been better. That was one of the downfalls of the conference and I heard that from a good number of the attendees. Our apologies and I think that having one person on the planning committee that can work more with the kitchen and what is expected for all meals and breaks is necessary and can be improved upon for 2013.

Item 5:
Looking forward to Canterbury and our work together during the coming year. It was decided that A&E 2013 will be held at Best Western Abbots Barton Hotel, Canterbury, UK.

Appendix 1: List of Attendees

John Amaral - USA
Curtis Amo - USA
Stephen Aronson - USA
Susan Aronson - USA
George Baker - USA
Paul Bakker - Netherlands
Christopher Barlow - USA
George Latura Beke - USA
Steven Biesmann - USA
David Brahinsky - USA
Larry Buckley - USA
Keith Buzzell - USA
Marlena Buzzell - USA
Adriana Calin - USA
Phobol Cheng - USA
Gloria Cuevas-Barnett - USA
Farzin Deravi - USA
George Donovan - USA
Debbie Elliot - UK
Carolina V. Esguerra - USA
Matt Frandsen - USA
Mani S. Gerlach - Germany
Irv Givot - USA
Bob Godon - USA
Dave Goodwin - Canada
Dean Greenberg - USA
Tay Haines - USA
Michael Hall - USA
Douglas Hall - Canada
William Halliburton - USA
Russell Harlow - USA
Robert Harwood - Canada
Evelee Hill - USA

Frankie Hutton - USA
Elaine Jacobs - USA
Kerry Judd - USA
Dave Kangas - USA
Linda Kangas - USA
Robert Knoke - USA
David Krizaj - USA
Greg Loy - Canada
Pat Lynch - USA
Stefan Maier - USA
Stephen Marino - USA
Will Mesa - USA
Robert Middleton - Canada
Richard Miller - Canada
Clare Mingins - UK
Julieanne Nielsen - USA
Teresa Paz - USA
Bonnie Phillips - USA
June Poulton - USA
Al Renton - Canada
Brian Russell - USA
Oyvind Ruud - Norway
Russell Schreiber - Canada
Derek Sinko - USA
Toddy Smyth - USA
Steffan Soule - USA
Tyler Speaks - Australia
Trevor Stewart - USA
Orjan Waldenstrom - USA
Mike Whelan - USA
Pamela Woodland - Canada
Mariette Yjsselmuiden - Netherlands

Index

A

Absolute, 45, 120, 134, 169, 183
accumulator, 184
active, 20, 49, 50, 70, 74, 76, 87, 93, 104, 150, 152, 158, 208, 212, 224, 226
affirming, 27, 31, 32, 93, 98, 224
Africa, 100
Ahoon, 39, 48, 52, 79, 80, 95
Aim, 22, 23, 24, 27, 29, 34, 77, 91, 120, 146, 147, 149, 154, 171, 193, 200, 205, 207
air, 25, 125, 166, 167, 183, 184, 220, 229
Akhaldan, 19, 41, 43, 50, 68, 141
Alchemy, 145, 213
alcohol, 93
Salzmann, de, Jean; Michel, 24, 25, 27, 31, 164, 169, 226, 234
Alla-attapan, 36, 40, 41, 42, 50, 54, 59
allegorical, 76, 89, 113, 143, 164, 165, 224
allegory, 81, 140, 193, 231
America, 35, 36, 37, 38, 39, 43, 48, 71, 88, 98, 157, 160, 178, 180, 193, 229, 230, 234, 236
Angel, 47, 51, 73, 102, 185, 192
Anklad, 40
Anodnatious, 74, 75
Ansanbaluiazar, 75
Antkooano, 27, 30
Anulios, 71, 72, 79, 82, 85
Archangel, 27, 53, 91, 113, 192
Armenian, 30
ascending, 160
Ashiata Shiemash, 20, 27, 29, 33, 177
Askokin, 79, 92
Assyrian, 160
Astrology, 229
Atarnakh, 94
Atlantis, 81, 129, 224, 226
atman, 169

Atom, 20, 84
Atomic, 108
Attention, 23, 28, 36, 39, 50, 61, 77, 81, 82, 83, 84, 88, 100, 101, 104, 106, 108, 114, 115, 117, 131, 133, 135, 155, 156, 157, 182, 193, 201, 203, 205, 206, 207, 213, 216, 217, 218, 220, 228, 229
Augustine, Saint, 102, 107
awareness, 54, 106, 112, 169, 175, 194, 206, 207, 208, 212, 230

B

Babel, 43
Babylon, 43, 44, 138, 139, 142
Beekman Taylor, Paul, 18
Beelzebub, 3, 4, 20, 22, 23, 24, 25, 26, 27, 28, 30, 31, 33, 34, 35, 36, 37, 38, 39, 40, 41, 42, 43, 44, 45, 46, 47, 48, 49, 50, 51, 52, 54, 55, 56, 57, 59, 61, 62, 64, 65, 67, 68, 69, 70, 71, 72, 73, 74, 75, 76, 77, 79, 80, 86, 87, 88, 89, 90, 92, 93, 95, 98, 99, 101, 102, 103, 105, 108, 110, 129, 130, 135, 138, 139, 141, 143, 144, 145, 146, 147, 149, 150, 151, 154, 155, 157, 158, 159, 160, 161, 165, 166, 168, 170, 178, 179, 183, 186, 188, 191, 210, 219, 222, 224, 225, 229, 231, 234, 235, 236, 237
Beelzebub's Tales
  The Tales, 24, 25, 30, 36, 38, 39, 40, 41, 42, 43, 45, 46, 47, 49, 50, 54, 56, 57, 59, 64, 66, 68, 70, 71, 72, 80, 81, 85, 86, 108, 113, 120, 128, 152, 162, 222, 225, 226, 235, 236, 237, 238
Being, 24, 25, 26, 27, 31, 32, 34, 36, 37, 38, 39, 40, 41, 42, 43, 45, 48, 49, 50, 52, 53, 54, 58, 61, 62, 63, 65, 68, 71, 72, 73, 76, 78, 82, 84, 85, 86, 87, 88, 90, 91, 93, 94, 96, 99, 100, 101, 102, 103, 105, 106, 107, 111, 112, 113, 132, 133, 134, 135,

Index

138, 141, 144, 148, 149, 150, 151, 153, 154, 155, 156, 159, 160, 163, 164, 165, 166, 167, 169, 170, 174, 175, 176, 177, 182, 183, 184, 185, 186, 187, 193, 194, 195, 196, 197, 198, 199, 201, 202, 204, 205, 206, 207, 208, 214, 215, 216, 217, 218, 222, 226, 227, 228, 229, 231, 235, 236
being-bodies, 71, 76
being-effort, 149
being-mentation, 90
Beke, George Latura, 1, 19, 137, 142, 239
Belcultassi, 150
Bennett, John G., 19, 25, 33, 81, 112, 113, 118, 153, 157, 182
Big Bang, 108, 124, 126
Bodhisattva, 35
Bokhara, 222
bone, 120, 224
Brain, 71, 72, 76, 77, 78, 79, 82, 84, 85, 100, 108, 112, 115, 116, 119, 120, 121, 128, 129, 131, 132, 133, 135, 136, 152, 153, 156, 166, 167, 169, 180, 182, 196, 197, 206, 229
breath, 93, 156, 212, 213, 220, 229, 230
breathe, 32, 167, 184, 228, 229, 230, 231
breathing, 32, 183, 184, 220, 221, 227, 228, 229, 230, 231, 232
Brook, Peter, 188
brother, 32, 36, 42, 181
Buddha, 26, 33, 186
Buddhism, 32, 169, 185, 197, 200
Buddhist, 169, 213, 230
Buzzell, Keith, 1, 18, 19, 70, 77, 78, 79, 80, 81, 82, 83, 84, 111, 118, 122, 127, 128, 129, 131, 135, 146, 147, 239

C

Canada, 5, 239
carbon, 113
Cathodnatious, 74, 75
Celestial, 19, 137, 140, 142
center, 20, 26, 27, 45, 61, 72, 73, 74, 76, 77, 78, 79, 81, 82, 83, 101, 126, 150, 156, 163, 164, 166, 167, 168, 169, 170, 173, 174, 175, 179, 187, 205, 206, 208, 216, 221, 225, 226, 227
Cerebellum, 189
cherubim, 45
Chi, 20, 137, 157
child, 26, 41, 42, 58, 82, 110, 187, 194, 197, 201, 202, 203, 209, 229
children, 47, 58, 83, 93, 101, 116, 131, 157, 180, 181, 187, 188, 196, 199, 201, 202, 203, 211
China, 20, 131, 135, 157, 158
Chinese, 36, 42, 69
Choon-Kil-Tez, 36, 42, 50, 236
Choon-Tro-Pel, 36, 42, 50, 236
Christ, 29, 59, 169
Christian, 138, 140, 153, 155, 157
Christianity, 197, 198
coat, 137
   coated, 54, 205
   coating, 76
comet, 53, 71
Commission, 95
compassion, 32, 33, 210, 216, 217, 218
concentrate, 41, 45, 75
concentration, 41, 45, 75
Conscience, 24, 25, 26, 73, 89, 94, 112, 115, 128, 136, 143, 168, 169, 186, 200, 203, 215, 224, 235
conscious, 27, 75, 106, 111, 153, 155, 160, 162, 165, 166, 168, 169, 182, 183, 196, 197, 198, 200, 207, 226
Conscious Labor, 106, 162, 198, 207, 226
consciousness, 3, 24, 32, 41, 78, 81, 89, 90, 150, 157, 163, 164, 165, 166, 167, 168, 170, 171, 175, 178, 192, 193, 194, 195, 196, 198, 200, 207, 217, 224, 227
constate
   constated, 90, 141
contemplate
   contemplation, 43, 93, 152

241

Cornelius, George, 104
Cortex, 78
cosmic, 20, 22, 30, 31, 34, 41, 42, 43, 45, 52, 53, 54, 74, 75, 76, 91, 92, 93, 94, 99, 100, 113, 135, 140, 141, 172, 174, 183, 187, 192, 193, 205, 207, 213, 215, 235, 236
cosmology, 92, 95, 142, 172
Creation, 34, 43, 45, 111, 123, 124, 127, 128, 129, 158, 164, 174, 226, 237
creative, 5, 111, 119, 150, 155, 156, 188
Creator, 140, 158
crystallize, 165, 167
   crystallization, 93, 163, 164, 166, 167, 168, 170, 171, 175, 213
   crystallized, 93, 108, 201

D

daughter, 24, 27, 88, 116
death, 19, 20, 23, 79, 102, 108, 128, 129, 134, 165, 169, 173, 178, 199, 200, 212
deflections, 46
Denying, 27, 31, 93, 98, 106, 203
Dervish, 65, 69, 221, 223, 227, 228, 229, 231, 236
descend, 156, 183
descending, 53, 230
descent, 22, 23, 25, 27, 51, 72, 81, 87, 89, 90, 91, 92, 95, 125, 179
Descent, 22, 23, 24, 26, 27, 28, 76
Deskaldino, 30, 52, 53, 234, 236, 237
devil, 51, 135, 172, 233, 234
Dharma, 35
die, 28, 94, 108, 120, 127, 184, 187
digest, 83, 116, 128, 129, 131, 236
digestion, 85, 104, 112, 116, 125, 223
dimension, 48, 158
dissonance, 152, 237
Djartklom, 236
DNA
   genes, 120
dog, 33, 139, 140, 143, 144, 222
dream, 151, 189, 207
dying, 104, 187

E

Earth, 23, 24, 27, 28, 29, 37, 42, 43, 44, 48, 50, 51, 55, 70, 71, 72, 73, 76, 79, 86, 90, 94, 96, 99, 102, 105, 108, 109, 113, 114, 118, 128, 129, 132, 133, 136, 138, 141, 143, 144, 147, 148, 149, 161, 179, 192, 219, 222
Ego, 89, 90, 97, 134
   egoism, 34, 108, 193
   egoistic, 77
Egolionopty, 52, 53
Egypt, 38, 41, 43, 54, 86, 87, 105, 145
Egyptian, 36, 41, 42, 43, 57, 64, 69, 86, 105, 118, 129, 139
Einstein, 118, 151
Ekim Bey, 97, 216, 220, 221, 222, 223, 224, 225, 226, 230, 231, 232
electricity, 70, 71, 76, 98, 134
electromagnetic, 76, 83, 111, 112, 122, 126, 136, 183
   EM, 108
electron, 84, 136
element, 36, 39, 41, 45, 49, 50, 60, 61, 66, 70, 74, 92, 93, 120, 140, 193, 204, 215, 227, 235
emanation, 93, 108, 122, 236
emotion, 49, 58, 79, 101, 120, 132, 145, 156, 171, 173, 176, 195, 197, 199, 201, 202, 203, 206, 208, 209, 214, 216, 217, 227
emotional, 35, 71, 72, 73, 74, 76, 77, 80, 81, 82, 85, 93, 101, 104, 112, 113, 153, 163, 165, 166, 167, 168, 169, 170, 171, 172, 174, 175, 176, 179, 180, 187, 191, 194, 195, 196, 201, 202, 203, 207, 210, 214, 227
Endlessness, 29, 40, 50, 51, 72, 89, 95, 99, 102, 103, 111, 112, 113, 118, 123, 129, 132, 161, 162
England, 23, 30, 82
Enneagram, 20, 84
esoteric, 19, 138, 139

Index

Essence, 32, 39, 74, 75, 88, 93, 95, 105, 106, 158, 159, 165, 169, 173, 188, 221, 228, 230
Essene, 144
Essentuki, 97
Ether, 141, 172
Etherokrilno, 45, 93, 166, 167, 168, 183
Etievan, Nathalie, 20, 24
Evil, 50, 51, 105, 128, 135
Evolution, 3, 25, 85, 163, 164, 165, 166, 168, 171, 172, 176, 191, 192, 193, 195, 197, 200, 201, 210
   evolutionary, 25, 27
Evolve, 107, 167, 173, 176, 185, 188, 192
Exercise, 26, 129, 137, 143, 153, 155, 156, 160, 183, 203, 206, 207, 210, 223, 228, 230, 232
Exioehary, 188, 189

F

Faith, 25, 33, 112, 115, 132, 135, 171, 186, 197, 200, 224
father, 76, 90, 113, 137, 146, 147, 156, 158, 161, 180, 181, 202, 209, 234
Feeling, 24, 32, 72, 74, 76, 79, 85, 89, 132, 135, 148, 149, 154, 156, 166, 169, 177, 184, 188, 196, 208, 209, 214, 216, 226, 230, 231, 235
Fire, 104, 114, 139
first being-food, 73, 238
First Conscious Shock, 168, 171, 182, 183
flatland, 113, 118
Food, 25, 38, 46, 78, 83, 85, 95, 113, 125, 127, 163, 164, 166, 167, 168, 170, 175, 188, 192, 198, 221, 222, 223, 227, 228, 232
force, 53, 72, 74, 76, 83, 93, 98, 99, 104, 106, 107, 112, 122, 127, 148, 150, 153, 156, 158, 194, 197, 201, 207, 214, 215, 217, 224, 226, 227
foreseeing, 50
Formatory, 58, 210, 213
Foundation, 19, 24

Fourth Way, 19, 24, 25, 176, 178
fractal, 46, 47
France, 82, 88, 98, 159, 234
Freud, 171, 172, 173
friction, 218
Fundamentalism, 199

G

genital, 174, 175, 176
Geometry, 122
Germany, 5, 98, 178, 239
Ginsburg, Seymour, 18
gland, 202
   Adrenal, 202
   Endocrine, 202
Gnostic, 24
God, 28, 29, 32, 51, 78, 92, 101, 102, 108, 111, 112, 113, 127, 128, 140, 151, 162, 172, 186, 189, 219, 231, 233, 236
Golden Rule, 27, 162
Good, 51, 60, 161
Gornahoor Harharkh, 33, 39, 40, 41, 54, 55, 60, 74, 75, 76, 82
Gornahoor Rakhoorkh, 74, 75, 76, 82, 84
Gospel, 24, 28
gravity, 23, 45, 141, 163, 164, 170, 225
Great Nature, 39, 193
Greece, 18
Greek, 19, 42, 67, 69, 138, 139, 140, 142, 143, 236
Gurdjieff, G. I., 3, 5, 19, 20, 22, 23, 24, 25, 26, 27, 28, 31, 32, 33, 34, 35, 36, 37, 39, 40, 43, 44, 45, 46, 47, 49, 54, 55, 57, 59, 60, 64, 65, 67, 71, 72, 73, 74, 75, 76, 77, 78, 79, 80, 81, 82, 83, 85, 88, 89, 90, 93, 94, 95, 97, 98, 99, 100, 101, 102, 103, 104, 106, 107, 108, 109, 110, 111, 112, 113, 116, 117, 118, 119, 120, 122, 127, 128, 129, 130, 131, 134, 135, 137, 138, 139, 140, 141, 142, 143, 144, 145, 146, 147, 148, 149, 151, 152, 154, 155, 156, 157, 159, 160, 163, 164, 165, 166, 167, 168, 169, 170, 171, 173, 174, 175, 176, 177,

178, 180, 181, 182, 183, 185, 186, 187, 188, 189, 190, 191, 192, 193, 194, 195, 197, 198, 199, 200, 201, 204, 205, 206, 207, 208, 210, 214, 215, 216, 217, 218, 221, 222, 223, 224, 225, 226, 227, 228, 230, 231, 232, 233, 234, 235, 236
Mr. G., 27
Guru, 226

H

Hamolinadir, 43, 160
Harahrahroohry, 74
Hariton, 27, 53
Harnel-Aoot, 25, 27, 153
Hartmann, Thomas and Olga de, 35, 67, 77
Hasnamuss, 66, 82
Head-Brain, 212, 216
Heap, Jane, 67
heart, 108, 155, 156, 167, 189, 230
heaven, 137, 140, 142
Heaven, 111, 127, 199, 234
Hell, 51, 97, 127, 199
Help, 22, 25, 37
Heptaparaparshinokh, 22, 23, 25, 36, 37, 45
hierarchical, 27
hierarchy, 27, 166
higher being-bodies, 48
higher being-body, 101, 162, 179
holistic, 165
Holy Affirming, 31
Holy Denying, 31
Holy Reconciling, 30, 31
Hope, 25, 27, 28, 29, 33, 54, 67, 88, 89, 104, 112, 114, 115, 119, 120, 129, 135, 197, 199, 200, 217, 218, 231
Howarth, Dushka, 27, 116, 137
hydrogen, 78, 83, 108, 125, 127, 235
Hypnosis, 222, 224, 225, 228
  hypnotised, 94, 97, 217
  hypnotism, 91, 217, 222, 228, 230, 231
  hypnotist, 222, 232

I

I Am, 111, 137, 228
Identification, 68, 102, 154, 163, 174, 200, 216
imagination, 104, 189, 195
impartial, 49, 55, 70
impressions, 45, 46, 54, 60, 62, 125, 132, 163, 164, 166, 167, 168, 169, 170, 174, 175, 191, 205, 206, 207, 210, 228, 230
In Search of the Miraculous, 24, 25, 28, 37, 55, 57, 64, 78, 164, 185, 192
India, 130, 177
Individual, 20, 67, 70, 75, 76, 89, 113, 128, 158, 160, 187, 190, 192, 194, 196, 197, 203
inexactitude, 44, 46, 56, 65, 66, 144
initiation, 20, 34, 71, 226
insight, 33, 61, 65, 78, 83, 85, 91
Instinctive, 78, 83, 96, 105, 196, 201, 203, 220
Institute, 95
Intellectual, 71, 74, 76, 77, 80, 81, 82, 84, 85, 93, 104, 172, 174, 201
intention, 26, 106, 156, 160, 193, 231
interconnected, 60, 62, 158
intuition, 33, 218
Involution, 33
  involutionary, 27
Involve, 33, 69, 122
Iraniranumange, 227
Ischmetch, 40, 73
Islam, 197, 198, 200
Itoklanoz, 85, 134, 205, 206, 207

J

Jerusalem, 222
Jesus, 29, 32, 33, 59, 144, 186
Jew, 222
Jewish, 222
Jobs, Steve, 3, 19, 108, 109, 110, 111, 114, 115, 116, 117, 118, 119, 120, 130, 131, 133, 134, 135

Judas, 215
Justice, 48, 71

K

Kal-da-sakh-tee, 73
Karatas, 52, 53, 70, 76, 90, 102, 143
Karnak, 30, 36, 39, 41, 52, 53, 54, 57, 67, 69, 90, 234
Kesdjan, 73, 76, 141, 142, 162, 205
Kondoor, 71
Konuzion, 42, 51
Koritesnokhnian, 36, 37, 38, 39, 42, 48
Korkaptilnian, 36, 43, 44, 150
Kundabuffer, 3, 50, 51, 61, 82, 84, 85, 91, 129, 150, 168, 191, 192, 193, 194, 195, 196, 197, 198, 203, 204, 210, 212, 213, 216, 217, 219

L

ladder, 122, 126
Lamaism, 197
Last Supper, 55
laugh, 230, 234
laughter, 96, 135, 143, 181, 182, 186, 230, 232
Law, 34, 45, 47, 60, 91, 95, 111, 123, 159, 164, 199, 200, 203, 209, 213, 222, 237, 238
Law of Seven, 23, 33, 44, 46, 48, 65, 66, 69
Law of Three, 27, 31, 94, 146, 155, 158, 224
Law-conformable, 75
lawful, 44, 46, 56, 65, 71, 76, 113, 152
Leary, Timothy, 90
Legominism, 23, 28, 29, 44, 56, 57, 65, 66, 95, 138, 142, 144, 160
Lentrohamsanin, 27, 33, 143
libido, 172
Life is Real, 104, 228
light, 28, 33, 36, 38, 41, 42, 45, 46, 47, 48, 49, 50, 51, 56, 59, 60, 61, 66, 72, 89, 93, 101, 108, 114, 115, 122, 137, 139, 148, 151, 155, 160, 174, 226

Limbic, 72
Looisos, 51, 91, 102
Love, 25, 29, 31, 32, 33, 34, 67, 81, 91, 107, 110, 111, 112, 115, 132, 134, 135, 148, 162, 169, 172, 176, 177, 187, 197, 200, 217, 227
Lucifer, 48, 49, 51

M

machine, 50, 53, 120, 204
Macrobius, 137, 140, 141
magic, 230
magnet
   magnetic, 40, 221
maintenance, 34, 45, 71, 111, 128, 164, 173, 192, 237
mammon, 29
Mars, 42, 48, 54, 62, 70, 71, 72, 73, 74, 76, 79, 89, 93
Martfotai, 23, 43
material, 20, 23, 24, 36, 38, 42, 55, 57, 105, 118, 124, 135, 140, 158, 172, 184, 196, 217, 224, 226, 227, 229, 231
matter, 23, 24, 38, 54, 61, 78, 94, 101, 107, 139, 144, 147, 156, 165, 166, 167, 168, 169, 170, 171, 174, 175, 180, 186, 189, 193, 215, 221, 235
Mdnel-In, 25
mechanical, 68, 135, 153, 159, 164, 193, 200, 203, 207
mechanicality, 214
meditation, 20, 26, 27, 31, 32, 169, 213
medulla, 78
Meetings with Remarkable Men, 3, 31, 93, 97, 130, 156, 220, 222, 224, 231
Megalocosmos, 45, 111, 112, 127
mentate, 75, 84, 182
mentation, 70, 87, 104, 108, 149, 150, 152, 208
Mesmer, 230
metanoia, 20
mind, 20, 23, 43, 56, 69, 81, 83, 90, 95, 99, 106, 108, 109, 113, 116, 117, 133, 134,

145, 151, 153, 165, 167, 169, 176, 194, 195, 212, 213, 221, 222, 224, 226, 231, 232
Mohammed, 34
monastery, 177
monk, 24, 25, 32, 176
Moon, 58, 62, 71, 72, 79, 94, 103, 108, 109, 113, 118, 192
Moore, James, 223
Moral, 48, 105, 107, 113, 201
  Morality, 32, 143, 152, 153, 169, 172, 186, 187, 201
Moscow, 28, 35
Moses, 186
mother, 102, 129, 181, 202, 209
Movements, 35, 80, 84, 238
Moving, 53, 66, 67, 72, 78, 79, 81, 83, 90, 111, 151, 170, 208, 226
Mullah Nassr Eddin, 38, 61
music, 18, 19, 25, 35, 67, 68, 69, 110, 114, 115, 116, 117, 118, 119, 120, 132, 134, 136, 141, 142, 145, 156, 160, 225, 227, 238
myth, 127, 129, 139, 140, 200
mythology, 21

N

Nature, 2, 23, 38, 49, 50, 53, 58, 61, 71, 72, 73, 74, 83, 94, 101, 107, 111, 127, 128, 146, 155, 158, 160, 165, 170, 174, 175, 177, 178, 183, 193, 194, 196, 198, 201, 203, 204, 205, 206, 207, 224, 227, 234
Negative emotion, 101, 110, 171, 191, 199, 212, 214, 215, 216
Neologism, 36, 40, 205
nerve, 57
nervous system, 167
  somatic, 20, 201, 230
  sympathetic, 43, 87, 91, 185
neural, 78
Newton, Isaac, 111, 187
Newton, Issac, 111, 114, 187
Nicoll, Maurice, 25, 92, 94, 167

nine, 30, 98, 106, 201
ninth, 162
Nirioonossian, 141, 142
nothing, 28, 31, 33, 36, 45, 59, 64, 69, 77, 78, 80, 83, 88, 102, 106, 127, 153, 169, 171, 186, 193, 206
Nott, Stanley and Rosemary, 25, 28
Nyland, W, 19, 20, 32

O

Objective, 30, 32, 46, 59, 64, 65, 67, 68, 75, 105, 128, 143, 145, 169, 186, 187, 192, 198, 200, 201
Obligatories, 225
Obligolnian, 149
Occasion, 39, 52, 69, 73, 76
octave, 27, 32, 44, 45, 46, 53, 56, 57, 59, 69, 89, 104, 106, 107, 126, 127, 159, 162
octavic, 125
Okidanokh, 20, 74, 75, 76, 77, 90, 93, 108, 109, 111, 122, 124
Omnipresent, 20, 52, 74, 76, 93
one-brained, 37, 205
Opium, 36, 42, 51
Orage, Alfred, 25, 28, 30, 99, 159, 160, 228, 230
Oragean Version, 228
organic, 24, 37, 71, 136, 165, 177, 184, 192, 200, 201, 203, 215
Orgone, 172, 174, 175, 183, 184, 185, 187, 231
Ors, 71, 72, 73, 76, 98
Ouspensky, P. D., 24, 25, 28, 55, 87, 94, 101, 102, 106, 122, 164, 167, 192, 212, 213, 214
oxygen, 184, 227, 229

P

pagan, 19
Parabola, 19, 137
paradise, 199
Parijrahatnatioose, 74, 75, 76, 77

Index

Paris, 20, 23, 24, 26, 27, 35, 88, 143, 225
Partkdolg-duty, 103, 106, 193
passive, 107, 158, 226
Pentland, John, 20
Peretzi, Dimitri, 18
Persian, 33, 88
personality, 39, 93, 95, 97, 133, 165, 173, 197, 224, 225, 230, 231, 237
Peters, Fritz, 189
Petersburg, 97
Philadelphia, 19, 31
photon, 83, 84, 122
physical, 51, 71, 73, 84, 93, 112, 115, 118, 120, 125, 165, 166, 171, 172, 174, 176, 192, 195, 196, 197, 199, 200, 209, 216, 222, 226, 231, 232
physics, 108, 112, 126, 228
pianola, 54, 153, 159, 160, 182
planet, 28, 30, 37, 38, 39, 41, 42, 43, 44, 48, 49, 52, 53, 54, 55, 62, 69, 71, 72, 73, 74, 75, 76, 86, 89, 90, 94, 95, 99, 100, 102, 105, 108, 113, 114, 143, 144, 145, 205
planetary, 73, 141, 142, 147, 192, 230, 234
Plato, 3, 19, 137, 138, 139, 140, 141, 142, 143, 185, 187, 234
Podkoolad, 40
Podobnisirnian, 76, 81
politics, 127, 211
ponder, 109, 114, 128, 129, 132, 203
pondering, 148
Pons, 78
Popoff, Irmis, 19
Pray, 102
Prayer, 102, 225
presence, 24, 37, 39, 41, 43, 45, 54, 73, 75, 88, 105, 132, 147, 154, 156, 161, 169, 201, 208, 217
Priest, 200
Prieuré, 23
prism, 42
psyche, 86, 91, 92, 97, 100, 106, 149, 150, 191, 192, 194, 197, 198, 203, 204, 205
psychological, 76, 92, 94, 95, 166, 172, 173, 175, 176, 191, 192, 193, 194, 195, 197, 198, 199, 202, 203, 204, 208, 210, 213, 215, 217, 218, 230
Psychological Commentaries, 167
psychologist, 20, 218, 230
psychology, 20, 79, 94, 95, 191, 198, 204, 208, 210
Purgatory, 30, 45, 49, 52, 53, 102, 160, 161, 237
Pyramid, 41, 43, 86, 114, 129
Pythagoras, 3, 55, 137, 138, 139, 142, 143, 144, 145, 185
Pythagorean, 139, 140, 141, 142, 144

Q

Quantum, 112, 151

R

radiation, 52, 87, 88, 99, 126, 192, 235
RAS, 78, 82
Ray of Creation, 108, 122, 125, 183
Real, 71
Reason, 30, 39, 40, 43, 50, 69, 70, 72, 74, 75, 76, 77, 89, 93, 96, 97, 99, 105, 108, 111, 112, 131, 132, 133, 143, 145, 147, 150, 151, 157, 160, 163, 164, 179, 187, 190, 192, 197, 200, 202, 204, 205, 207, 213, 217, 220
Reciprocal, 99, 100, 128, 208
Reconcile, 19, 71, 76, 108, 110, 113, 128, 132, 133, 135, 210
  Reconciliation, 77, 132, 135, 225
  Reconciling, 27, 74, 75, 76, 77, 98, 99, 100, 106, 112, 136, 214, 217
Reich, Dr., 19, 136, 163, 164, 165, 168, 170, 171, 172, 173, 174, 175, 177, 179, 180, 181, 183, 184, 185, 187, 188, 189, 231
Relativity, 108, 168
religion, 19, 32, 51, 102, 127, 172, 186, 198, 199, 200, 215

Remember, 24, 26, 27, 34, 65, 79, 81, 82, 89, 92, 95, 96, 99, 103, 104, 130, 144, 147, 148, 154, 156, 168, 181, 183, 184, 188, 205, 212, 224, 225, 231
    Remembering, 106, 108, 148, 231
Remorse, 92, 128, 148, 149, 169, 186
repetition, 47, 150
resonate, 156, 159
restorials, 42
Reticular, 78
Ropp, Robert de, 212, 213
Rosary, 223, 225
Rumi, Jalaluddin, 187
Russia, 25, 35, 60, 86, 88, 90, 91, 93, 95, 97, 98, 99, 231, 234

S

Sacred, 22, 23, 25, 30, 37, 40, 45, 49, 50, 71, 73, 74, 93, 138, 146, 149, 155, 177, 224, 227
sacrifice, 34, 154, 179, 180
    sacrificed, 180
    sacrificial, 95, 179, 180
Saint Lama, 33
Salzmanino, 30, 52, 53, 234, 235, 236, 237
Saturn, 70, 71, 72, 73, 74, 76, 79, 93, 145
Science, 50, 68, 69, 112, 113, 118, 127, 128, 131, 135, 164, 172, 200, 228, 229
Scientific, 54, 78, 113, 122, 125, 128, 151, 163, 164, 183, 229
second being-food, 228, 229
Second Conscious Shock, 163, 164, 168, 169, 170, 171, 176, 183, 186, 187
seeing, 36, 38, 39, 46, 58, 59, 61, 84, 115, 121, 192, 200, 207, 212, 218
Self, 20, 169, 193, 207, 208, 216
Self Observation, 20, 168, 207, 209
Self Remembering, 137, 168, 169, 207
Self-consciousness, 193
sensation, 108, 195, 207, 226
senses, 85, 195, 228
Sensing, 96, 159, 207, 216
Sensory, 61

seraphim, 45
seven, 23, 26, 32, 37, 42, 44, 45, 47, 48, 52, 53, 57, 60, 66, 68, 69, 72, 96, 98, 99, 111, 143, 159, 215, 230, 234
seventh, 23, 99
Sex, 32, 163, 164, 167, 168, 169, 170, 171, 172, 173, 174, 175, 176, 177, 178, 180, 181, 182, 183, 187, 188, 189, 199, 232
    sexual, 143, 163, 164, 169, 170, 172, 173, 174, 175, 176, 177, 180, 181, 186, 199
    sexuality, 3, 163, 164, 166, 168, 169, 171, 173, 174, 175, 176, 177, 179, 180, 181
shock, 62, 71, 104, 106, 168, 169, 170, 171, 182, 183, 226
sin, 75, 136
singing, 159
sister, 20
Sitting, 26, 31, 32, 35, 81, 97, 185, 213, 220, 221, 226, 228
Skull, 78
Sleep, 91, 147, 153, 154, 165, 170, 173, 174, 192, 196, 199, 224
solar plexus, 212, 217
Solioonensius, 86, 89, 92, 94, 99, 100, 103
Soloviev, 223
son, 75, 76, 82, 101, 140, 146, 147, 148, 156, 158, 161, 178, 181, 218, 221, 225, 233, 234
Soorptakalknian, 43
Sophia, 98
Soul, 43, 49, 66, 101, 141, 142, 160, 165, 186, 199, 200, 219
sound, 36, 42, 53, 54, 59, 60, 69, 96, 117, 134, 135, 141, 142, 159, 205, 226
sounding, 155
spinal column, 51, 193
Spirit, 20, 26, 51, 222, 232
    spiritual, 27, 134, 141, 142, 151, 153, 163, 176
    spirituality, 169
St. Petersburg (also Petersburg), 97, 99
Staveley, A.L., 19, 20, 32, 65, 96, 104, 152, 154, 160

Index

Stopinder, 27, 34, 46, 98
subconscious, 81, 90, 168, 195, 200, 215, 225
subjective, 24, 26, 187, 201, 234
substance, 38, 45, 74, 75, 124, 137, 166, 192
Suffer, 103, 110, 196, 197, 200, 215, 217, 230
   Intentional Suffering, 19, 26, 162, 198, 207, 226
   suffered, 27, 148, 198, 215
   suffering, 103, 110, 181, 200, 207, 232
Sufis, 138
suggestibility, 50, 91, 107, 134, 149
Sun, 45, 59, 64, 71, 72, 93, 102, 108, 111, 123, 139, 140, 145, 152, 236
Sun Absolute, 45, 93, 102, 108, 111, 123, 236
Symbol, 53, 126, 167, 170
   symbolic, 46, 51, 58, 149, 163, 164, 165, 167, 170, 225
   symbology, 64

T

Tail, 49, 51, 96
Teleoghinoora, 36, 40, 43, 44
Tenikdoa, 141
Thalamus, 78
Thanatos, 173
The Fourth Way, 25, 171
Theomertmalogos, 93
third being-food, 228
Third Force, 74, 75, 93, 106, 107, 112, 158
   3rd Force, 82, 84
three-brained, 28, 36, 37, 38, 39, 40, 43, 44, 50, 51, 70, 71, 72, 73, 74, 75, 86, 100, 105, 106, 113, 159, 175, 192, 194, 198, 201, 205, 207, 222
Tibet, 138
Tikliamish, 81
Timaeus, 140, 141
time, 23, 24, 25, 26, 27, 35, 38, 39, 41, 42, 43, 45, 48, 49, 51, 54, 55, 56, 59, 67, 70, 72, 76, 80, 81, 83, 86, 87, 88, 89, 91, 92, 93, 95, 96, 98, 99, 100, 102, 103, 104, 105, 106, 108, 110, 111, 112, 113, 115, 116, 117, 118, 119, 120, 121, 127, 129, 131, 132, 133, 134, 135, 136, 137, 140, 141, 144, 147, 148, 149, 150, 151, 152, 153, 154, 157, 158, 159, 160, 162, 174, 177, 178, 180, 181, 184, 190, 192, 196, 199, 202, 205, 206, 207, 209, 210, 212, 214, 215, 216, 217, 219, 220, 221, 222, 225, 226, 229, 230, 231, 232, 234, 235, 236, 237, 238
tolerance, 184
Toof-Nef-Tef, 3, 70, 71, 73, 75, 77, 78, 79, 87, 89, 90
Tracol, Henri, 20, 24, 225
Traditional Studies Press, 55
transform, 210, 236
transformation, 52, 104, 127, 135, 170, 207, 208, 213, 214, 217, 235
transmutation, 20, 34, 171, 176, 177, 205
transmute, 165
Triad, 98, 104, 152
Triamazikamno, 37, 45, 146, 155
Trinity, 107, 148, 152, 155, 158, 159
Trogoautoegocrat, 30, 234, 237
   Trogoautoegocratic, 52, 235
two-brained, 37, 71, 205, 207, 222

U

unconscious, 94, 131, 192, 195, 196, 197, 207, 209
understanding, 26, 42, 61, 64, 65, 69, 77, 87, 93, 94, 104, 107, 110, 112, 117, 128, 129, 136, 140, 146, 147, 148, 150, 151, 152, 155, 163, 165, 166, 171, 173, 175, 177, 191, 195, 198, 199, 200, 203, 209, 210, 216, 217, 224, 229
universe, 39, 40, 45, 53, 54, 55, 68, 74, 75, 83, 93, 111, 112, 113, 135, 136, 140, 150, 151, 155, 156, 166, 169, 172, 174, 183, 205, 235
USA, 5, 18, 239

V

Vacuum, 40, 54, 66
Vedanta, 178
Venus, 72
vibration, 44, 45, 54, 57, 58, 60, 65, 69, 72, 87, 92, 94, 97, 106, 151, 154, 192, 205, 207, 222
vivifyingness, 155, 163, 164, 166, 167, 174, 175
Vznooshlitzval, 74

W

Walker, Kenneth, 166
Washington, 193
Water, 39, 49, 62, 73, 88, 113, 181, 221, 223, 225
Wellbeloved, Sophia, 98
Will, 1, 20, 22, 23, 29, 30, 31, 34, 89, 94, 98, 100, 103, 106, 111, 129, 161, 162, 239
Wisdom, 50, 112, 155
wiseacre, 235
    wiseacring, 229, 237
Work, 3, 5, 19, 20, 22, 23, 24, 26, 27, 29, 30, 31, 32, 77, 80, 146, 148, 150, 152, 153, 154, 156, 158, 163, 164, 165, 168, 171, 173, 182, 183, 186, 188, 190
world, 5, 30, 34, 35, 44, 45, 51, 53, 66, 68, 71, 74, 80, 81, 85, 89, 91, 92, 100, 101, 108, 110, 111, 112, 113, 114, 116, 118, 123, 124, 126, 127, 132, 133, 134, 135, 138, 140, 141, 142, 149, 158, 164, 166, 172, 173, 181, 187, 192, 194, 197, 198, 208, 209, 214, 218, 224, 225, 230, 232, 237

Y

Yoga, 213, 221
    Tantra, 178

Z

Zen, 23, 27, 32, 177, 185
Zilnotrago, 30, 32, 52, 234, 235, 236, 237
Zirlikner, 73
Zodiac, 137, 140
    Cancer, 172

www.ingramcontent.com/pod-product-compliance
Lightning Source LLC
Chambersburg PA
CBHW080334170426
43194CB00014B/2559